WRITTEN CHINESE
MADE EASY

How to Download the Audio Recordings for this Book

1. Make sure you have an Internet connection.
2. Type the URL below into your web browser.

https://www.tuttlepublishing.com/written-chinese-made-easy

For support, you can email us at info@tuttlepublishing.com.

WRITTEN CHINESE MADE EASY

A Beginner's Guide to Learning 1,000 Chinese Characters

MICHAEL L. KLUEMPER AND KIT-YEE YAM NADEAU 任潔儀

TUTTLE Publishing

Tokyo | Rutland, Vermont | Singapore

Published by Tuttle Publishing, an imprint of Periplus Editions (HK) Ltd.

www.tuttlepublishing.com

Library of Congress Control Number: 2016939558

ISBN 978-0-8048-5551-8
(Previously published under ISBN 978-0-8048-4385-0)

"Books to Span the East and West"

Tuttle Publishing was founded in 1832 in the small New England town of Rutland, Vermont [USA]. Our core values remain as strong today as they were then—to publish best-in-class books which bring people together one page at a time. In 1948, we established a publishing office in Japan—and Tuttle is now a leader in publishing English-language books about the arts, languages and cultures of Asia. The world has become a much smaller place today and Asia's economic and cultural influence has grown. Yet the need for meaningful dialogue and information about this diverse region has never been greater. Over the past seven decades, Tuttle has published thousands of books on subjects ranging from martial arts and paper crafts to language learning and literature—and our talented authors, illustrators, designers and photographers have won many prestigious awards. We welcome you to explore the wealth of information available on Asia at **www.tuttlepublishing.com**.

Distributed by

North America, Latin America & Europe
Tuttle Publishing
364 Innovation Drive, North Clarendon
VT 05759-9436 U.S.A.
Tel: 1 (802) 773-8930; Fax: 1 (802) 773-6993
info@tuttlepublishing.com
www.tuttlepublishing.com

Japan
Tuttle Publishing
Yaekari Building, 3rd Floor, 5-4-12 Osaki
Shinagawa-ku, Tokyo 141 0032
Tel: (81) 3 5437-0171; Fax: (81) 3 5437-0755
sales@tuttle.co.jp
www.tuttle.co.jp

Asia Pacific
Berkeley Books Pte. Ltd.
3 Kallang Sector #04-01, Singapore 349278
Tel: (65) 6741-2178; Fax: (65) 6741-2179
inquiries@periplus.com.sg
www.tuttlepublishing.com

26 25 24 23 22 6 5 4 3 2 1 2204TP
Printed in Singapore

CONTENTS

A GUIDE TO THE ILLUSTRATIONS

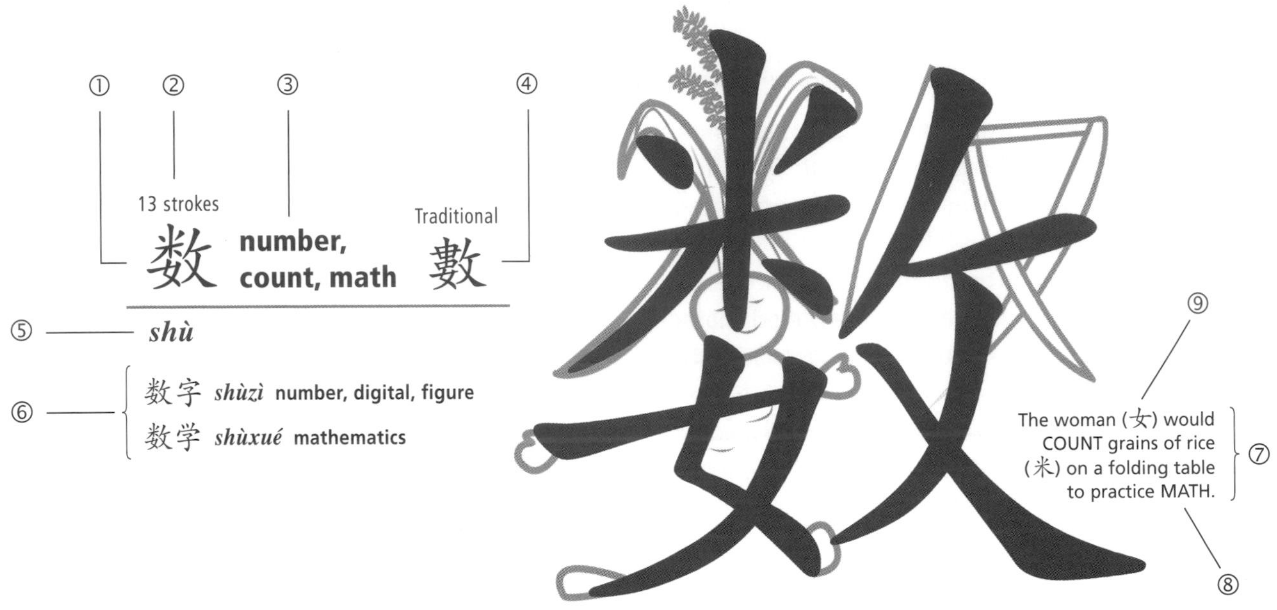

1. The simplified character. In this book we use simplified characters and where is a traditional character, we will list it at the right top corner for each entry.
2. The number of writing strokes for the character.
3. English meanings of the character.
4. The traditional form of the character.
5. The common pronunciation of the character in *pinyin*. All pronunciation is given in italics in this book.
6. Examples of common vocabulary words. These are given with *pinyin* pronunciations (in italics), followed by English meaning(s).
7. A tip with each illustration to help remember the meaning of the character.
8. The meaning of the character is written in capital letters.
9. Many characters contain elements that can be stand-alone characters, or elements that are common radicals closely associated with a particular meaning. These stand-alone characters and radicals are highlighted in the tip accompanying each illustration.

CHAPTER 1

NUMBERS and COLORS

13 strokes

数 number, count, math Traditional 數

shù

数字 ***shùzì*** **number, digital, figure**

数学 ***shùxué*** **mathematics**

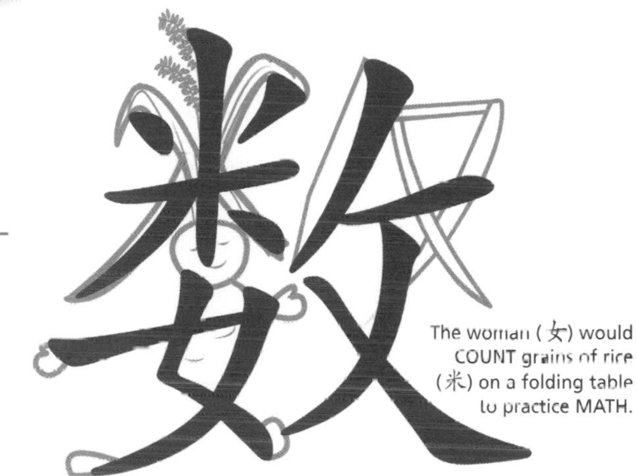
The woman (女) would COUNT grains of rice (米) on a folding table to practice MATH.

A snake has patterns of COLOR and a forked tongue.

6 strokes

色 color

sè

颜色 ***yánsè*** **color**

Numbers 数

1 stroke

一 one

yī

第一 *dìyī* **No. 1**

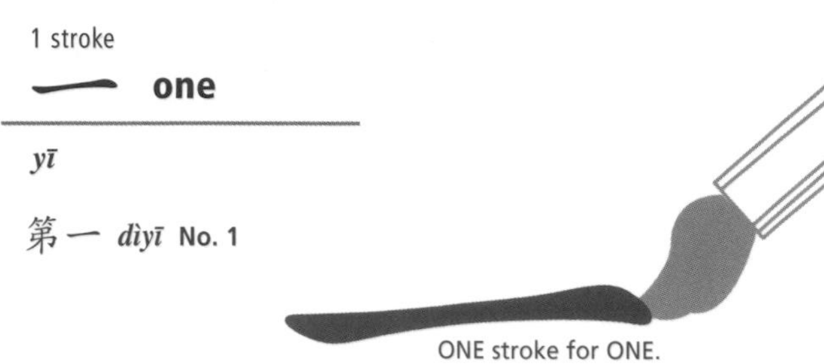

ONE stroke for ONE.

2 strokes

二 two

èr

二手货 *èrshǒuhuò*
secondhand goods

TWO strokes for TWO.

3 strokes

三 three

sān

三角形 *sānjiǎoxíng*
triangle

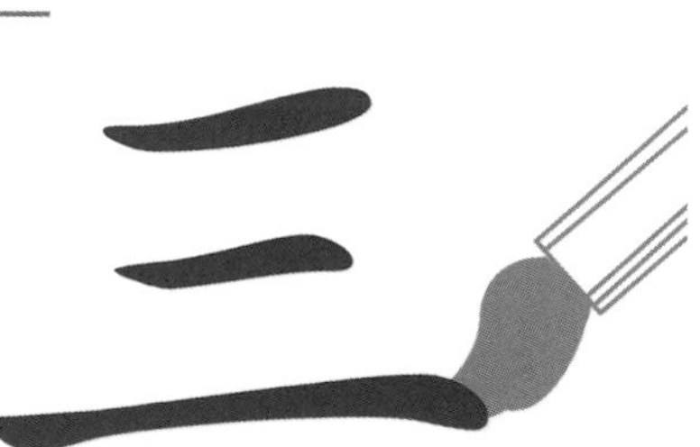

THREE strokes for THREE.

5 strokes

四 four

sì

四月 *sìyuè* **April**

A FOUR-sided sheet of paper is held up by two hands at the top corners.

4 strokes

五 five

wǔ

五行 *wǔxíng*
the five elements (i.e. 木 wood, 火 fire, 土 earth, 金 metal, and 水 water)

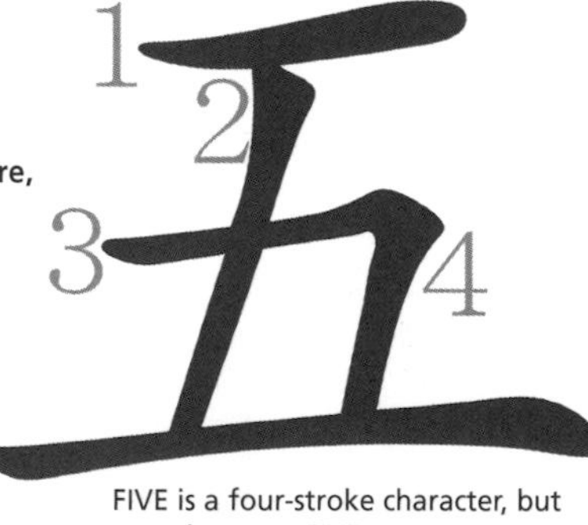

FIVE is a four-stroke character, but there are FIVE segments.

4 strokes

六 **six**

liù

六个 *liùgè* **six pieces**

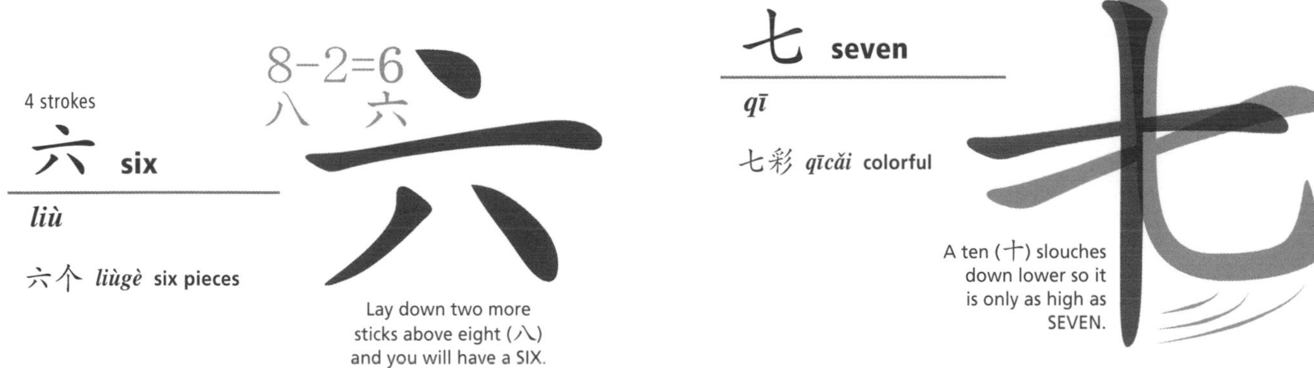

Lay down two more sticks above eight (八) and you will have a SIX.

2 strokes

七 **seven**

qī

七彩 *qīcǎi* **colorful**

A ten (十) slouches down lower so it is only as high as SEVEN.

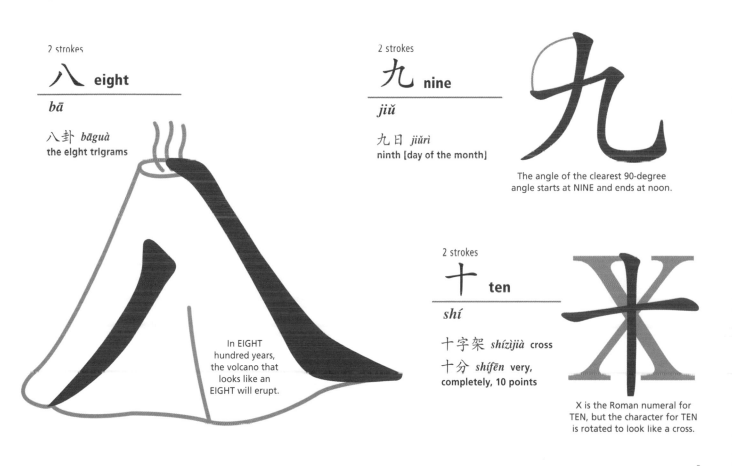

2 strokes

八 **eight**

bā

八卦 *bāguà*
the eight trigrams

In EIGHT hundred years, the volcano that looks like an EIGHT will erupt.

2 strokes

九 **nine**

jiǔ

九日 *jiǔrì*
ninth [day of the month]

The angle of the clearest 90-degree angle starts at NINE and ends at noon.

2 strokes

十 **ten**

shí

十字架 *shízìjià* **cross**

十分 *shífēn* **very, completely, 10 points**

X is the Roman numeral for TEN, but the character for TEN is rotated to look like a cross.

6 strokes

百 **hundred**

bǎi

百万 ***bǎiwàn*** million

百姓 ***bǎixìng*** common people

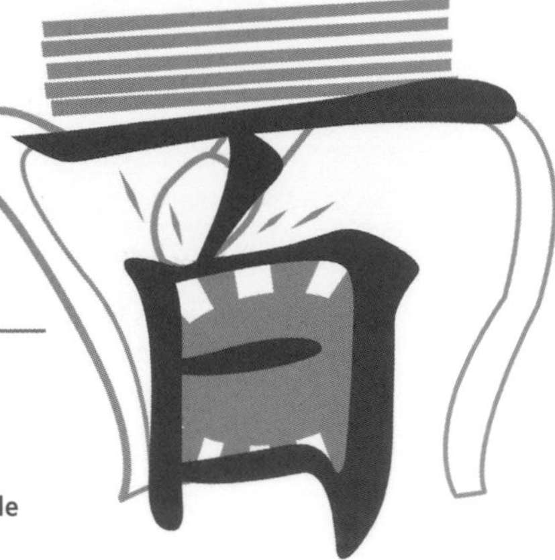

A white (白) band of paper wraps around one HUNDRED one dollar bills.

3 strokes

万 **ten thousand** Traditional 萬

wàn

一万 ***yīwàn*** ten thousand

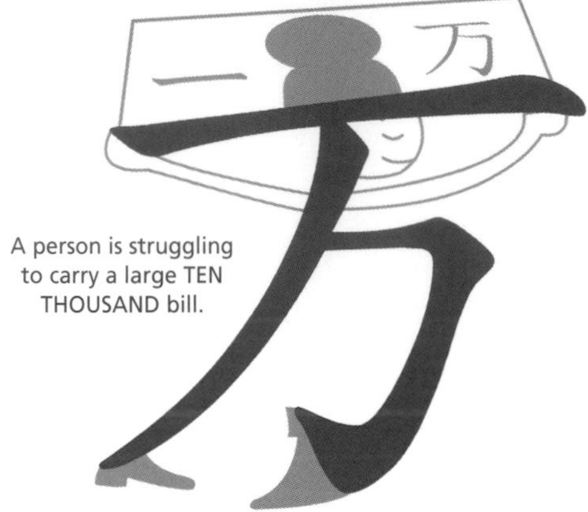

A person is struggling to carry a large TEN THOUSAND bill.

3 strokes

 **thousand**

qiān

一千 ***yīqiān*** one thousand

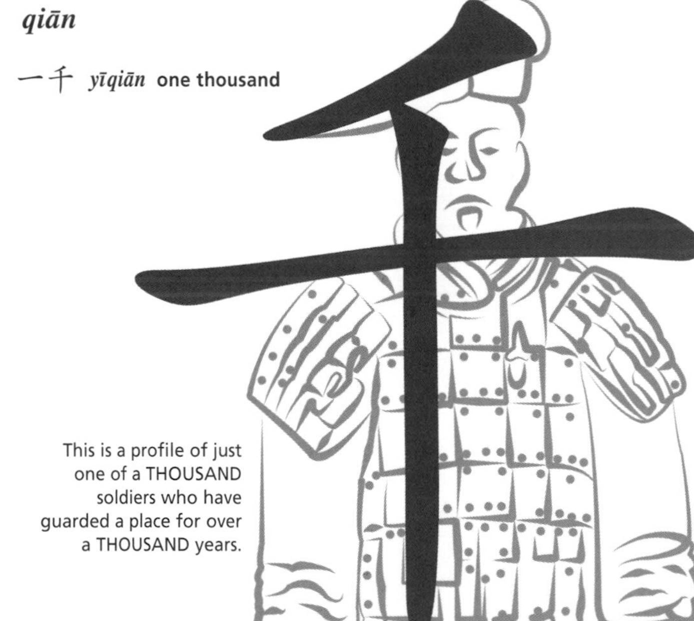

This is a profile of just one of a THOUSAND soldiers who have guarded a place for over a THOUSAND years.

4 strokes

元 **primary, original, currency (dollar)**

yuán

元老 ***yuánlǎo*** senior statesman

元旦 ***yuándàn*** New Year Day

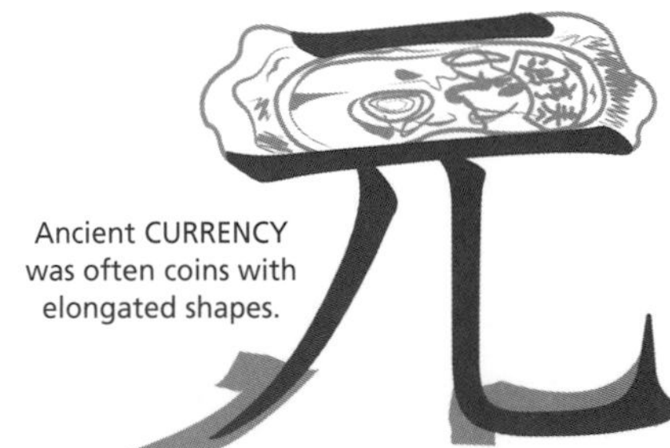

Ancient CURRENCY was often coins with elongated shapes.

5 strokes

号 number, item, mark

Traditional 號

hào

号码 *hàomǎ* number

记号 *jìhào* mark, sign

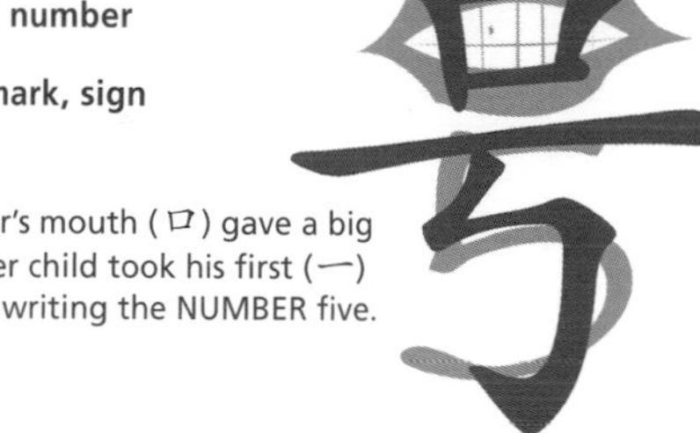

The mother's mouth (口) gave a big smile as her child took his first (一) attempt at writing the NUMBER five.

5 strokes

半 half, middle

bàn

一半 *yībàn* half

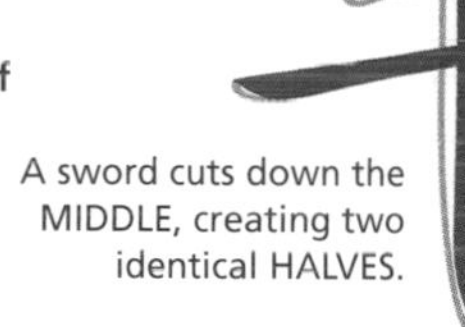

A sword cuts down the MIDDLE, creating two identical HALVES.

8 strokes

单 simple, single, list, bill, odd number

Traditional 單

dān

单独 *dāndú* alone, individual

菜单 *càidān* menu

The SIMPLE addition of two bits of knowledge about how to plant a field (田) can reap benefits tenfold (十).

6 strokes

协 assist, help, cooperation

Traditional 協

xié

协助 *xiézhù* to help

协力 *xiélì* to work together, cooperation, collaboration

协会 *xiéhuì* association, society, organization

When ten (十) or more people multiply their power (力) through COOPERATION, they are stronger.

12 strokes

博 plentiful, extensive

bó

广博 *guǎngbó* extensive, general

博士 *bóshì* doctorate, PhD

博物馆 *bówùguǎn* museum

A RICH person can grow crops in ten (十) fields (田) and has EXTENSIVE knowledge of small things that can be measured (寸).

Colors 色

13 strokes

蓝 **blue** Traditional 藍

lán

蓝色 *lánsè* **blue**

蓝天 *lántiān* **blue sky**

蓝图 *lántú* **blueprint**

The BLUE grasses (艹) and structures are a popular pattern on plates (皿) of BLUE Willow china.

8 strokes

青 **blue, blue-green**

qīng

青绿 *qīnglǜ* **green, dark green**

青春 *qīngchūn* **youth, bloom, prime**

青蛙 *qīngwā* **frog**

During a BLUE moon (月), plants sprout a second set of branches and BLUE-GREEN leaves.

11 strokes

绿 **green** Traditional 綠

lǜ

绿色 *lǜsè* **green**

绿茶 *lǜchá* **green tea**

The grass is like layers of GREEN threads that have been hosed with water (水).

11 strokes

黄 **yellow** Traditional 黃

huáng

黄色 *huángsè* **yellow**

黄豆 *huángdòu* **soybean**

黄油 *huángyóu* **butter**

A grill has tens (十) of people ready to eat the organic YELLOW (黄) squash and other veggies.

12 strokes

紫 **purple**

zǐ

紫色 *zǐsè* **purple**

紫罗兰 *zǐluólán* **violet (flower)**

When mixing PURPLE grapes for juice with a ladle (匕), stop (止) if you spill any on your clothes, as the silk (糸) will stain.

16 strokes

橙 orange

chéng

橙色 *chéngsè* orange (color)

橙汁 *chéngzhī* orange juice

Beside a tree (木), a jagged mountain can be climbed (登) to see the ORANGE sunset, but take plenty of beans (豆) for energy.

5 strokes

白 white

bái

白色 *báisè* white

明白 *míngbái* to understand, realize, to be clear

Striking a match on the sun (日) might initially produce a WHITE light.

12 strokes

黑 black

hēi

黑色 *hēisè* black

黑暗 *hēi'àn* dark, without light

When the floodgates open to the fields (田), rich BLACK soil (土) pours free.

6 strokes

红 red, crimson

Traditional 紅

hóng

红色 *hóngsè* red

红茶 *hóngchá* black tea

口红 *kǒuhóng* lipstick

The worker (工) sewed the CRIMSON silk (糸).

6 strokes

灰 gray, ashes

huī

灰色 *huīsè* gray, gloomy

骨灰 *gǔhuī* bone ashes, ashes of the dead

In the shade of a GRAY cliff, ASHES of a fire (火) were found.

12 strokes

棕 **brown**

zōng

棕色 *zōngsè* brown

棕榈 *zōnglǘ* palm

The structure with the wooden (木) roof (宀) was BROWN.

The roots hanging from the ceiling above the table will BECOME tasty after being cooked.

8 strokes

的 **possessive article, self, aim**

de/dì

我的 *wǒde* my, mine

目的 *mùdì* purpose, aim, intent, goal

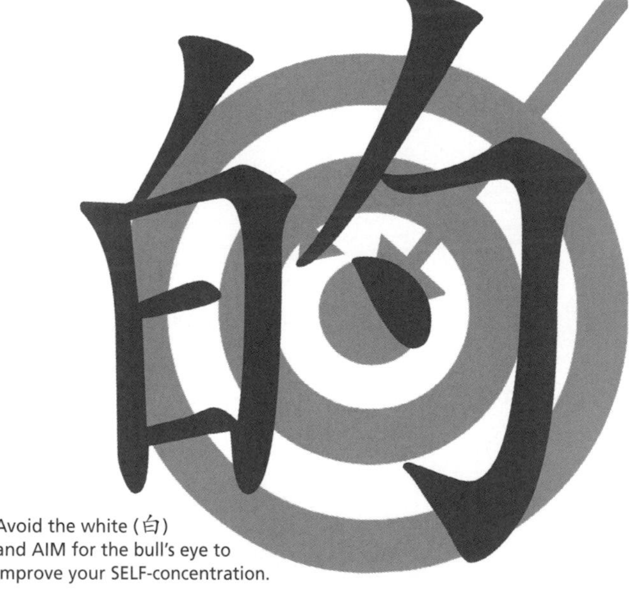

Avoid the white (白) and AIM for the bull's eye to improve your SELF-concentration.

8 strokes

变 **change, alter, become**

Traditional 變

biàn

变更 *biàngēng* to change, alter, modification

转变 *zhuǎnbiàn* to change, transform, conversion

9 strokes

皇 **emperor**

huáng

皇帝 *huángdì* emperor

皇后 *huánghòu* empress

皇宫 *huánggōng* palace

The EMPERORS and kings (王) of foreign lands sometimes wear white (白).

CHAPTER 2

PERSON

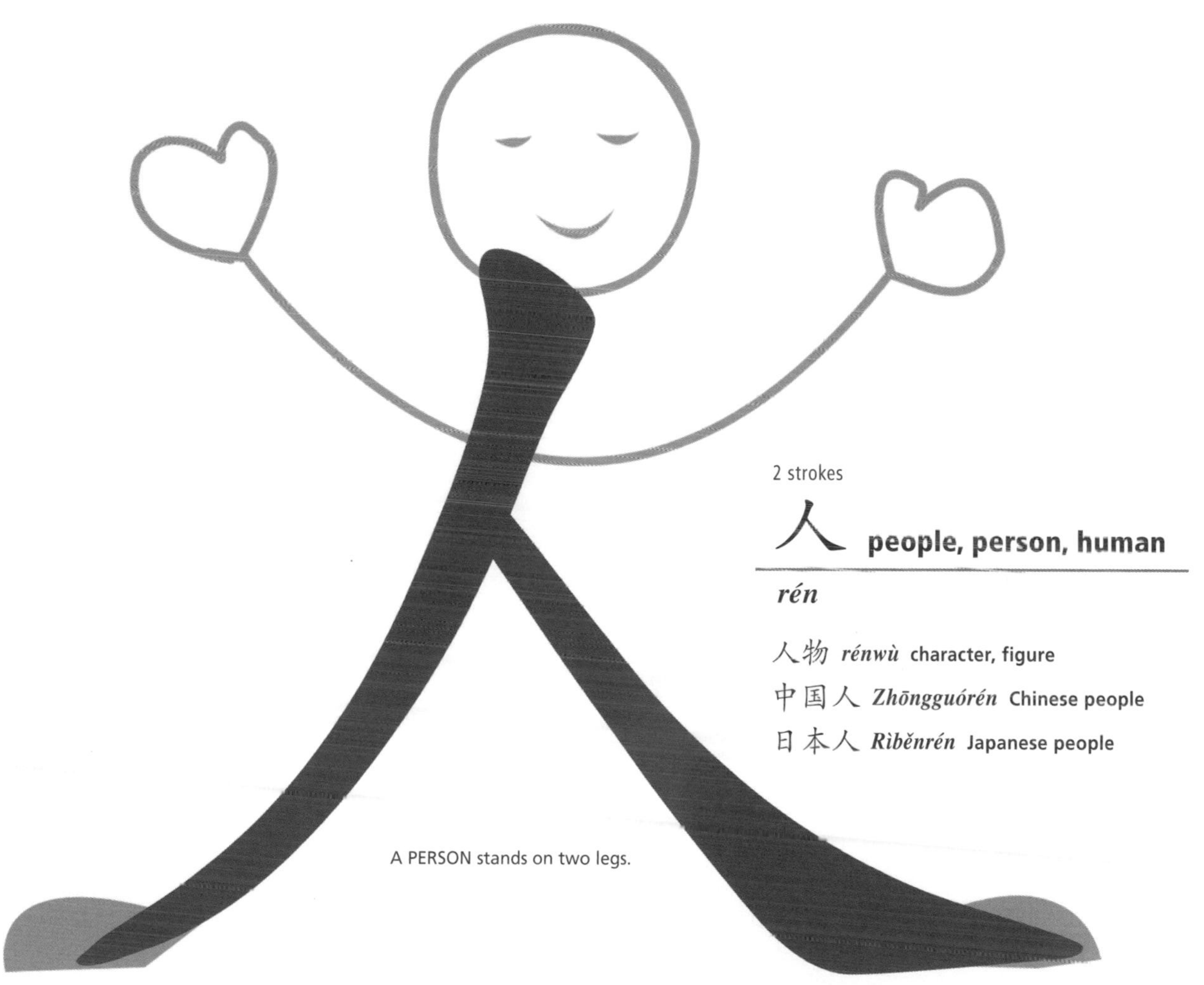

A PERSON stands on two legs.

2 strokes

人 **people, person, human**

rén

人物 ***rénwù*** **character, figure**

中国人 ***Zhōngguórén*** **Chinese people**

日本人 ***Rìběnrén*** **Japanese people**

Person 人/亻

4 strokes

从 **accompany, obey, submit to, comply**

Traditional 從

cóng

服从 ***fúcóng*** **obedience, submission**

从前 ***cóngqián*** **before, previously, in the past**

Two people (人) were told to ACCOMPANY each other and they OBEYED the request to do so.

6 strokes

 **many, numerous, crowd**

Traditional 

zhòng

众多 ***zhòngduō*** **numerous, multiple**

群众 ***qúnzhòng*** **the masses, crowd**

观众 ***guānzhòng*** **audience**

MANY people (人) consider three a CROWD.

8 strokes

 **serve, waiter, wait upon**

shì

服侍 ***fúshì*** **to wait upon, serve**

侍候 ***shìhòu*** **to wait upon, serve**

An attendant is there to SERVE monks and others at a temple (寺).

5 strokes

 **immortal, hermit, wizard**

xiān

神仙 ***shénxiān*** **immortal**

仙女 ***xiānnǚ*** **fairy, female celestial**

A HERMIT lives on a mountain (山) and is thought to be a WIZARD.

7 strokes

佐 assist; aid

zuǒ

辅佐 *fǔzuǒ* **assistant**

The person on the left (左) will ASSIST the other climb upon an I-beam.

7 strokes

佑 bless, help, protect, assist

yòu

保佑 *bǎoyòu* **to bless, protect**

天佑 *tiānyòu* **god bless**

The person on the right (右) will HELP the other climb upon a box.

4 strokes

仁 benevolence, humanity, charity

rén

仁慈 *réncí* **kindness, charity**

仁爱 *rén'ài* **benevolence, humanity**

A good person (亻) should have at least two (二) strong values: CHARITY and BENEVOLENCE.

9 strokes

信 faith, truth, trust, message, letter

xìn

相信 *xiāngxìn* **to believe**

信息 *xìnxī* **information, message**

信号 *xìnhào* **signal**

A person you TRUST, says (言) the TRUTH.

8 strokes

供 supply, provide, offer

gōng

供应 *gōngyìng* **supply, provision**

提供 *tígōng* **to provide, offer**

A person (亻) made an OFFER to help two (二) friends get down from a table.

4 strokes

内 inside, within

Traditional 內

nèi

内地 *nèidì* **inland, outback**

内向 *nèixiàng* **introverted, diffidence**

This person (人) is INSIDE or WITHIN this enclosure.

6 strokes

休 rest, stop, cease

xiū

休息 ***xiūxí*** to rest

退休 ***tuìxiū*** to retire; retirement

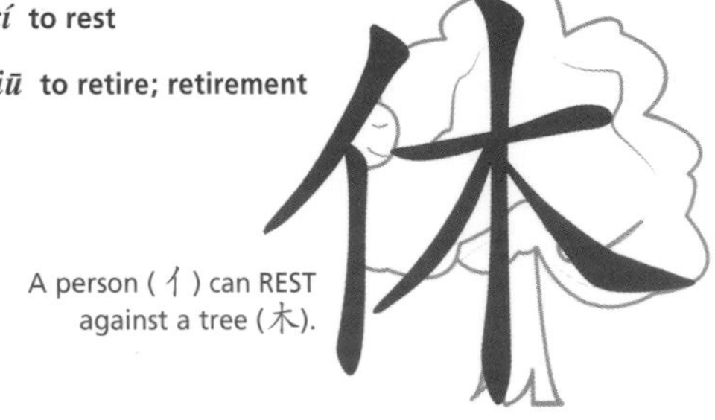

A person (亻) can REST against a tree (木).

10 strokes

候 await, climate, weather

hòu

气候 ***qìhòu*** climate, atmosphere

等候 ***děnghòu*** to await, waiting, expect

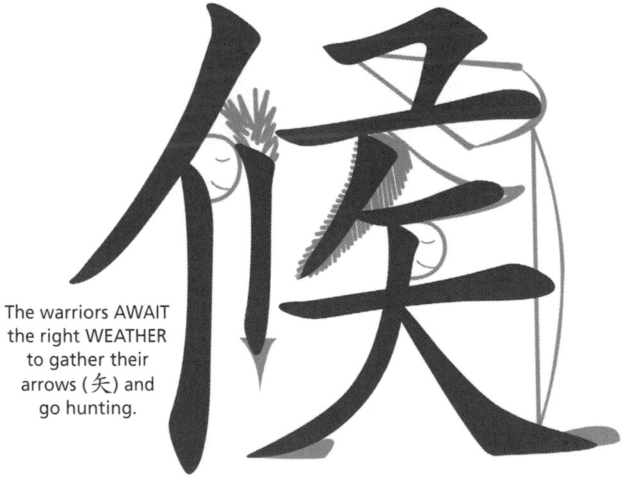

The warriors AWAIT the right WEATHER to gather their arrows (矢) and go hunting.

5 strokes

代 substitute, replace, time, era, generation

dài

替代 ***tìdài*** substitute, to replace

时代 ***shídài*** time, age, era

A person (亻) takes down the character for 10 (十), at the end of an ERA, ready to REPLACE it with a new TIME.

5 strokes

们 plural for pronouns or nouns

Traditional 們

men

我们 ***wǒmen*** we, us, ourselves

人们 ***rénmen*** people, folk

A man waits by a gate for friends to make their numbers PLURAL.

6 strokes

优 excellent, superior, outstanding

Traditional 優

yōu

优秀 ***yōuxiù*** excellent, outstanding

优胜 ***yōushèng*** winning, victorious

A person (亻) who himself (自) is kind and places his heart (心) on the table has OUTSTANDING character and compassion.

7 strokes

你 you

nǐ

你们 *nǐmen* you (plural)

你好 *nǐhǎo* hello, hi

YOU have waved your hands in excitement since YOU were little (小).

7 strokes

但 but, however, yet

dàn

但是 *dànshì* but, however

但愿 *dànyuàn* if only

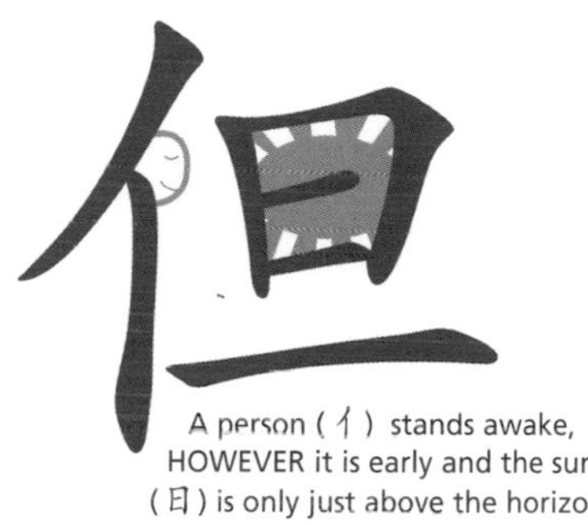

A person (亻) stands awake, HOWEVER it is early and the sun (日) is only just above the horizon.

10 strokes

倒 collapse, fall down

dǎo

倒塌 *dǎotā* to collapse, topple down

摔倒 *shuāidǎo* to fall down, drop

When a person arrives (至) at the end of his day after using a knife (刂) to till his land, he might COLLAPSE from exhaustion.

6 strokes

价 value, price

Traditional 價

jià

价值 *jiàzhí* value, worth

价钱 *jiàqián* price, cost

减价 *jiǎnjià* on sale

A person (亻) must sometimes look behind the scenes to find out the real VALUE or PRICE.

4 strokes

什 what, why

Traditional 甚

shén

什么 *shénme* what?

为什么 *wèishénme* why?

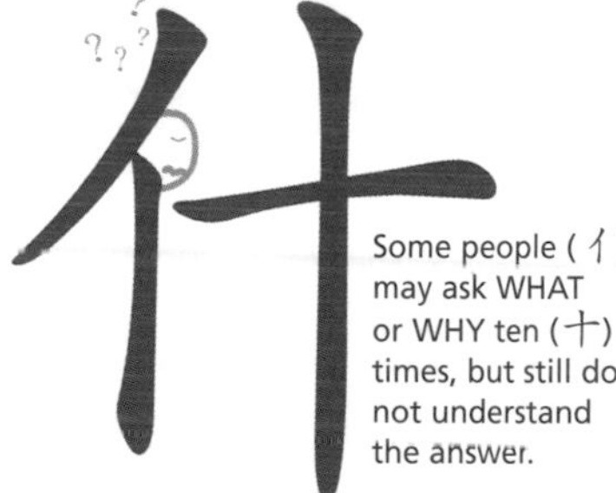

Some people (亻) may ask WHAT or WHY ten (十) times, but still do not understand the answer.

6 strokes

传 pass, transmit

Traditional 傳

chuán

传染 *chuánrǎn* to infect, transmit

宣传 *xuānchuán* to publicize, propagate

A person (亻) had to TRANSMIT two (二) lines of a message to me, crossing them off as he did.

7 strokes

伸 **expand, stretch, extend**

shēn

伸展 *shēnzhǎn* **to extend**

A person (亻) needs to STRETCH the size of his advertisements to EXPAND his business.

5 strokes

付 **pay, commit, handover**

fù

付出 *fùchū* **to pay, disbursement**

应付 *yìngfù* **to deal with, cope with, handle**

A person (亻) may COMMIT to PAY ten (十) percent of the fee until the HANDOVER of the purchased item.

2 strokes

 **enter, insert**

rù

入口 *rùkǒu* **entrance**

进入 *jìnrù* **to go in**

A person (人) might turn around to ENTER a room to say goodbye.

7 strokes

作 **to make, work, product**

zuò

工作 *gōngzuò* **work, job, task**

合作 *hézuò* **to work togther, cooperate**

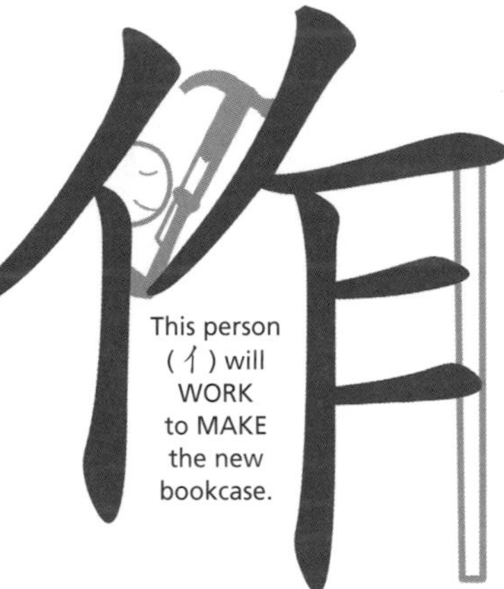

This person (亻) will WORK to MAKE the new bookcase.

8 strokes

 **to use, make**

shǐ

行使 *xíngshǐ* **perform, exercise**

使用 *shǐyòng* **to use, employ, apply**

A person (亻) starts TO USE a table saw to cut one piece of wood.

9 strokes

 **how, what**

zěn

怎样 *zěnyàng* **how, what**

怎么办 *zěnmebàn* **what should be done**

WHAT has he made with all his heart (心)?

9 strokes

保 protect, guarantee, keep

bǎo

保存 ***bǎocún*** **to keep, preservation, conservation**

保险 ***bǎoxiǎn*** **insurance, safety, secure**

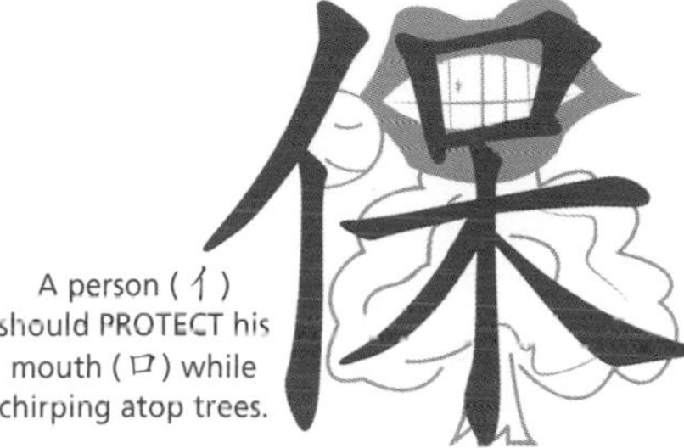

A person (亻) should PROTECT his mouth (口) while chirping atop trees.

7 strokes

 position, place, seat

wèi

位置 ***wèizhì*** **position**

座位 ***zuòwèi*** **seat, place**

The POSITION of the person standing (立) is closest to the SEAT.

A woman uses a mirror to help her appear SIMILAR to the image she wants to RESEMBLE.

6 strokes

似 like, similar, to resemble

sì

相似 ***xiāngsì*** **similar, like**

9 strokes

 repair, mend, study; embellish, decorate

xiū

修理 ***xiūlǐ*** **repairing, mending**

修饰 ***xiūshì*** **to modify, qualify**

After her archery STUDY, she put down her arrow and grabbed the comb that she would DECORATE her hair with.

4 strokes

 by means of, thereafter

yǐ

所以 ***suǒyǐ*** **so, therefore, thus**

以后 ***yǐhòu*** **after, later, hereafter**

BY MEANS OF a mirror, a person (人) views the present, but cannot see what happens THEREAFTER.

7 strokes

何 what, how, why

hé

如何 ***rúhé*** how

为何 ***wèihé*** why

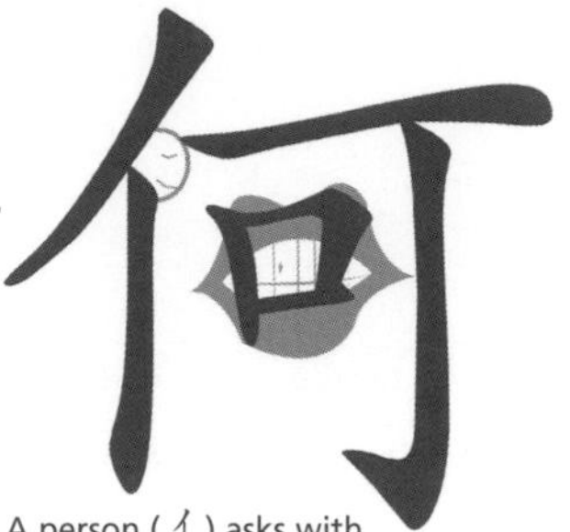

A person (亻) asks with their mouth (口) WHAT something can (可) be.

9 strokes

便 convenient, easy

biàn

方便 ***fāngbiàn*** convenient

轻便 ***qīngbiàn*** light, portable, easy and convenient

It is EASY and more CONVENIENT for a person (亻) to determine how to make soil from a field (田) more profitable by examining it on a table.

A person (亻) uses a spoonful (匕) of spice to TRANSFORM the flavor of a dish.

4 strokes

化 melt, transform, convert

huà

融化 ***rónghuà*** melting, thaw

文化 ***wénhuà*** culture, civilization, literacy

化学 ***huàxué*** chemistry

7 strokes

更 more, further, change

gèng

更加 ***gèngjiā*** more, even more

更好 ***gènghǎo*** better

更改 ***gēnggǎi*** to change, alter, modify

Taking a lid off of a soil sample from the field (田) and examining it on a table, we can determine how to CHANGE it to make it better.

A person (亻) standing (立) on a box can be heard TWICE as loud and can see DOUBLE the distance.

10 strokes

倍 times as many

bèi

倍数 ***bèishù*** multiple

5 strokes

他 he, him, other, another

tā

其他 *qítā* other

他们 *tāmen* they, them

A person (亻) looks at his fishing bobber to see if he has caught ANOTHER fish.

11 strokes

停 stop, cease, pause, halt, stopping

tíng

停止 *tíngzhǐ* to stop, cease, halt

暂停 *zàntíng* to pause, suspend

A person (亻) HALTS at a bus STOP to read the posted bus schedule.

5 strokes

仔 young, offspring

zǐ

仔细 *zǐxì* careful, detailed

The child (子) of a person (亻) is their OFFSPRING.

8 strokes

侧 side

Traditional 側

cè

侧面 *cèmiàn* side, side face

A person (亻) will slip his knife (刂) into one SIDE of a shellfish (贝) to open it.

7 strokes

低 low, beneath

dī

低级 *dījí* low level, elementary, low class

最低 *zuìdī* lowest

Because the table was too LOW on one side, the man put a block BENEATH one leg.

6 strokes

伤 wound, hurt, injure

Traditional 傷

shāng

伤害 *shānghài* to harm, hurt, injure

伤心 *shāngxīn* sad, grieved, broken-hearted

A person (亻) may become HURT or INJURED when exercising too much power (力) with shears.

8 strokes

例 example, case

lì

例子 *lìzi* example

例行 *lìxíng* routine

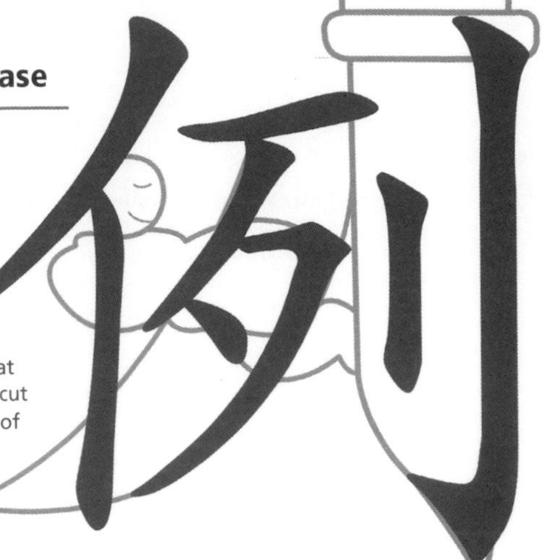

To that person (亻), one EXAMPLE of something that looks as though it has been cut with a knife (刂) is a sliver of the evening (夕) moon.

6 strokes

全 all, entire, whole

quán

完全 *wánquán* complete, entirely

全部 *quánbù* entire, all, everything

ALL the people in the ENTIRE realm of the king (王) supported him.

7 strokes

住 live, reside, stop

zhù

居住 *jūzhù* to live

住宅 *zhùzhái* residence, housing

住口 *zhùkǒu* shut up, stop talking

A man had to ask the master (主) for permission to LIVE in the building where he wanted to RESIDE.

6 strokes

会 can, see, meeting, to meet, association

Traditional 會

huì

会面 *huìmiàn* to meet, get together

社会 *shèhuì* society, community

教会 *jiàohuì* church

A person (人) is going to MEET another to SEE if they could do a couple (二) of exercises.

4 strokes

今 now, the present

jīn

今天 *jīntiān* today

如今 *rújīn* now, nowadays

Look at the person (人) who is NOW in mid-air, jumping a hurdle.

5 strokes

order, command, ancient laws

lìng

指令 *zhǐlìng* orders, command, instructions

命令 *mìnglìng* to order, command

A person's (人) ORDERS were to jump far.

8 strokes

think, idea

niàn

信念 *xìnniàn* belief, faith

概念 *gàiniàn* concept, notion

Now (今) when we put our hearts (心) into something, we might WISH for luck or have a SENSE of our fortunes

3 strokes

individual, unit for articles

Traditional 個

gè

个别 *gèbié* individual, specific

三个 *sāngè* three pieces

A satisfied INDIVIDUAL becomes one with himself.

6 strokes

umbrella

Traditional

sǎn

雨伞 *yǔsǎn* umbrella

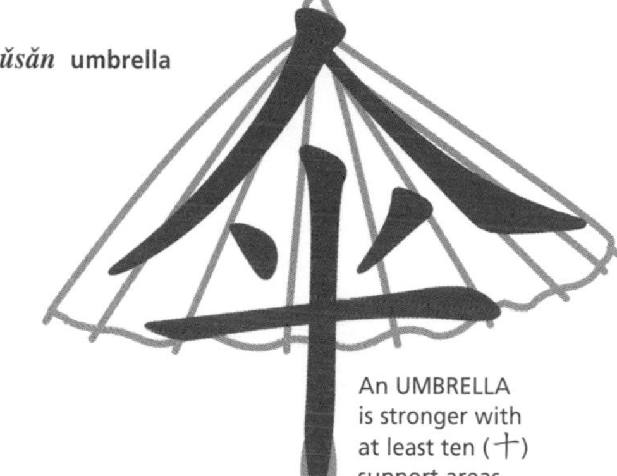

An UMBRELLA is stronger with at least ten (十) support areas.

4 strokes

between

jiè

介绍 *jièshào* to introduce

介入 *jièrù* intervention

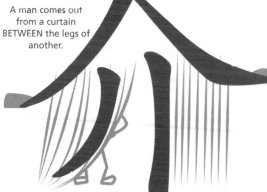

A man comes out from a curtain BETWEEN the legs of another.

10 strokes

拿 take, hold, seize

ná

拿走 *názǒu* to take away, walk off with

捉拿 *zhuōná* to arrest, catch

One person (人) used his hand (手) to TAKE an object that he hopes to HOLD indefinitely.

6 strokes

件 item, piece

jiàn

事件 *shìjiàn* event, case, incident

件数 *jiànshù* number [of things]

A person (亻) with a cow (牛) also needs at least one PIECE of equipment to farm.

10 strokes

借 borrow, lend

jiè

借款 *jièkuǎn* loan

借用 *jièyòng* to borrow, for another purpose

We can BORROW ten things for ten days (日) but must return them before they LEND us more.

6 strokes

任 responsibility, duty, appoint, assign

rèn

责任 *zérèn* responsibility

委任 *wěirèn* to appoint

The DUTY of a warrior (士) was to his leader and they had a RESPONSIBILITY to protect their people.

10 strokes

病 ill, sick

bìng

生病 *shēngbìng* ill, sick

疾病 *jíbìng* illness, disease

流行病 *liúxíngbìng* epidemic disease

A person caught two ailments while climbing up a cliff, and now ILL, resting inside (内) under a blanket.

Family 家族

10 strokes

家 house, home, family

jiā

家人 ***jiārén*** family members

专家 ***zhuānjiā*** expert, specialist

In many places, they kept pigs under the HOUSE to eat scraps and keep things clean.

11 strokes

族 tribe, family

zú

家族 ***jiāzú*** family, household, clan

民族 ***mínzú*** ethnic group, people

种族 ***zhǒngzú*** race, ethnicity

An archer focuses his attention in the direction (方) of taking care of his FAMILY and protecting his TRIBE.

4 strokes

父 father

fù

父亲 ***fùqīn*** father, dad

父母 ***fùmǔ*** parents

My FATHER has big arms and strong legs.

5 strokes

母 mother

mǔ

母亲 ***mǔqīn*** mother

母语 ***mǔyǔ*** mother tongue, native language

This MOTHER is very Picasso-esque in her pose.

5 strokes

兄 older brother

xiōng

兄弟 ***xiōngdì*** brothers, siblings

Sometimes an OLDER BROTHER has a big mouth (口) and struts around with his long legs.

7 strokes

弟 younger brother

dì

弟弟 ***dìdi*** younger brother

弟子 ***dìzǐ*** disciple, pupil, follower

My YOUNGER BROTHER had a bow, arrow, sword, and warrior's helmet.

8 strokes

爸 dad, father

bà

爸爸 ***bàba*** dad, father

爸妈 ***bàmā*** mom and dad, parents

A good DAD or FATHER holds his child in his hand and anxiously wishes (巴) that she will be safe.

8 strokes

姐 elder sister

jiě

姐姐 ***jiějie*** elder sister

姐妹 ***jiěmèi*** sisters

小姐 ***xiǎojiě*** Miss

My ELDER SISTER has lots of shelves for books and clothes.

6 strokes

妈 mom, mother

Traditional 媽

mā

妈妈 ***māma*** mom

婆婆妈妈 ***pópomāmā*** maudlin, overly sensitive, mawkish

8 strokes

妹 younger sister

mèi

妹妹 ***mèimei*** younger sister

妹夫 ***mèifū*** brother-in-law (husband of younger sister)

Dad made a tree house for my YOUNGER SISTER.

The MOTHER had a female (女) horse (马).

11 strokes

婚 marriage

hūn

结婚 *jiéhūn* **to marry, get married**

离婚 *líhūn* **to divorce**

The woman (女) had planned her MARRIAGE for many days (日).

6 strokes

妇 lady, woman

Traditional 婦

fù

妇女 *fùnǚ* **woman**

主妇 *zhǔfù* **housewife, homemaker**

A WOMAN (女) sits beside a large stack of folded clothes.

4 strokes

夫 husband, man

fū

丈夫 *zhàngfū* **husband**

夫妇 *fūfù* **married couple**

If there is a HUSBAND, there are usually two (二) people together who are in love.

7 strokes

男 male

nán

男性 *nánxìng* **male[s]**

男子汉 *nánzǐhàn* **a manly man, man**

Traditionally, MALES were the ones who exerted strength [力] planting rice fields [田].

8 strokes

规 rule, custom

Traditional 規

guī

规则 *guīzé* **rule, regulation**

规矩 *guījǔ* **custom, well-disciplined**

规模 *guīmó* **scale, scope**

The husband (夫) had a CUSTOM of looking at anything that was around.

3 strokes

女 female, woman

nǚ

女人 ***nǚrén*** woman

女孩 ***nǚhái*** girl

女儿 ***nǚér*** daughter

This WOMAN is relaxing, legs crossed, hands openly welcoming.

10 strokes

娘 mother, girl

niáng

姑娘 ***gūniáng*** girl, young woman

A female (女) GIRL often brings good (良) smiles to her MOTHER.

8 strokes

姑 aunt

gū

姑母 ***gūmǔ*** aunt (father's sister)

姑息 ***gūxí*** to appease, tolerate

An AUNT can be a woman (女) possessing age-old (古) knowledge.

6 strokes

孙 grandchild, descendants

Traditional 孫

sūn

孙儿 ***sūnér*** grandson

子孙 ***zǐsūn*** descendants, offspring

A GRANDCHILD is a special little (小) child (子) born into the family.

6 strokes

好 good, well, like, fond

hǎo/hào

很好 ***hěn hǎo*** very good

爱好 ***àihào*** hobby, interest, hiking

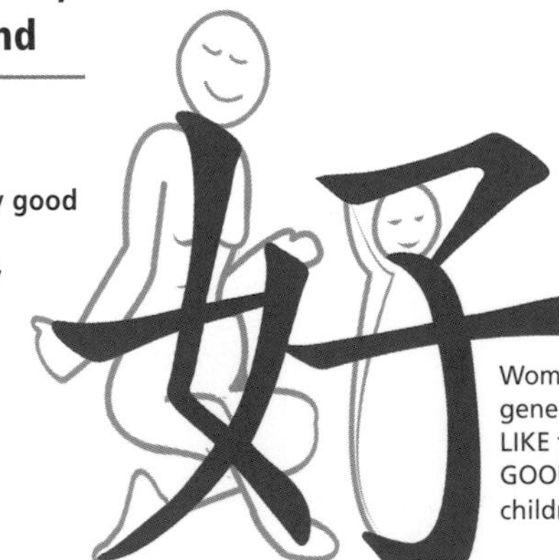

Women (女) generally LIKE taking GOOD care of children (子).

6 strokes

如 as, if

rú

如同 *rútóng* as, like

如果 *rúguǒ* if, in case

如此 *rúcǐ* so, in this way

A woman (女) opens her mouth (口) IF she sees something she needs to mention.

9 strokes

姿 posture, manner, figure

zī

姿态 *zītài* attitude, posture, stance

姿势 *zīshì* posture, position

姿色 *zīsè* pretty, good-looking

After fanning herself in a vigorous MANNER, a woman (女) next (次) adjusts her POSTURE.

8 strokes

始 commence, begin, start

shǐ

开始 *kāishǐ* start, beginning

始创 *shǐchuàng* pioneer, to create

When the woman (女) had a platform (台) she would BEGIN to tell a story.

6 strokes

次 secondary, next, order, sequence

cì

次要 *cìyào* secondary, minor, subordinate

次序 *cìxù* order

其次 *qícì* next, secondary

After a SEQUENCE of events causing beads of persperation, she NEXT vigorously fanned herself.

10 strokes

资 money, invest

Traditional 資

zī

资金 *zījīn* funds

资产 *zīchǎn* assets, property

投资 *tóuzī* to invest, investment

After the next (次) successful INVESTMENT, you can afford to eat oysters and other shellfish (贝).

8 strokes

妻 **wife, spouse**

qī

妻子 ***qīzi*** wife

夫妻 ***fūqī*** husband and wife

The artist loves his WIFE but grips his favorite brush almost as tightly as he does the woman (女) he loves.

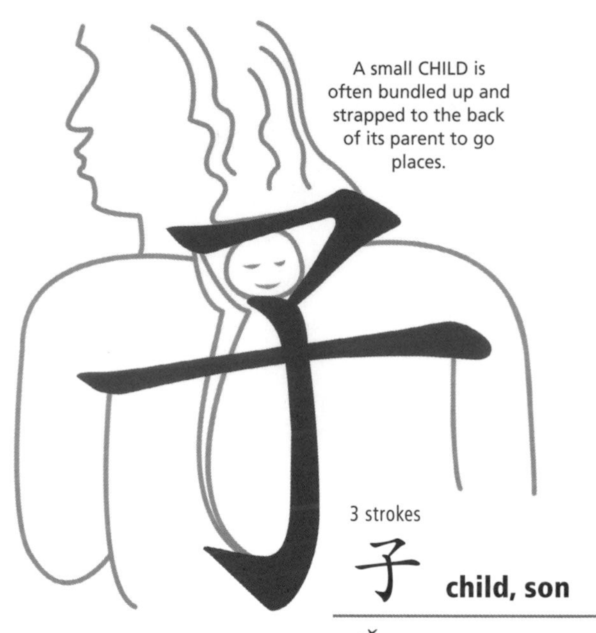

A small CHILD is often bundled up and strapped to the back of its parent to go places.

3 strokes

子 **child, son**

zǐ

孩子 ***háizi*** child, children

儿子 ***érzi*** son

9 strokes

要 **need, want, demand**

yào/yāo

需要 ***xūyào*** to need, want

要求 ***yāoqiú*** to request, require, demand

The NEED to make a DEMAND by the woman (女) led her to pull down a screen on the west (西) wall to explain exactly what she WANTED.

2 strokes

了 **end, finish; verb particle for a new situation or a completed action**

le

好了 ***hǎole*** well, ok

我饿了 ***wǒèle*** I am hungry

做好了 ***zuòhǎole*** to complete, finish

To FINISH first, the child will stand on his own without being strapped to his mother's back in the END.

8 strokes

委 **appoint, committee, entrust to**

wěi

委任 ***wěirèn*** to appoint

委员会 ***wěiyuánhuì*** committee, commission

委屈 ***wěiqu*** grievance

A wealthy woman (女) decided to APPOINT a preservation COMMITTEE to care for these trees (木).

9 strokes

孩 child

hái

小孩 *xiǎohái* child

男孩 *nánhái* boy

女孩 *nǚhái* girl

When two people lie together under coverings, they may produce a CHILD (子).

6 strokes

字 character, letter

zì

汉字 *hànzì* Chinese character

文字 *wénzì* writing, script

Children (子) learned to write their LETTERS and CHARACTERS at home under their parents' roof (宀).

6 strokes

 存 deposit, keep, retain

cún

储存 *chúcún* deposit, to store

存在 *cúnzài* to exist, existence, presence

保存 *bǎocún* to save, keep, preserve

To RETAIN knowledge is difficult for some children (子) as they jump over hurdles to KEEP up.

6 strokes

 共 common, general, together

gòng

公共 *gōnggòng* public, common, community

一共 *yīgòng* altogether

Friends stand TOGETHER atop a volcano.

5 strokes

 民 people, nation

mín

人民 *rénmín* people

公民 *gōngmín* citizen

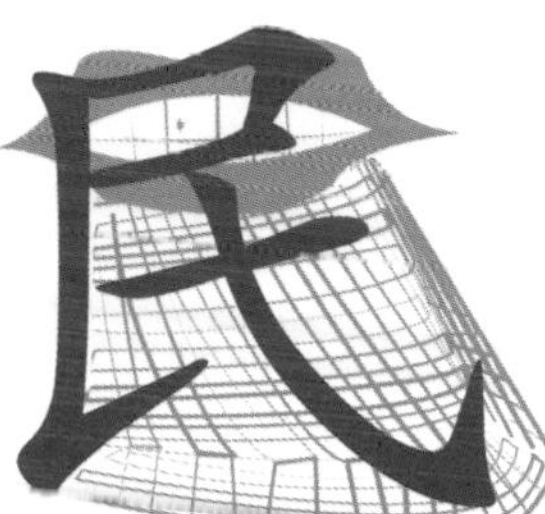

Mouths (口) of PEOPLE and languages are woven together to make up a NATION.

7 strokes

孝 filial piety, respect for elders

xiào

孝顺 ***xiàoshùn*** **filial piety**

不孝 ***bùxiào*** **unfilial to one's parents**

Families with RESPECT FOR ELDERS would return with their children (子) to the land (土), cut and tilled by their parents, once a year.

11 strokes

教 teach, instruct; religion, faith

jiào

教师 ***jiàoshī*** **teacher**

教科书 ***jiàokēshū*** **textbook**

宗教 ***zōngjiào*** **religion**

We TEACH children (子) at folding tables as ground (土) is broken with a sword for a new school in which to INSTRUCT them.

The child (子) reaches into the PLUM tree (木) for fruit.

7 strokes

李 plum, common Chinese last name (Li)

lǐ

李子 ***lǐzi*** **plums**

行李 ***xínglǐ*** **luggage, baggage**

8 strokes

 study, learn, imitate

Traditional

xué

学习 ***xuéxí*** **to learn, study**

学生 ***xuéshēng*** **student, scholar**

学校 ***xuéxiào*** **school**

Three bits of knowledge trickle down through the roof above a child (子) for him/her to STUDY and LEARN.

8 strokes

 seasons

jì

季节 ***jìjié*** **season, period**

四季 ***sìjì*** **four seasons**

Trees (木) help children (子) learn about colors and SEASONS.

Man on the Move 彳

This man on the move (彳) uses a brush to record LAWS.

9 strokes

律 **law, discipline, control, rhythm**

lǜ

法律 ***fǎlǜ*** law

纪律 ***jìlǜ*** discipline

旋律 ***xuánlǜ*** melody, rhythm

8 strokes

径 **path, diameter** Traditional 徑

jìng

途径 ***tújìng*** path, way

捷径 ***jiéjìng*** shortcut

直径 ***zhíjìng*** diameter

A moving man (彳) moves in a circular PATH as he rotates around a table on a pedestal to measure its DIAMETER.

8 strokes

往 **go, toward, past**

wǎng

前往 ***qiánwǎng*** to go, proceed, leave for

往昔 ***wǎngxī*** in former times, early times, yore

A moving man (彳) walks TOWARD his lord (主) to seek favors.

15 strokes

 **ethics, virtue, morality**

dé

道德 ***dàodé*** morals, virtue, ethics

美德 ***měidé*** virtue

A moving man (彳) with good ETHICS has a VIRTUOUS heart (心) and looks at things ten (十) times from all sides before making a decision.

9 strokes

待 wait, depend on

dài

等待 *děngdài* **to wait, await**

招待 *zhāodài* **to entertain, serve; reception**

Moving men (彳) WAIT at a temple (寺) when they DEPEND ON someone to answer their requests for favors.

11 strokes

得 gain, acquire, can

dé

得到 *dédào* **to gain, obtain, receive**

得意 *déyì* **proud, pleased, self-satisfied**

A man on the move (彳) at break of day (日) takes measures of what he can GAIN and ACQUIRE.

10 strokes

徒 disciple, follower; on foot

tú

学徒 *xuétú* **apprentice, learner, trainee**

教徒 *jiàotú* **follower, believer**

徒步 *túbù* **on foot**

A man on the move (彳) with his FOLLOWER walk the lands (土) of national parks.

12 strokes

街 boulevard, street, town

jiē

街道 *jiēdào* **street, neighborhood**

逛街 *guàngjiē* **shopping**

A moving man (彳) walks down a BOULEVARD in the TOWN with land (土) on both sides.

5 strokes

术 art, technique, skill

Traditional 術

shù

艺术 *yìshù* **the arts**

美术 *měishù* **fine art, painting**

技术 *jìshù* **technology, technique, skill**

ART often has a wooden (木) armature or pedestal.

9 strokes

复 repeat, restore, return to

Traditional 復

fù

恢复 *huīfù* **to resume, renew, recover**

复原 *fùyuán* **restoration, rehabilitation**

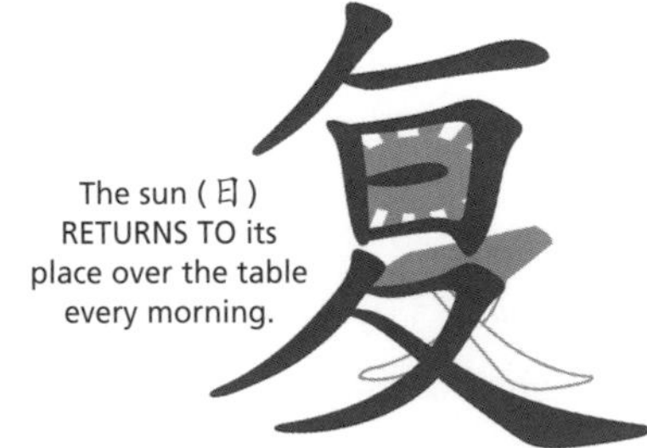

The sun (日) RETURNS TO its place over the table every morning.

Self 自/厶/己

10 strokes

stinking, ill-smelling, odor

chòu

恶臭 *èchòu* stink, stench

口臭 *kǒuchòu* bad breath, halitosis

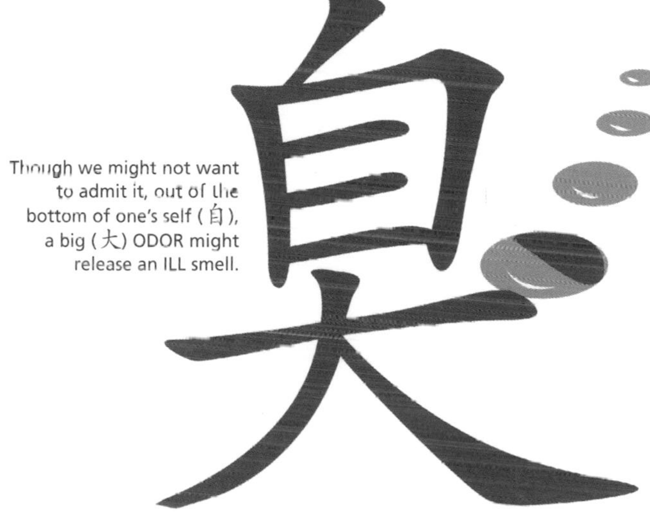

Though we might not want to admit it, out of the bottom of one's self (自), a big (大) ODOR might release an ILL smell.

6 strokes

oneself, self

zì

自己 *zìjǐ* self, oneself, myself

自由 *zìyóu* freedom, liberty

Look here, closely into my eye (目), to see the SELF I've become.

A person stands with his BODY up tall, a sword and scabbard at his side.

7 strokes

身 **body, oneself**

shēn

身体 *shēntǐ* body

身份 *shēnfèn* identity, status

7 strokes

Buddha

fó

佛教 *fójiào* Buddhism

佛像 *fóxiàng* the Buddha

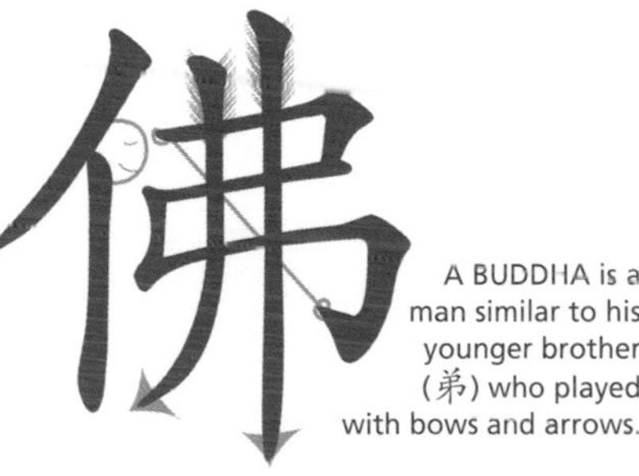

A BUDDHA is a man similar to his younger brother (弟) who played with bows and arrows.

4 strokes

公 public, fair, common

gōng

公平 *gōngpíng* fair, equality, just

公园 *gōngyuán* public park

公共 *gōnggòng* public, community

In a PUBLIC bureaucracy, it is COMMON to need the approval of eight (八) council members for something I write.

3 strokes

 self, oneself

jǐ

自己 *zìjǐ* self, oneself

知己 *zhījǐ* close friend

The snakelike shape of this character can easily turn and look back upon ITSELF.

8 strokes

 participate, join, attend

Traditional 參

cān

参加 *cānjiā* to participate, join, take part

参考 *cānkǎo* to consult, refer

I will PARTICIPATE in three big (大) events that I plan to ATTEND.

8 strokes

 scroll, volume, to roll

juǎn/juàn

春卷 *chūnjuǎn* spring roll

试卷 *shìjuàn* examination/test paper

The man made big (大) arm motions as the snake began to ROLL itself up like a long SCROLL.

CHAPTER 3

THE BODY

7 strokes

体 **body, form** Traditional 體

tǐ

体育 *tǐyù* **sports, physical training**

体重 *tǐzhòng* **body weight**

The BODY is the trunk of a person's physical FORM.

Body 体

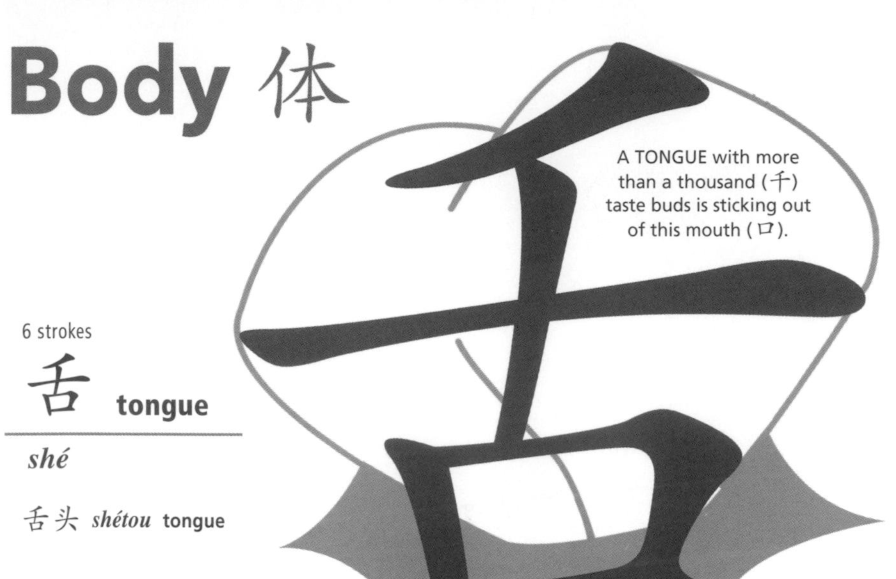

A TONGUE with more than a thousand (千) taste buds is sticking out of this mouth (口).

6 strokes

舌 tongue

shé

舌头 ***shétou*** tongue

17 strokes

臂 arm

bì

手臂 ***shǒubì*** arm

膀臂 ***bǎngbì*** arm, upper arm, reliable helper

His ARM muscles got bigger as he worked out by the light of the moon (月) in a laborious (辛) way, standing and balancing on a pole.

9 strokes

 back

bèi

背面 ***bèimiàn*** back, rear

背景 ***bèijǐng*** background, scenery

BACK in the winter, the moon (月) seemed to provide most of the light at the North (北) Pole.

14 strokes

精 spirit, precise, excellent

jīng

精神 ***jīngshén*** spirit

精确 ***jīngquè*** accurate, precise

精彩 ***jīngcǎi*** wonderful, excellent

The EXCELLENT rice (米) that grew by the light of the moon (月) was awarded a blue (青) ribbon.

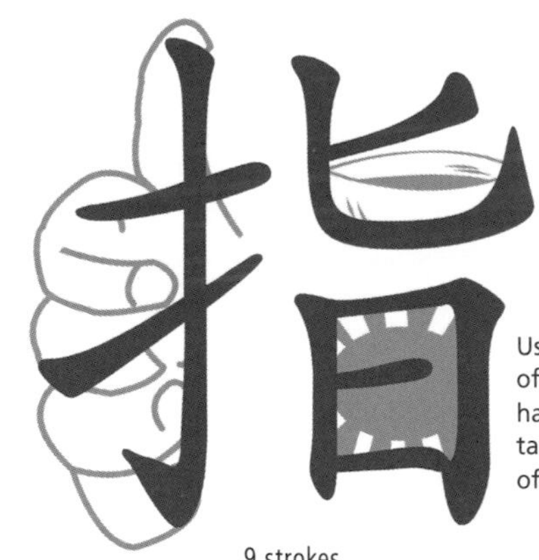

Use a FINGER of your clean hand (扌) to taste the soup of the day (日).

9 strokes

指 finger, point to, indicate

zhǐ

手指 ***shǒuzhǐ*** finger

指导 ***zhǐdǎo*** to direct, instruct, guide; leadership

9 strokes

胃 stomach

wèi

肠胃 ***chángwèi*** intestines and stomach

胃痛 ***wèitòng*** stomach-ache

胃癌 ***wèi'ái*** stomach cancer

If you eat too much, your STOMACH grows like a fertile field (田) under the moon.

11 strokes

趾 toes

zhǐ

脚趾 ***jiǎozhǐ*** toes

拇趾 ***mǔzhǐ*** big toe, hallux

You want to be doubly vocal in telling someone to stop (止) if they are about to step on your TOES.

7 strokes

 leg, foot, enough, satisfy

zú

足球 ***zúqiú*** soccer

充足 ***chōngzú*** adequate, sufficient

This is a profile of a person with a mouth (口) atop a body with a forward facing arm and an exaggerated FOOT.

4 strokes

心 heart, mind

xīn

心脏 ***xīnzàng*** heart

中心 ***zhōngxīn*** center, core

小心 ***xiǎoxīn*** careful

The character for HEART has four lines and the heart has four chambers.

13 strokes

 follow, heel

gēn

跟随 ***gēnsuí*** to follow, tack

跟踪 ***gēnzōng*** to track, scout

脚跟 ***jiǎogēn*** heel

Stop (止) and FOLLOW on the HEEL of another.

4 strokes

 hand

shǒu

拍手 ***pāishǒu*** to clap hands, applaud

选手 ***xuǎnshǒu*** athlete, contestant, player [in a game]

This HAND has four strokes and four fingers (plus a thumb).

Head 头

5 strokes

头 **head, counter for animals** Traditional 頭

tóu

头部 ***tóubù*** **head**

一头牛 ***yītóuniú*** **a cow**

A bean counter might count large animals, adding up the HEADS of cows and horses, as he writes totals on the pages of a ledger.

11 strokes

脸 **face** Traditional 臉

liǎn

洗脸 ***xǐliǎn*** **to wash up, wash the face**

丢脸 ***diūliǎn*** **humiliation, loss of face, embarrassing**

The moon is refected on the slated roof like a FACE.

15 strokes

颜 **color, face** Traditional 顏

yán

颜色 ***yánsè*** **color**

容颜 ***róngyán*** **face**

A FACE looking up on the right, a top hat with flowing hair below, his neck on the left.

5 strokes

发 **hair** Traditional 髮

fà

头发 ***tóufà*** **hair (on the head)**

理发 ***lǐfà*** **haircut, hairdressing**

My friend (友) always plays with her long HAIR.

10 strokes

脑 **brain** Traditional 腦

nǎo

动脑筋 ***dòngnǎojīn*** **thinking, to think hard**

头脑 ***tóunǎo*** **mind, brains**

电脑 ***diànnǎo*** **computer**

Once a month (月), my BRAIN feels like it is in a pot about to be cooked like noodles.

5 strokes

目 **eye, look, insight**

mù

目的 ***mùdì*** **purpose, aim, goal**

目录 ***mùlù*** **directory, catalog, table of contents**

A sleepy EYE sees things sidewise.

3 strokes

口 mouth

kǒu

人口 *rénkǒu* population

入口 *rùkǒu* entrance; to import

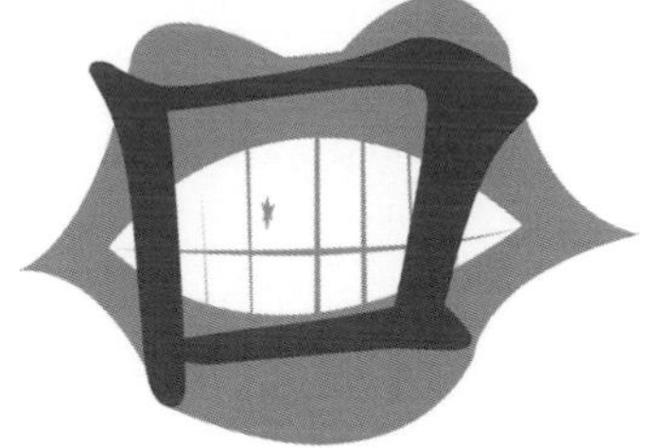

This is an open MOUTH.

6 strokes

耳 ear

ěr

耳朵 *ěrduo* ear

This is an EAR with a dangling earring.

9 strokes

首 head, first, chief

shǒu

首先 *shǒuxiān* first

首长 *shǒuzhǎng* senior official, principal

首都 *shǒudū* capital [city]

I myself (自) have a little NECK below a fancy collar.

11 strokes

眼 eye

yǎn

眼睛 *yǎnjing* eye

眼泪 *yǎnlèi* tear

To make my left eye (目) good (良), my EYES need glasses.

14 strokes

鼻 nose

bí

鼻子 *bízi* nose

鼻水 *bíshuǐ* dripping nose

鼻涕 *bítì* snivel, nasal mucus

I use my NOSE to take a whiff myself (自) and smell the fragrance of the field (田) by the gate.

11 strokes

颈 neck

Traditional 頸

jǐng

颈部 *jǐngbù* neck, throat

长颈鹿 *chángjǐnglù* giraffe

The muscled NECK of a laborer (工) is much thicker than the core of a rolled up sheet of paper (页) or hanging scroll.

Mouth 口

8 strokes

call out to, shout, breathe

hū

呼吸 *hūxī* **breathing, respiration**

呼叫 *hūjiào* **to call, shout, yell**

This little person stands tall, waving his arms to CALL OUT TO a friend.

8 strokes

and, peace, harmony

hé

和平 *hépíng* **peace**

和谐 *héxié* **harmony**

柔和 *róuhé* **soft, mild, gentle**

A tree seems to whisper messages of PEACE and HARMONY as it is blown by the wind.

9 strokes

what, where

nǎ

哪 *nǎ* **what? which one?**

哪儿 *nǎer* **where?**

在哪儿 *zàinǎer* **where? in which place?**

A person wants to ask WHAT is happening and WHERE that child who climbed to the moon (月) came from.

9 strokes

sound, noise

Traditional

xiǎng

音响 *yīnxiǎng* **sound**

响亮 *xiǎngliàng* **loud and clear**

影响 *yǐngxiǎng* **to influence, affect**

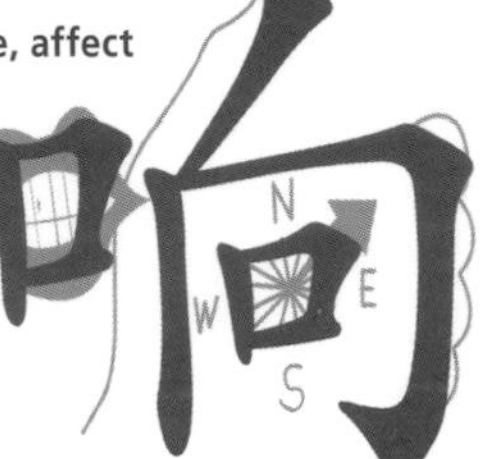

When a mouth (口) makes a SOUND or you hear a loud NOISE, turn toward (向) its direction to see what it is.

6 strokes

吗 **interrogative particle**

Traditional

嗎

ma

你好吗? *nǐhǎoma* **How are you?/ Are you good?**

好吗? *hǎoma* **Is it okay?**

A horse whisperer murmurs calming interrogatives to horses (马).

7 strokes

吧 used at the end of sentence to indicate a suggestion

ba

走吧 *zǒuba* let's go

好吧 *hǎoba* Okay, well

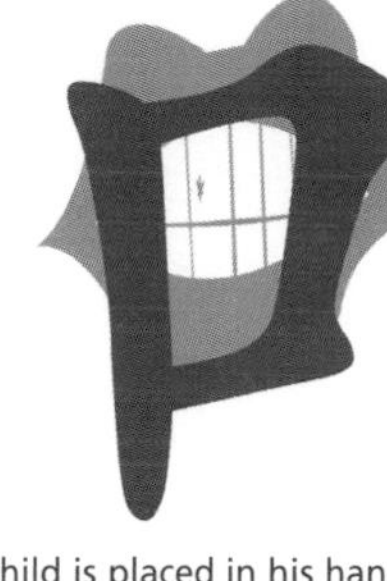

When a child is placed in his hand, he might anxiously wish (巴) that the mother will vocally INDICATE A SUGGESTION or two about what to do.

6 strokes

吃 eat

chī

吃饭 *chīfàn* to eat, have a meal

小吃 *xiǎochī* snack, refreshment

吃素 *chīsù* vegetarian

Both men and animals open their mouths (口) wide to EAT.

6 strokes

吸 inhale, breathe

xī

吸收 *xīshōu* to absorb

吸烟 *xīyān* to smoke

吸引 *xīyǐn* to attract

Use your mouth (口) to BREATHE when exercising on a platform or when climbing anything that looks like stairs.

5 strokes

另 other, besides

lìng

另外 *lìngwài* other, additional

另类 *lìnglèi* alternative

OTHER than being a good speaker, he has a lot of power (力) backing him.

12 strokes

喝 drink; shout

hē/hè

喝茶 *hēchá* to drink tea

喝彩 *hècǎi* to applaud, cheer

喝令 *hèlìng* to order, shout a command

After being wrapped up in his work all day (日), the small boy asked for something to DRINK.

5 strokes

只 just, only, merely

zhǐ

只是 *zhǐshì* just, only, merely

只好 *zhǐhǎo* have to, be forced to

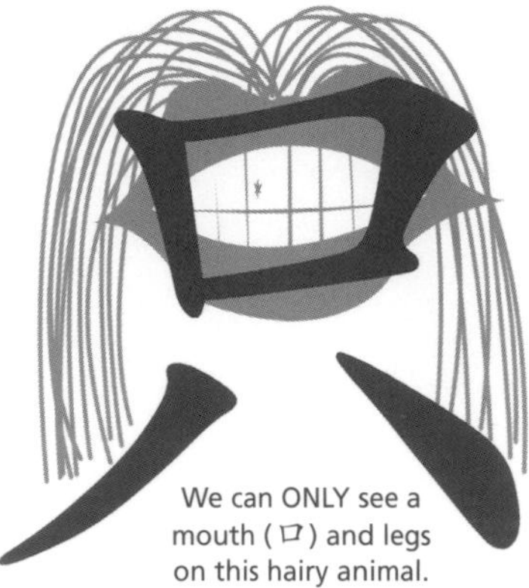

We can ONLY see a mouth (口) and legs on this hairy animal.

5 strokes

可 can

kě

可以 *kěyǐ* can

可爱 *kě'ài* lovely

Put a tack on a location on a map to say where we CAN go.

5 strokes

句 phrase, sentence

jù

句子 *jùzi* sentence

句法 *jùfǎ* sentence structure

A mouth (口) uses the occasional PHRASE and SENTENCE to talk around a topic.

2 strokes

丁 man, population, fourth heavenly stem (used in Chinese calendar), cubes (of food)

dīng

人丁 *réndīng* population

鸡丁 *jīdīng* diced chicken

5 strokes

司 department, director, administer

sī

公司 *gōngsī* company, firm, corporation

司令 *sīlìng* commander

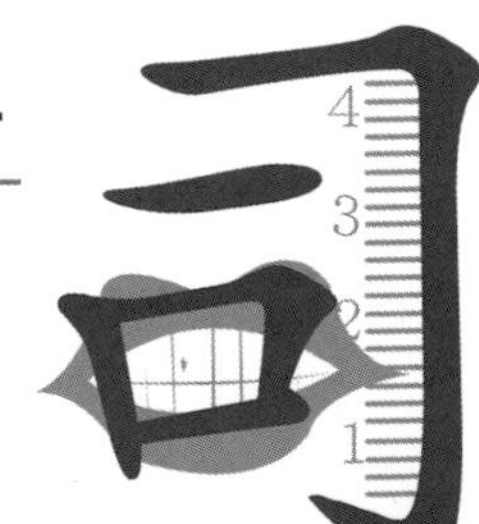

The DIRECTOR had to mouth (口) the orders to his DEPARTMENT in a voice at a higher level than normal.

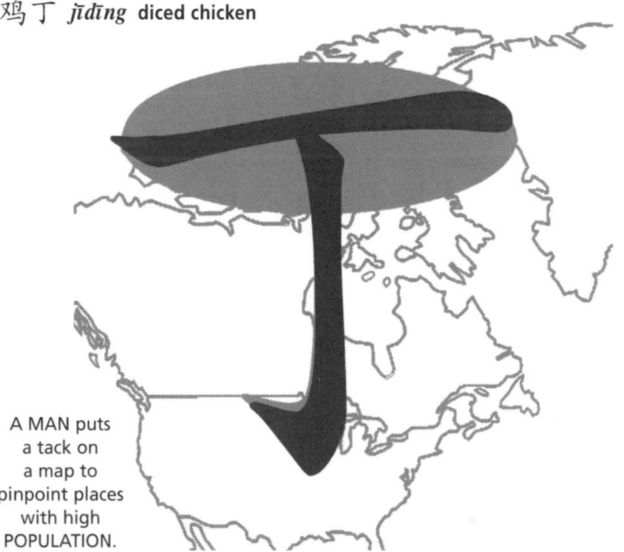

A MAN puts a tack on a map to pinpoint places with high POPULATION.

5 strokes

台 a stand, pedestal, platform

tái

平台 *píngtái* platform, terrace

舞台 *wǔtái* stage [theater]

Sometimes I say things with my mouth (口) as though I am standing on a PEDESTAL.

6 strokes

吏 officer, minor official

lì

公吏 *gōnglì* public officials

An OFFICER must train you to use (使) the equipment.

11 strokes

 send, post

jì

邮寄 *yóujì* to post, send by post

寄托 *jìtuō* to place, consign, repose

Under a roof with a chimney (宀), a big (大) group gathers to listen to one (一) mouth (口) talk about another person before they SEND him off.

6 strokes

向 direction, face, toward

xiàng

方向 *fāngxiàng* direction

This hand is holding a compass FACING the DIRECTION of northeast.

6 strokes

 after, behind

Traditional 後

hòu

后面 *hòumiàn* back, behind, rear

后果 *hòuguǒ* aftermath, consequence

A highly ranked person from BEHIND made an announcement.

6 strokes

各 each, every

gè

各人 ***gèrén*** **everyone, each person; individual, personal**

各样 ***gèyàng*** **every, many ways, various methods**

EACH and EVERY way you look at a folding table from the top, it might still look like a square.

6 strokes

合 close, fit, suit, join

hé

适合 ***shìhé*** **to suit, fit**

联合 ***liánhé*** **to unite, joint**

联合国 ***liánhéguó*** **United Nations**

When a man (人) tries on one (一) thing that SUITS him, his mouth (口) will say happy things if it actually FITS.

As a child, I remember hearing my mother's mouth (口) calling my NAME to come in for the evening (夕).

6 strokes

名 name, reputation

míng

名字 ***míngzì*** **name**

有名 ***yǒumíng*** **famous, well-known**

Looking at a situation, you must AGREE to say (口) that things are the SAME on all sides and totally EQUAL.

6 strokes

同 with; together; agree; same, equal

tóng

相同 ***xiāngtóng*** **same, identical, equal**

同意 ***tóngyì*** **to agree, consent, approve**

7 strokes

告 say, inform, tell, accuse, notify

gào

告诉 ***gàosu*** **to tell, to inform**

控告 ***kònggào*** **to accuse, sue, charge**

广告 ***guǎnggào*** **advertisement**

NOTIFY me if the soil (土) sprouts new life and SAY something to others too.

7 strokes

君 **monarch, ruler, gentleman**

jūn

君权 ***jūnquán*** **monarchy**

君子 ***jūnzǐ*** **gentleman**

Speak politely when addressing a GENTLEMAN or a RULER who wears an official rank on his sleeve.

8 strokes

命 **life, fate**

mìng

生命 ***shēngmìng*** **life**

命运 ***mìngyùn*** **fate**

A man (人) said that FATE has dictated the path of his LIFE as if it were a row furrowed by a hoe in a field

13 strokes

群 **group, crowd**

Traditional 羣

qún

人群 ***rénqún*** **crowd**

群体 ***qúntǐ*** **group, community**

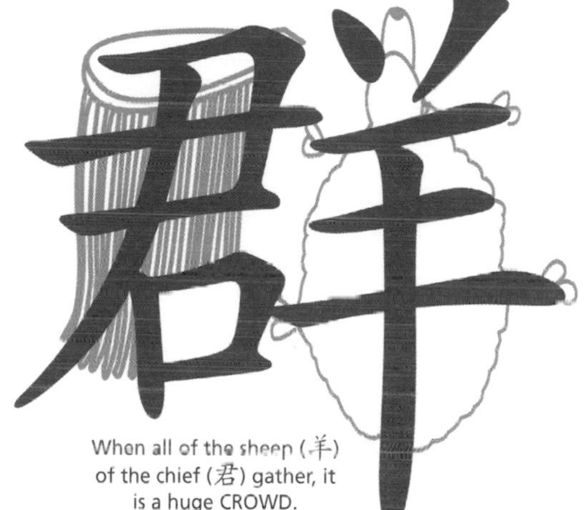

When all of the sheep (羊) of the chief (君) gather, it is a huge CROWD.

7 strokes

否 **negative; no; refuse, decline**

fǒu

否认 ***fǒurèn*** **to deny, denial**

否则 ***fǒuzé*** **otherwise**

To DECLINE or REFUSE, say NO (不) clearly with your mouth (口).

4 strokes

不 **negative, non–**

bù

不好 ***bùhǎo*** **not good**

不要 ***búyào*** **don't want**

Roots exist, but only in the NEGATIVE space we don't see below ground.

8 strokes

周 circumference, circuit

zhōu

周围 *zhōuwéi* around, surrounding

周全 *zhōuquán* thorough, comprehensive

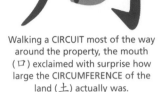

Walking a CIRCUIT most of the way around the property, the mouth (口) exclaimed with surprise how large the CIRCUMFERENCE of the land (土) actually was.

8 strokes

味 flavor, taste, smell

wèi

味道 *wèidào* flavor, taste

趣味 *qùwèi* interest, hobby, liking

The fruit from the upper branches of the tree has the best FLAVOR.

11 strokes

营 operate, trade, conduct (business)

Traditional

營

yíng

营业 *yíngyè* to do business, trade, operate

经营 *jīngyíng* to run a business

When you CONDUCT business in adverse conditions, you may need to rely on word of mouth (口) to cut through the weeds and tall grass (艹) to OPERATE efficiently.

9 strokes

品 goods, article(s), quality

pǐn

食品 *shípǐn* food, foodstuffs

品质 *pǐnzhí* quality

物品 *wùpǐn* goods, articles

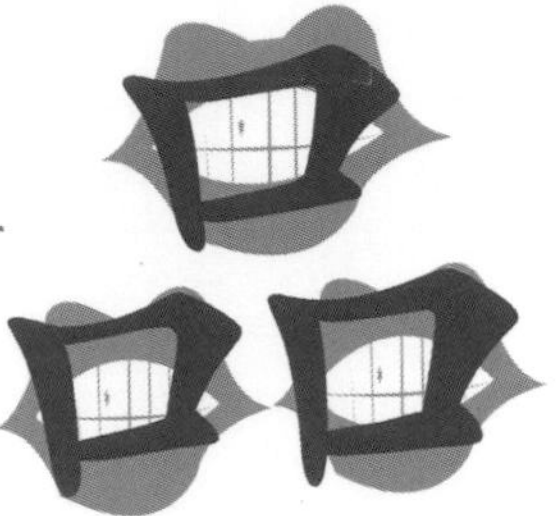

With three mouths (口) to feed, one must purchase a lot of GOODS or ARTICLES.

14 strokes

歌 sing, song

gē

歌曲 *gēqǔ* song

唱歌 *chànggē* to sing a song

歌手 *gēshǒu* singer

The mouths (口) of the choir SING as the conductor directs.

11 strokes

唱 to sing, to recite, to chant

chàng

唱歌 *chànggē* to sing a song

合唱团 *héchàngtuán* chorus, choir

I SING a CHANT about the sun (日).

16 strokes

器 utensil, implement, instrument

qì

器具 ***qìjù*** appliance, utensil, implement, ware

器材 ***qìcái*** equipment, materials

Four mouths (口) sitting around a big (大) table need UTENSILS to eat dinner.

12 strokes

喜 like, joy, rejoice, take pleasure in

xǐ

喜欢 ***xǐhuan*** to like, fond of

喜剧 ***xǐjù*** comedy, funny show

欢喜 ***huānxǐ*** to be delighted, to be glad, joyful

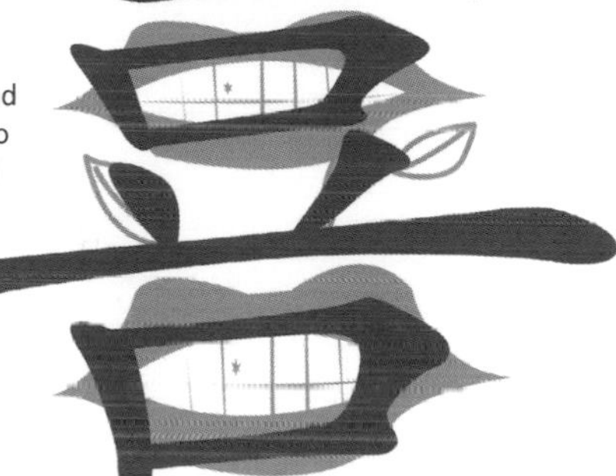

A warrior used the soil (士) to plant his crops, and his mouth (口) opened to REJOICE in PLEASURE IN seeing what he grew.

13 strokes

辞 word, resign, term

Traditional 辭

cí

言辞 ***yáncí*** words

辞职 ***cízhí*** to resign, quit [job]

If a naughty child stands (立) up and says a bitter (辛) WORD or uses bad TERMS, he might also stick out his tongue (舌).

5 strokes

古 old, ancient

gǔ

古老 ***gǔlǎo*** old, ancient

古董 ***gǔdǒng*** antique, curio

An OLD cross tops off an ANCIENT headstone.

9 strokes

故 intentionally, the late

gù

故事 ***gùshì*** story, tale, narrative

故乡 ***gùxiāng*** hometown

故意 ***gùyì*** intentionally, deliberately

Do not INTENTIONALLY sit on the old (古) folding table THE LATE woodworker made.

Eye 目 and Ear 耳

11 strokes

着 **wear, used after a word to form a preposition**

Traditional 著

zhuó

穿着 *chuānzhuó* clothes, apparel

着重 *zhuózhòng* to focus, emphasize

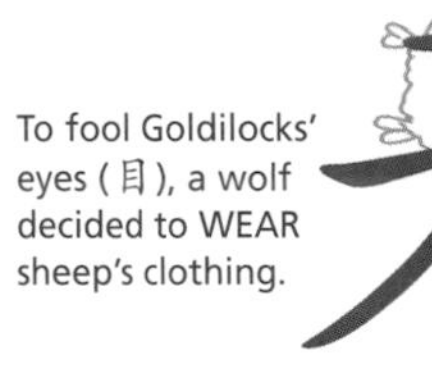

To fool Goldilocks' eyes (目), a wolf decided to WEAR sheep's clothing.

9 strokes

省 **province, save, omit**

shěng

省份 *shěngfèn* province

节省 *jiéshěng* to save, economize, thrift

Use ones eye (目) to OMIT a few (少) details and SAVE the situation as if with a sword.

9 strokes

看 **watch over, see, look**

kàn/kān

看见 *kànjiàn* to see, sight

看守 *kānshǒu* to watch over, guard

A person who WATCHES OVER another who is sick will often cast an eye (目) over the patient and check for a fever with one hand (手).

Using your eyes (目), you can see the details of wood (木) and how they MUTUALLY blend together to form a tree.

9 strokes

相 **mutually; minister**

xiāng/xiàng

互相 *hùxiāng* mutual, each other

相信 *xiāngxìn* to believe, trust

首相 *shǒuxiàng* Prime Minister

A MASK for one eye (目) lies on its side.

9 strokes

面 **surface, face, mask**

miàn

表面 *biǎomiàn* surface

面具 *miànjù* mask

13 strokes

署 sign, signature, office

shǔ

签署 *qiānshǔ* to sign, undersign

署名 *shǔmíng* signature

事务署 *shìwùshǔ* services department

One day (日), a person who used a blade to till his neighbor's land (土) had to go to an OFFICE to SIGN some papers.

8 strokes

直 straight, directly, vertical, straightaway

zhí

正直 *zhèngzhí* upright, honesty

直接 *zhíjiē* direct, firsthand

A VERTICAL eye (目) stares DIRECTLY at a target for ten (十) seconds.

13 strokes

罪 guilt, sin, crime

zuì

犯罪 *fànzuì* crime, offense, to commit a crime

有罪 *yǒuzuì* guilty, culpability

罪犯 *zuìfàn* criminal

People who are GUILTY of a serious CRIME have bars in their slotted cell doors.

10 strokes

值 worth, value

zhí

价值 *jiàzhí* worth, value, price

值得 *zhídé* to deserve, merit

A person (亻) sometimes knows that the VALUE of goods is actually ten (十) times the price and buying it would be WORTH the price paid.

13 strokes

置 placement, put, set

zhì

放置 *fàngzhì* to put/place/leave [behind]

设置 *shèzhì* to set up, install

位置 *wèizhì* location, place, position

PUT an object down and look at it with your eyes (目) ten (十) different ways to before you determine the best PLACEMENT for it.

10 strokes

真 true, genuine, true reality

zhēn

真正 *zhēnzhèng* real, true, genuine

真诚 *zhēnchéng* sincere

Ten (十) eyes (目) look to examine the table and see what the TRUE REALITY might be.

9 strokes

闻 hear, listen

Traditional  聞

wén

听闻 *tīngwén* heard, to listen, hear

新闻 *xīnwén* news

闻名 *wénmíng* famous, well-known

Put your ear (耳) to the gate to LISTEN.

8 strokes

 具 tool, utensil

jù

工具 *gōngjù* tool, equipment, utensil

家具 *jiājù* furniture

Use your eyes (目) to look for TOOLS that can be used on the table to prepare the ingredients for dinner.

11 strokes

职 position, employment

Traditional 職

zhí

职业 *zhíyè* profession, occupation

职位 *zhíwèi* post, position

When looking for EMPLOYMENT or a new POSITION, keep your ears (耳) open and put in at least eight (八) applications.

5 strokes

 且 moreover, also, furthermore

qiě

而且 *érqiě* and also, but also

况且 *kuàngqiě* moreover, besides

I knew you were ALSO there, and FURTHERMORE, I saw your eye (目) peek out from over the horizon.

15 strokes

题 topic, subject

Traditional  題

tí

问题 *wèntí* problem, trouble

主题 *zhǔtí* theme, topic, motif

He has big shoes for his feet (足) to fill as he examines pages (页) on a TOPIC of a SUBJECT being studied that day (日).

Nape of the Neck 项

9 strokes

顺 **obey, order, turn, along** Traditional 順

shùn

顺从 ***shùncóng*** **to obey, defer**

顺利 ***shùnlì*** **smoothly, successfully, favorably**

The natural ORDER of river (川) is to flow downhill just as we TURN pages (页) of a book from front to back.

11 strokes

领 **collar, to lead** Traditional 領

lǐng

领子 ***lǐngzi*** **collar**

领导 ***lǐngdǎo*** **leadership, guidance**

本领 ***běnlǐng*** **ability, skill**

The command on the sheet of paper (页) requested him TO LEAD the others over hurdles.

9 strokes

类 **sort, variety; genus** Traditional 類

lèi

种类 ***zhǒnglèi*** **kinds, variety, types**

类别 ***lèibié*** **category, classification**

There is a VARIETY of rice (米) that has quite big (大) grains.

6 strokes

页 **page, leaf** Traditional 頁

yè

第五页 ***dìwǔyè*** **page 5**

网页 ***wǎngyè*** **web page**

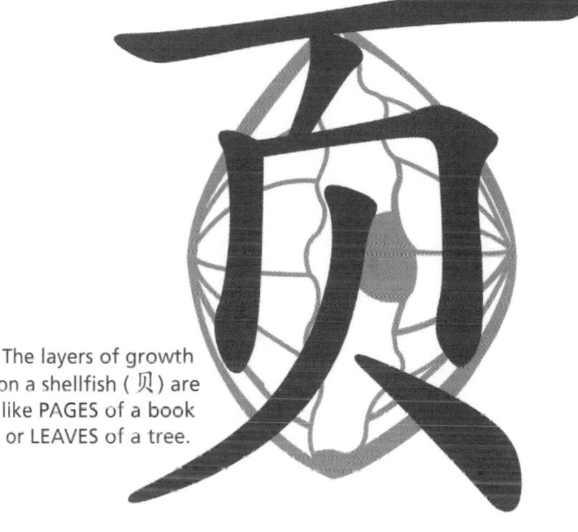

The layers of growth on a shellfish (贝) are like PAGES of a book or LEAVES of a tree.

10 strokes

预 **advance, beforehand, previous** Traditional 預

yù

预备 ***yùbèi*** **preparations, to get ready**

预定 ***yùdìng*** **plans, arrangements**

预约 ***yùyuē*** **to reserve, reservation**

I (予) considered options in ADVANCE by looking at PREVIOUS attempts recorded on sheets of paper (页).

Heart 心/忄

13 strokes

 **emotion, feeling, sensation**

gǎn

感觉 ***gǎnjué*** **to feel, sense**

感动 ***gǎndòng*** **to move (emotionally), affection, emotion**

感谢 ***gǎnxiè*** **thanks, gratitude**

When one (一) has a burst of EMOTION in one's heart (心) the FEELING is like having a cliff to climb.

11 strokes

情 **feelings, emotion, passion**

qíng

感情 ***gǎnqíng*** **feeling, emotion, affection**

同情 ***tóngqíng*** **pity, sympathy, compassion**

情报 ***qíngbào*** **intelligence, information**

FEELINGS of sadness and being blue (青) may lead to a sudden release of EMOTION.

14 strokes

 **wish, hope, desire**

Traditional 願

yuàn

愿望 ***yuànwàng*** **wish**

愿意 ***yuànyì*** **willing**

My HOPE is that under the cliff I will be able to clear my heart (心) and to discover the source (原) of my DESIRE.

9 strokes

 **overall, general, chief**

Traditional 

zǒng

总之 ***zǒngzhī*** **overall**

总数 ***zǒngshù*** **total, sum**

总统 ***zǒngtǒng*** **president**

The CHIEF stated that he had taken to heart (心) the OVERALL situation.

8 strokes

态 **attitude, condition, appearance**

Traditional 態

tài

态度 ***tàidù*** **attitude, manner**

姿态 ***zītài*** **stance, posture**

状态 ***zhuàngtài*** **current status, condition**

It is of greatest (太) importance to put your heart (心) into having a positive ATTITUDE and APPEARANCE.

12 strokes

悲 grieve; sad

bēi

悲伤 ***bēishāng*** **sad, sorrow**

悲剧 ***bēijù*** **tragedy, disaster**

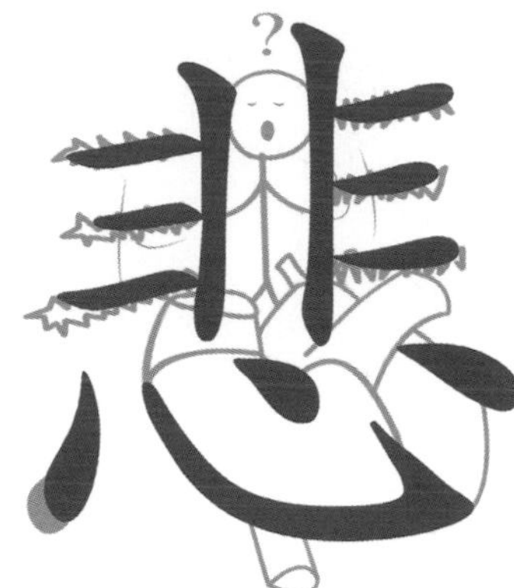

It's no use to GRIEVE before attempting to get through a spiked gate. Just put your heart (心) into it and don't be SAD if you fail the first time.

8 strokes

 loyalty, fidelity, faithfulness

zhōng

忠实 ***zhōngshí*** **faithful, loyal, true, honest**

忠告 ***zhōnggào*** **advice, warning**

LOYALTY and FAITHFULNESS come from the center (中) of one's heart (心).

8 strokes

非 mistake; negative, non–

fēi

非法 ***fēifǎ*** **illegal**

非常 ***fēicháng*** **very, extreme**

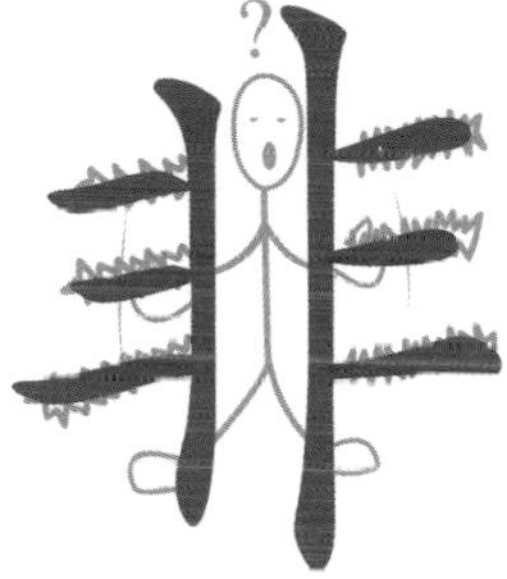

Going through this spiked gate might be a MISTAKE.

11 strokes

 surprise

Traditional 驚

jīng

吃惊 ***chījīng*** **surprised, be amazed**

震惊 ***zhènjīng*** **to shock, astonishment**

惊动 ***jīngdòng*** **disturb, alert**

The SURPRISE that they were approaching the capital (京) city caused her heart (忄) to beat quickly.

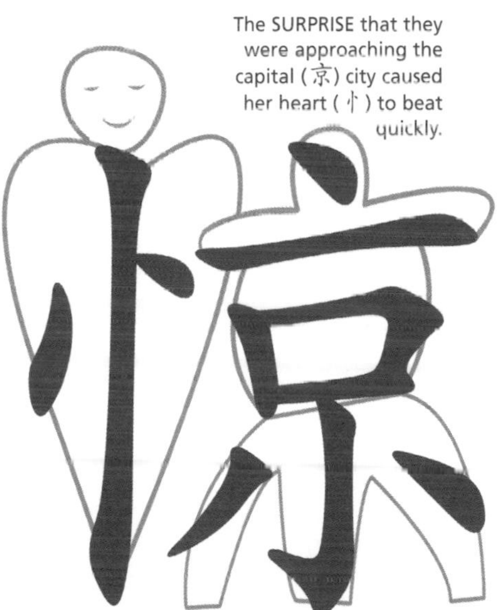

8 strokes

 fear, afraid

pà

害怕 ***hàipà*** **be afraid, scared**

可怕 ***kěpà*** **terrible, awful**

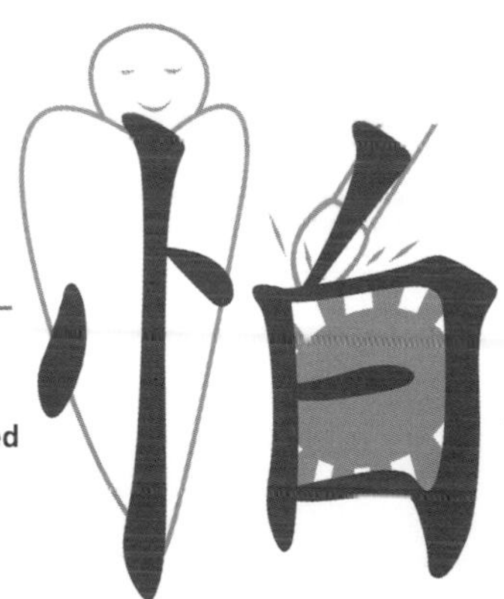

When you FEAR something, your heart (忄) pounds and your face might turn white (白), but don't be AFRAID.

7 strokes

 **fast, cheerful**

kuài

快速 *kuàisù* **fast, rapid, high-speed**

赶快 *gǎnkuài* **immediately, hurry up**

快乐 *kuàilè* **happy, joyful, cheerful**

This CHEERFUL man holding a broken box must put his heart (忄) into working FAST to keep the contents from spilling.

10 strokes

 **grace, kindness, favor**

ēn

恩惠 *ēnhuì* **grace, favor, kindness**

恩人 *ēnrén* **benefactor**

感恩节 *Gǎn'ēnjié* **Thanksgiving**

The reason (因) for such GRACE and KINDNESS can only be seen when one has an open heart (心).

7 strokes

 **bored, stuffy** Traditional 

mèn

苦闷 *kǔmèn* **depressed, gloomy**

闷热 *mēnrè* **muggy, hot and stuffy**

Being BORED in a STUFFY home all day, one wishes with all his heart (心) to exit the gate for some fresh air.

7 strokes

 **endure, bear, conceal**

rěn

容忍 *róngrěn* **to endure, tolerate**

忍耐 *rěnnài* **patience, sufferance, restraint**

A small blade (刀) is CONCEALED close to the heart (心) to help one ENDURE struggles.

10 strokes

 **repent, regret**

huǐ

后悔 *hòuhuǐ* **to regret, repent, remorse**

A person will show REGRET every (每) day until he has a clear heart (忄).

10 strokes

恶 fierce, wickedness, evil

Traditional 惡

è

凶恶 *xiōng'è* fierce, brutal

恶梦 *èmèng* nightmare

The weight of Asia pressing down on one's heart (心) would be FIERCE.

A farmer will THINK about his field (田) with all of his heart (心).

9 strokes

思 think

sī

思想 *sīxiǎng* to think, thought, idea

思量 *sīliáng* to consider, ponder

6 strokes

亚 Asia, second

Traditional 亞

yà

东亚 *dōngyà* East Asia/the Orient

亚洲 *yàzhōu* Asia

亚军 *yàjūn* 2nd place [runner-up]; to rank next to

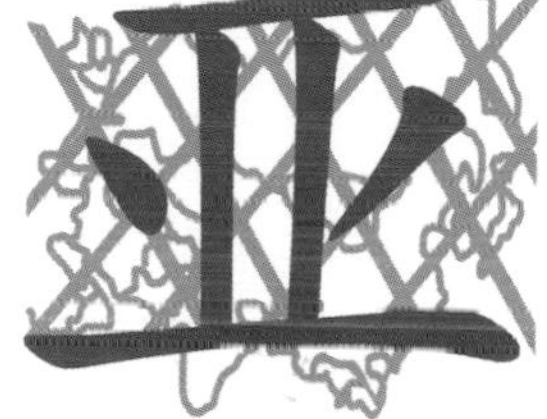

EAST ASIA stretches out over latticework to cover a wall.

3 strokes

亡 deceased, dying, perish

wáng

死亡 *sǐwáng* death, deceased; deadly

逃亡 *táowáng* fugitive, escape, getaway

An urn for the DECEASED sits broken.

7 strokes

忘 forget, overlook

wàng

忘记 *wàngjì* to overlook, forget

备忘 *bèiwàng* memo, reminder

The lid was put on the pot, but the owner FORGOT that it was broken on one side and his heart (心) began to race as the soup poured out.

9 strokes

怒 angry, be offended

nù

愤怒 ***fènnù*** anger, rage, wrath

The woman (女) at the table was OFFENDED and ANGRY when someone tried to break her heart (心).

9 strokes

急 hurry, emergency, sudden

jí

紧急 ***jǐnjí*** **urgent, pressing; emergency**

危急 ***wéijí*** **critical, desperate**

急忙 ***jímáng*** **to hurry/rush**

A SUDDEN twist of the top leaves it broken in an EMERGENCY and the heart (心) races.

7 strokes

 aspiration, will, ambition

zhì

志向 ***zhìxiàng*** **ambition**

意志 ***yìzhì*** **will, determination**

志愿 ***zhìyuàn*** **ambition, to volunteer**

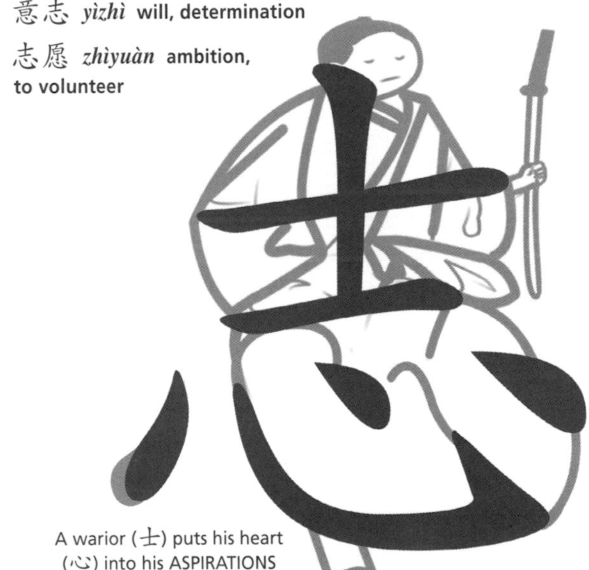

A warior (士) puts his heart (心) into his ASPIRATIONS to protect his lord.

6 strokes

 busy, occupied, restless

máng

忙碌 ***mánglù*** **busy, bustling**

匆忙 ***cōngmáng*** **hurry, hastiness**

帮忙 ***bāngmáng*** **to help, do a favor, lend a hand**

A RESTLESS heart (忄) is BUSY being OCCUPIED with fixing a broken pot.

14 strokes

 slow

màn

缓慢 ***huǎnmàn*** **slow, tardy**

傲慢 ***àomàn*** **arrogant, haughty, pride**

On a hot day (日), sit down at a table, close your eyes, and SLOW down.

8 strokes

in a moment, instantly, all of a sudden

hū

忽然 ***hūrán*** **sudden, unexpected**

忽略 ***hūlüè*** **to ignore, neglect, overlook**

One must not (勿) all of a SUDDEN retreat from what one's heart (心) has felt.

5 strokes

must, necessary, essential

bì

必须 ***bìxū*** **must, need**

必要 ***bìyào*** **necessary**

You MUST cross your heart (心) and swear to do the things that are NECESSARY.

13 strokes

think, thought, concept

xiǎng

想像 ***xiǎngxiàng*** **imagination; to visualize**

思想 ***sīxiǎng*** **thinking, thought, ideology**

The CONCEPT of focusing on a lone tree (木) will calm the heart (心) and turn the mind to THOUGHTS of serenity.

13 strokes

idea, meaning, intent, thought

yì

意思 ***yìsi*** **meaning, sense**

意味 ***yìwèi*** **meaning, to mean, imply**

意图 ***yìtú*** **intent, intention, objective**

The IDEA of standing (立) above the sun (日) with an open heart (心) and mind would allow for deep THOUGHT.

10 strokes

breath, respiration

xí

气息 ***qìxí*** **breath, flavor**

消息 ***xiāoxi*** **news [from someone]**

A BREATH of oxygen to one's self (自) helps the heart (心) keep beating.

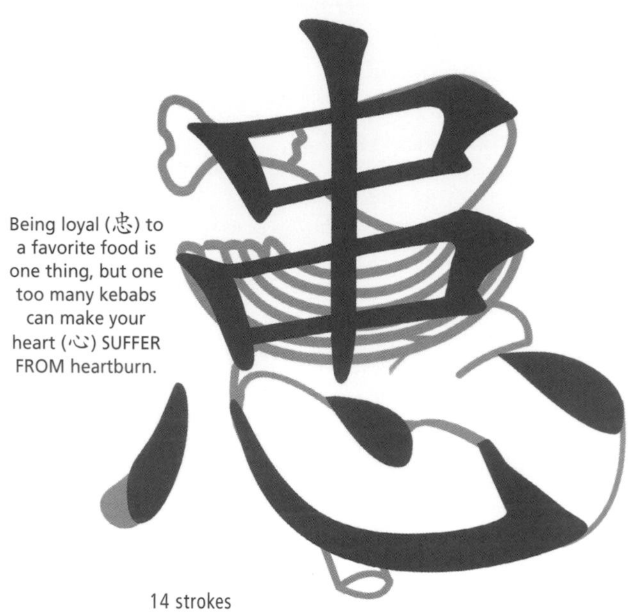

Being loyal (忠) to a favorite food is one thing, but one too many kebabs can make your heart (心) SUFFER FROM heartburn.

14 strokes

患 suffer from

huàn

患病 ***huànbìng*** **to fall sick**

患难 ***huànnàn*** **adversity, trouble**

8 strokes

性 sex, gender, nature

xìng

性别 ***xìngbié*** **gender**

人性 ***rénxìng*** **human nature**

女性 ***nǚxìng*** **woman, female**

The male GENDER goes through many stages of life (生) as does the female SEX.

5 strokes

生 raw; life, birth

shēng

生命 ***shēngmìng*** **life**

出生 ***chūshēng*** **birth, to be born**

生日 ***shēngrì*** **birthday, date of birth**

Both plants and people from BIRTH go through many stages of LIFE, sometimes marked on a wall.

9 strokes

 constitution, law

Traditional 

xiàn

宪法 ***xiànfǎ*** **constitution, law of the land**

Below a roof (宀), lawmakers had previously (先) written a CONSTITUTION.

5 strokes

失 lose, miss, fail

shī

遗失 ***yíshī*** **to lose, lost**

失败 ***shībài*** **failure**

She thought she could carry the plant, but she would FAIL because it obstructed her sight and caused her to LOSE her balance.

Blood 血

6 strokes

血 blood

xuè

血压 *xuèyā* **blood pressure**

捐血 *juānxuè* **blood donation**

A broken plate (皿) might draw BLOOD.

9 strokes

盆 basin, bowl, pot, tub, tray

pén

盆栽 *pénzāi* **bonsai, miniature potted plant**

盆地 *péndì* **basin**

During different parts (分) of a meal we use POTS, plates (皿), and cups, and then wash them in a BASIN.

5 strokes

皿 dish, plate

mǐn

器皿 *qìmǐn* **container**

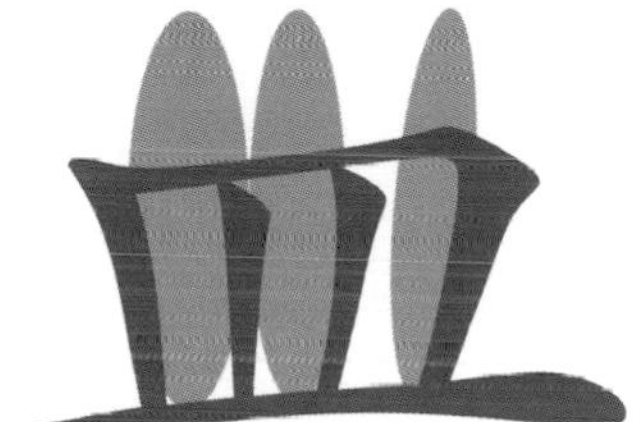

A DISH-drying rack is ready for someone to do the DISHES.

13 strokes

盟 alliance, oath

méng

同盟 *tóngméng* **alliance, league, union**

加盟 *jiāméng* **participation, affiliation**

誓盟 *shìméng* **oath**

The sun (日) and moon (月) form an ALLIANCE each year, working together and looking like large plates (皿) in the sky.

11 strokes

盛 hold, bloom, prosper

shèng

盛大 **shèngdà majestic, grand**

旺盛 **wàngshèng vigorous**

We will PROSPER by defending the cliff with spears (戈) so that people can HOLD many plates (皿) of food and fresh produce.

Hand 手/扌

10 strokes

捉 catch, capture

zhuō

捉拿 *zhuōná* to capture, arrest

捕捉 *bǔzhuō* capture, seizure

To successfully CAPTURE someone who is fast on their feet (足), you might have to use your hands (扌).

7 strokes

扶 support, aid; help, assist

fú

扶助 *fúzhù* to support, help, assistance

扶养 *fúyǎng* to raise, bring up

Use both hands (扌) to ASSIST a tall person carrying a big (大) package to AID others.

7 strokes

批 criticism, strike

pī

批评 *pīpíng* criticism, to criticize, pick on

Compared (比) to using dialog, using the STRIKE of a hand (扌) to resolve something would receive CRITICISM.

5 strokes

打 strike, hit, knock

dǎ

敲打 *qiāodǎ* to beat [a drum], to hit/punch, tap, rap

打击 *dǎjí* blow, strike, knock

Use a hand (扌) to HIT and STRIKE a tack.

10 strokes

捐 donate, contribute, give away

juān

捐助 *juānzhù* donation, contribution

捐款 *juānkuǎn* to contribute money

Say that you will DONATE money or volunteer to give a hand (扌) to CONTRIBUTE time for the work necessary to finish the project this month (月).

7 strokes

技 skill, craft, ability

jì

技术 *jìshù* skill, technology

技师 *jìshī* technician, engineer

The SKILL of one's hands (扌) gives one the ABILITY to sit at a table and CRAFT ten (十) or more identical figures.

8 strokes

 bear, undertake

Traditional 擔

dān

承担 *chéngdān* to bear, assume the responsibility

担保 *dānbǎo* guarantee, to assure

A person raises his hand (扌) to UNDERTAKE the one (一) challenge of the day (日).

8 strokes

 Latin, pull, drag, haul

lā

拉丁 *Lādīng* Latin

拖拉 *tuōlā* to pull, drag, haul

A person standing (立) DRAGS his hand (扌) to PULL open drawers and doors.

9 strokes

按 press, push; according to; hold

àn

按照 *ànzhào* according to, on the basis of

按钮 *ànniǔ* to push buttons

按摩 *ànmó* to massage

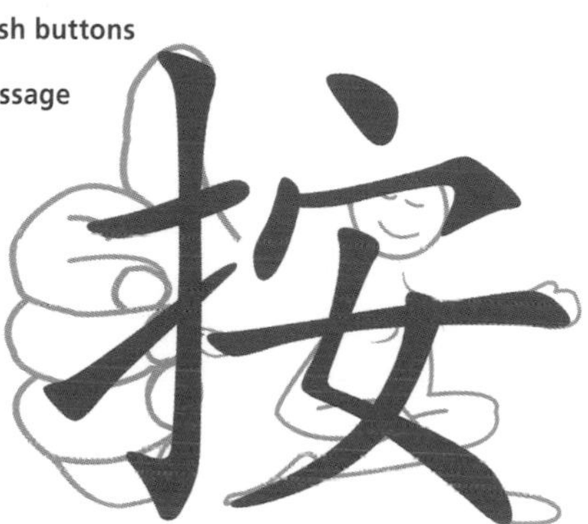

A woman's (女) hands (扌) signal that she is safe (安) after she decided to HOLD onto something to avoid falling.

After EXPLORING the land to find a nice table by a tree (木), a hand (扌) signals to the others that the SEARCH is over and they should come to VISIT him.

11 strokes

 explore, visit, search, grope

tàn

探测 *tàncè* to grope, survey

探索 *tànsuǒ* to explore, search

密探 *mìtàn* spy, secret agent

11 strokes

推 push, promote, infer

tuī

推测 *tuīcè* to speculate, guess, conjecture

推荐 *tuījiàn* to recommend, recommendation

推断 *tuīduàn* to infer, deduce

On the one hand (扌), one could INFER that the bird (隹) was yellow, but maybe not.

7 strokes

找 search, find

zhǎo

寻找 *xúnzhǎo* to search, seek

找到 *zhǎodào* to find

找换 *zhǎohuàn* money exchange

He uses his hand (扌) as if wielding a spear (戈), to SEARCH for what he needed until it was FOUND.

12 strokes

提 raise, propose, take along

tí

提议 *tíyì* proposal, suggestion

提高 *tígāo* to improve, increase, enhance

She RAISED her hand (扌) to PROPOSE seizing the day (日).

11 strokes

据 receipt, evidence; according to

Traditional 據

jù

收据 *shōujù* receipt

证据 *zhèngjù* evidence, proof

根据 *gēnjù* according to

Get a RECEIPT as EVIDENCE when you hand (扌) over something old (古) through a door.

7 strokes

把 hold, grasp

bǎ

把手 *bǎshǒu* handle, grip, knob

把握 *bǎwò* certainty, assurance

It is good to HOLD onto hopes (巴) and reach with your hands (扌) to GRASP your dreams.

As he went over the shellfish (贝) with his hand (扌), he realized that it was DAMAGED and said something about the LOSS.

10 strokes

损 damage, loss, injure

Traditional 損

sǔn

损害 *sǔnhài* **to damage, harm, injury**

损失 *sǔnshī* **to lose, loss**

16 strokes

操 maneuver, manipulate, operate

cāo

操纵 *cāozòng* **to manipulate, rig, control**

操行 *cāoxíng* **conduct, behavior**

体操 *tǐcāo* **gymnastics**

A hand (扌) directs a figure as it MANEUVERS boxes around the room.

8 strokes

招 beckon, recruit, attract

zhāo

招募 *zhāomù* **to recruit, enlist**

招待 *zhāodài* **to entertain, serve, host**

招呼 *zhāohū* **to greet, call**

He chose to BECKON others to do his will with his hand (扌) and sword (刀) rather than using his mouth (口) to call them.

9 strokes

持 hold, maintain, have (possession of)

chí

保持 *bǎochí* **to maintain, keep, retain**

持有 *chíyǒu* **to hold, have**

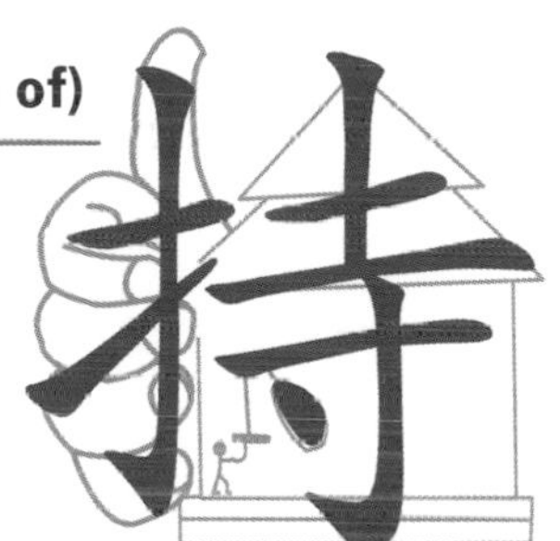

He HOLDS in his hands (扌) offerings for a temple (寺).

11 strokes

接 connect, piece together, contact

jiē

连接 *liánjiē* **connection, to link, attach**

接受 *jiēshòu* **to accept, receive**

直接 *zhíjiē* **direct, firsthand, immediate**

A hand (扌) stretched out to CONNECT to a woman (女).

6 strokes

扩 **extend, spread, enlarge**

Traditional 擴

kuò

扩大 ***kuòdà*** **to expand, extend, widen, enlargement**

扩散 ***kuòsàn*** **to spread, diffuse**

I EXTEND my hands (扌) to measure the height of the dotted cliff.

12 strokes

掌 **palm**

zhǎng

手掌 ***shǒuzhǎng*** **palm [of hand]**

掌握 ***zhǎngwò*** **to grasp, predominate**

鼓掌 ***gǔzhǎng*** **to clap, applaud**

When you are supposed to learn something in school, your teacher may ask to see the PALM of your hand (手) to ensure you are not cheating.

11 strokes

 **trace, draw, sketch, describe**

miáo

描写 ***miáoxiě*** **to describe, draw**

描绘 ***miáohuì*** **to depict, portray, describe**

素描 ***sùmiáo*** **sketch**

A skillful hand (扌) would SKETCH the grass (艹) behind a field (田) as it was DESCRIBED.

10 strokes

 **fist**

quán

拳头 ***quántóu*** **fist**

拳击 ***quánjí*** **boxing**

太极拳 ***Tàijíquán*** **Tai Chi**

The first signs of spring appeared as a FIST breaking through winter in the third month.

11 strokes

 **impart, instruct, grant**

shòu

传授 ***chuánshòu*** **to teach, impart, pass on**

教授 ***jiàoshòu*** **professor, to teach**

Teachers have a hand (扌) in how they IMPART information or INSTRUCT various aspects of knowledge under a roof at tables and desks.

8 strokes

 **support, undertake, receive**

chéng

承认 ***chéngrèn*** **recognition/ acknowledgment**

承担 ***chéngdān*** **to undertake, bear, assume**

I myself UNDERTAKE to use my hand (手) to RECEIVE water (水) as it falls.

Foot 足

7 strokes

go, run, move

zǒu

走路 *zǒulù* to walk, go on foot

逃走 *táozǒu* to flee, run off

Lots of earth (土) will GO past underfoot as one continues to MOVE.

15 strokes

interest, inclination

qù

有趣 *yǒuqù* interesting, amusing

趣味 *qùwèi* interest, delight, liking

If you take long strides across the land (土), you might have an INTEREST in listening to the crickets and birds as you sit to rest at a table.

9 strokes

proceed, get, to attend

fù

前赴 *qiánfù* to proceed, depart

赴任 *fùrèn* moving to a new post

If worried, PROCEED on foot to GET a good fortune teller (卜) to help.

12 strokes

exceed, go beyond; the more…

yuè

超越 *chāoyuè* to exceed, surpass

越南 *Yuènán* Vietnam

10 strokes

rise, start

qǐ

起来 *qǐlái* to wake/get up

起点 *qǐdiǎn* starting point

You can engage in focusing the self (己) when you START meditating after you wake up, to keep the mind from walking (走).

THE MORE you walk (走) through the lands (土) the MORE you might want to carry a spear (戈).

13 strokes

路 road, path, route

lù

路 *dàolù* road, path, way

路线 *lùxiàn* route, itinerary

直路 *zhílù* straight road

A person stops (止) at the end of a ROAD where the picnic table stands and people sit and talk.

6 strokes

先 before, previous

xiān

预先 *yùxiān* advance, beforehand

优先 *yōuxiān* priority

先生 *xiānshēng* Mister (Mr.), sir

The leaf from that plant in the soil (土) sprouted PREVIOUSLY, just BEFORE you walked away.

2 strokes

儿 child, son

Traditional 兒

ér

儿童 *értóng* child

儿子 *érzi* son

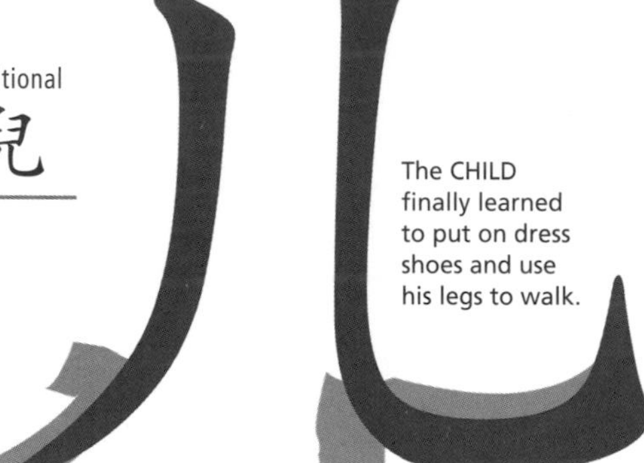

The CHILD finally learned to put on dress shoes and use his legs to walk.

10 strokes

 party, gang, society, faction

Traditional 

dǎng

党派 *dǎngpài* faction, partisan

民主党 *Mínzhǔdǎng* Democrat Party

共和党 *Gònghédǎng* Republican Party

My older brother (兄) learned bits of knowledge from books about a political PARTY and its FACTIONS.

9 strokes

 ghost, spirit

guǐ

鬼魂 *guǐhún* ghost, spirit, apparition

鬼鬼祟祟 *guǐguǐsuìsuì* stealthy, sneaking

Popping its head up from a field (田), a GHOST stood on its huge legs to scare me.

6 strokes

光 light, bright, ray, shine

guāng

光辉 *guānghuī* radiance, shine

阳光 *yángguāng* sunlight, sunshine

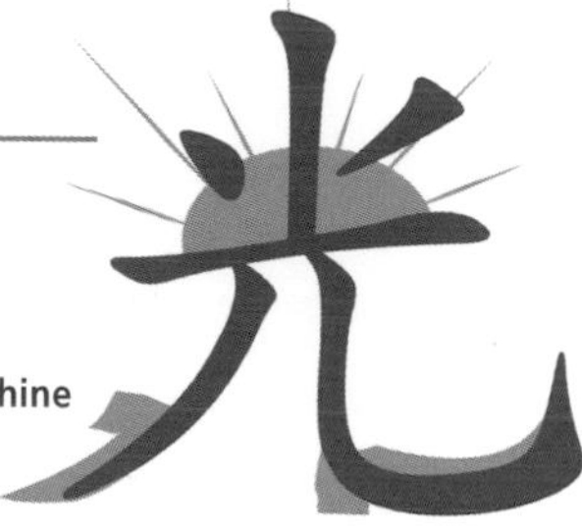

The rays of LIGHT from the sun were like long legs stretching down in a BRIGHT glow across the land.

One of the final STEPS in putting this ladder together is to place it on a table and use your legs to help put it together.

9 strokes

段 segment, paragraph, steps

duàn

阶段 *jiēduàn* phrase, stage, level

段落 *duànluò* paragraph, part, stage

6 strokes

当 right, appropriate

Traditional 當

dāng/*dàng*

当然 *dāngrán* of course, certainly

适当 *shìdàng* appropriate, suitable

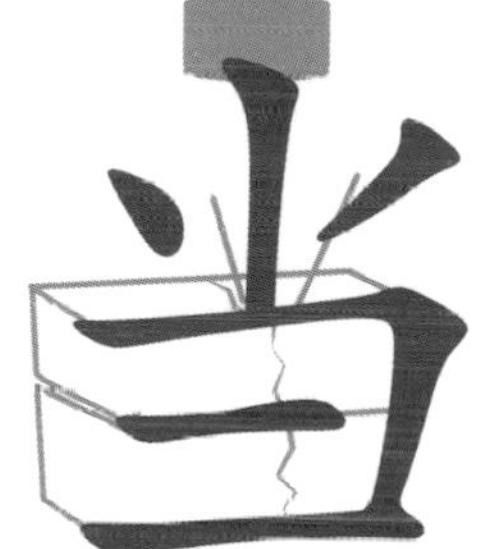

When trying to break a stack of boards, it is sometimes APPROPRIATE to hit straight down at the target.

7 strokes

投 throw, discard, abandon

tóu

投资 *tóuzī* investment, to invest

投降 *tóuxiáng* to surrender

The legs standing on the table broke it, so use your hands (扌) to THROW it away.

6 strokes

 杀 kill, murder

Traditional  殺

shā

谋杀 *móushā* to murder

屠杀 *túshā* massacre, slaughter

He spun around and then fell to the ground after the KILL.

A man standing with his arm lifted up directs others to HALT with a STOP sign.

4 strokes

止 stop, halt

zhǐ

停止 *tíngzhǐ* **to stop, halt, cease**

禁止 *jìnzhǐ* **prohibition, to ban, forbid**

6 strokes

此 this, here, and now

cǐ

如此 *rúcǐ* **so, in this way**

从此 *cóngcǐ* **from now on, thereupon**

You stop HERE because of the aroma AND NOW use the spoon to taste some of the soup.

8 strokes

 step, pace, walk

bù

步行 *bùxíng* **to walk**

散步 *sànbù* **to take a walk**

步骤 *bùzhòu* **step, procedure**

When WALKING stop (止) a few (少) times to watch your STEP.

8 strokes

 some, a few, a little

xiē

一些 *yīxiē* **some, a few**

这些 *zhèxiē* **these**

Stop (止) A FEW times to take a ladle (匕) to sample A LITTLE of the soup.

5 strokes

正 correct, straight

zhèng

改正 *gǎizhèng* **correct/right**

正常 *zhèngcháng* **normal**

The one (一) CORRECT way to do something is to stop (止) and think about the challenge ahead.

CHAPTER 4

ACTIONS

A moving man (彳) hovers before finally deciding to GO.

6 strokes

行 **go, walk, travel**

xíng

进行 *jìnxíng* in progress, execute

旅行 *lǚxíng* trip, travel

行为 *xíngwéi* behavior, conduct

If he will COME early someone will be waiting with a welcome sign.

7 strokes

来 **come, arrive**

Traditional 來

lái

过来 *guòlái* come, come up, come over

Stride 辶

5 strokes

边 edge, side, boundary

Traditional

biān

边界 *biānjiè* boundary, border

海边 *hǎibiān* seaside, seashore

Power (力) is centered in the BOUNDARY path around the EDGE of the city.

9 strokes

追 chase, drive away, follow, pursue

zhuī

追求 *zhuīqiú* to pursue, chase, seek

追逐 *zhuīzhú* to chase, run after

追究 *zhuījiù* to investigate

Mouths (口) give directions to FOLLOW the path closely.

7 strokes

返 return

fǎn

返回 *fǎnhuí* to return, come back

If you borrow the table, RETURN it to the end of the path at the base of the cliff (厂).

10 strokes

速 quick, fast

sù

快速 *kuàisù* fast, quickly, high-speed

急速 *jísù* rapid [progress, etc.]

速度 *sùdù* speed, velocity, pace

9 strokes

送 send, deliver, escort

sòng

发送 *fāsòng* to send, transmit, send out

传送 *chuánsòng* to deliver, convey

After a long walk (辶) to the mountain pass (关), SEND pictures and have the postman DELIVER a letter or two.

Make QUICK work of bundling the tree to take it down the path.

7 strokes

进 advance, proceed, progress

Traditional 進

jìn

前进 ***qiánjìn*** to advance, go forward

进步 ***jìnbù*** progress, improvement

ADVANCE down the path and you will see the well (井).

7 strokes

运 carry, transport, luck, destiny

Traditional 運

yùn

运输 ***yùnshū*** transport, carriage

幸运 ***xìngyùn*** lucky, fortunate

Using his legs as TRANSPORT, he went along the path, past the cloud (云), to meet his DESTINY.

6 strokes

 accomplished, reach

Traditional 達

dá

到达 ***dàodá*** to reach, arrive, get to

达成 ***dáchéng*** to accomplish, reach (an agreement)

Your path will lead you to become ACCOMPLISHED and to REACH many big (大) goals.

We decided to follow THIS path because information was written in the literature (文) scrolls right HERE.

12 strokes

 roadway, street, method, teachings

dào

道路 ***dàolù*** road, street

道理 ***dàolǐ*** reason, principle, theory

Use the TEACHINGS your leader shared to navigate the ROADWAYS ahead.

7 strokes

 this, here

Traditional 

zhè

这是 ***zhèshì*** this is

这儿 ***zhèr*** here

这些 ***zhèxiē*** these

6 strokes

过 **pass, cross, exceed**

Traditional 過

guò

经过 ***jīngguò*** **to pass through**

超过 ***chāoguò*** **to exceed, surpass**

过程 ***guòchéng*** **process, procedure**

As you walk a path to CROSS something unknown, measure every inch (寸) of your tracks to ensure that you can return and PASS your destination.

7 strokes

还 **still, yet, return**

Traditional 還

hái/huán

还是 ***háishì*** **still, or**

还有 ***háiyǒu*** **also, besides, likewise**

退还 ***tuìhuán*** **to return, send back**

If you have not (不) YET reached the end of the path, you may still RETURN early.

7 strokes

违 **violate, disobey, to go against**

Traditional 違

wéi

违反 ***wéifǎn*** **violation [of law]**

违抗 ***wéikàng*** **to disobey, defy**

If you DISOBEY any of the three (三) directions on this sign post on the path, you could be in trouble.

10 strokes

造 **make, manufacture**

zào

制造 ***zhìzào*** **manufacture, made in**

建造 ***jiànzào*** **to build, construct**

If you walk away from the land (土) where you were born, you will have to inform (告) many people that you have MADE the decision.

12 strokes

游 **travel, play**

Traditional 遊

yóu

游戏 ***yóuxì*** **game, play, recreation**

旅游 ***lǚyóu*** **travel, tour, trip, journey**

游行 ***yóuxíng*** **to parade, demonstration**

We TRAVEL to places near water where the children (子) can safely PLAY.

7 strokes | Traditional

远 distant, far 遠

yuǎn

遥远 *yáoyuǎn* far, distant

远方 *yuǎnfāng* a distant place

From the origin (元) of the path it is sometimes difficult to travel to the DISTANT future.

LEAD your ox (牛) down the path that CONNECTS to the field.

7 strokes | Traditional

连 connect, lead, continuously 連

lián

连接 *liánjiē* connection, link

连绵 *liánmián* continuous, unbroken

9 strokes | Traditional

选 elect, select, prefer 選

xuǎn

选择 *xuǎnzé* to choose, select

选手 *xuǎnshǒu* athlete, contestant, player [in a game]

选举 *xuǎnjǔ* election

People walk (辶) to previous (先) polling places to SELECT names on ballot papers to ELECT leaders.

10 strokes

 通 pass through, commute

tōng

沟通 *gōutōng* to link up

通知 *tōngzhī* to notify, advice, notifiation

通过 *tōngguò* to go past, go by

During your COMMUTE, you might use (用) tunnels under scaffolding or other passages you can PASS THROUGH.

Stand 立

This man STANDS tall.

5 strokes

立 stand up, stand, set up

lì

起立 ***qǐlì*** **to stand up, rise**

立刻 ***lìkè*** **immediately, prompt**

公立 ***gōnglì*** **public [institution]**

10 strokes

竞 compete with, race Traditional 競

jìng

竞争 ***jìngzhēng*** **to compete, competition**

竞赛 ***jìngsài*** **contest, race**

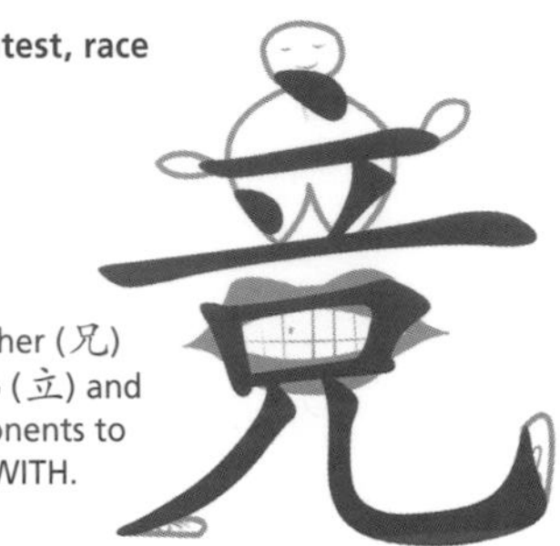

My older brother (兄) often stands up (立) and looks for opponents to COMPETE WITH.

Stand (立) still while the fortune teller divines (占) your future at his STAND.

10 strokes

站 stand, station

zhàn

站立 ***zhànlì*** **standing**

车站 ***chēzhàn*** **station, stop**

11 strokes

章 badge, chapter

zhāng

徽章 ***huīzhāng*** **badge, insignia**

章节 ***zhāngjié*** **chapter, section**

文章 ***wénzhāng*** **article, essay**

Standing (立) up tall, early (早) in the day (日), ten (十) times in a row and you may earn a BADGE for perserverance.

11 strokes

竟 actually, unexpectedly

jìng

究竟 ***jiùjìng*** **exactly, actually**

竟然 ***jìngrán*** **unexpectedly**

If a man stands up (立) tall in exactly the right place, he might UNEXPECTEDLY be rewarded with a beautiful sunrise.

12 strokes

童 child, juvenile

tóng

儿童 *értóng* **child**

童话 *tónghuà* **fairy tale**

The CHILD, being young and JUVENILE, stood on the rice fields (田) of the village (里) without realizing that he was crushing the plants.

6 strokes

产 products, produce, give birth

Traditional 産

chǎn

生产 *shēngchǎn* **to produce, manufacture, give birth**

产量 *chǎnliàng* **productivity, output**

Standing (立) on a cliff (厂) will PRODUCE a wonderful view.

11 strokes

商 business, trade, commerce

shāng

商业 *shāngyè* **commerce, trade, business**

商人 *shāngrén* **businessman**

An auctioneer will TRADE for goods while standing up (立) on a podium and conducting BUSINESS with his voice.

9 strokes

音 sound, noise

yīn

音乐 *yīnyuè* **music**

声音 *shēngyīn* **sound, voice**

If you were to stand (立) on the sun (日), you'd make a very loud, short SOUND before being incinerated.

3 strokes

亿 hundred million

Traditional 億

yì

一亿 *yīyì* **one hundred million**

亿万 *yìwàn* **hundreds of millions**

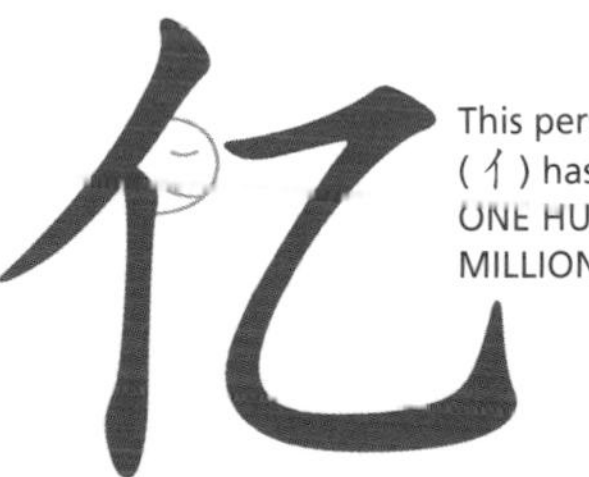

This person (亻) has won ONE HUNDRED MILLION yuan.

4 strokes

见 **see/look, opinion** Traditional 見

jiàn

看见 *kànjiàn* sight, to look/see

意见 *yìjiàn* opinion, view, idea

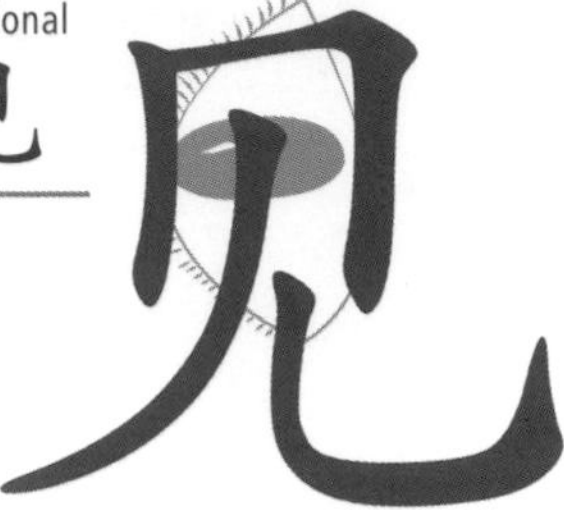

Walk around and LOOK at things around you.

9 strokes

亲 **parent, familiarity** Traditional 親

qīn

亲人 *qīnrén* relatives

亲切 *qīnqiè* cordial, kindness, close

A PARENT stands (立) tall when a child earns a high rank (朩).

8 strokes

视 **inspection, look at** Traditional 視

shì

视力 *shìlì* vision, eyesight

视察 *shìchá* to inspect, observe, watch

LOOK AT the spirit cult (礻) carefully and you can see (见) more details.

6 strokes

观 **outlook, appearance** Traditional 觀

guān

参观 *cānguān* to visit, look around, inspect

观光 *guānguāng* sightseeing

Look (见) carefully at your APPEARANCE at the dressing table before leaving.

9 strokes

觉 **feel, sense, sleep** Traditional 覺

jué/jiào

感觉 *gǎnjué* sense, feeling, intuition

睡觉 *shuìjiào* to sleep, go to sleep

Study bits of knowledge and you may FEEL that you are able to see (见) more than before.

7 strokes

严 **stern, strictness, rigidity** Traditional 嚴

yán

严格 *yángé* strict, rigorous

威严 *wēiyán* dignity, majesty, prestige

Many places in Asia (亚) STRICT policies protecting technologies in their factories (厂).

Sliding Up and Down 阝

6 strokes

阳 **sunshine, positive** Traditional 陽

yáng

太阳 ***tàiyáng*** sun, solar

阳光 ***yángguāng*** sunlight, sunshine, brightness

A child should climb up and down outside on days (日) full of SUNSHINE.

院

A child can assend to a future of wealth (元) if he works hard in SCHOOL and at higher INSTITUTIONS of learning.

8 strokes

降 **descend, reduce, fall**

jiàng

下降 ***xiàjiàng*** to decline, go down

降低 ***jiàngdī*** to lower, reduce, drop

A child DESCENDS down a pole as smoothly as snow FALLS to the ground.

9 strokes

院 **institution, school, courtyard**

yuàn

医院 ***yīyuàn*** hospital

寺院 ***sìyuàn*** temple, monastery

学院 ***xuéyuàn*** college, institute, faculty

6 strokes

 **rank, step, stair** Traditional 

jiē

阶级 ***jiējí*** class, rank

阶层 ***jiēcéng*** social stratum, social class

A child ascended up a pole to demonstrate that he was ready for the next STEP in his challenges in the club house.

7 strokes

 **border, edge, boundary** Traditional 

jì

实际 ***shíjì*** practical, realistic

国际 ***guójì*** international

A child is on the EDGE of a new land as he sees a sign announcing the BORDER.

7 strokes

陈 **display, explain, stale, common Chinese last name**

Traditional 陳

chén

陈列 ***chénliè*** to display, exhibit

陈述 ***chénshù*** statement, to explain

陈旧 ***chénjiù*** obsolete, out-of-date

After sliding down the pole, the child twirled (朩) and swung side-to-side in an awkward DISPLAY, trying to EXPLAIN what he had done.

6 strokes

那 **that**

nà

那个 ***nàgè*** that

那些 ***nàxiē*** those

那么 ***nàme*** so, then, in that way

A child climbs up a pole to get a better view of a moon THAT doesn't quite look right.

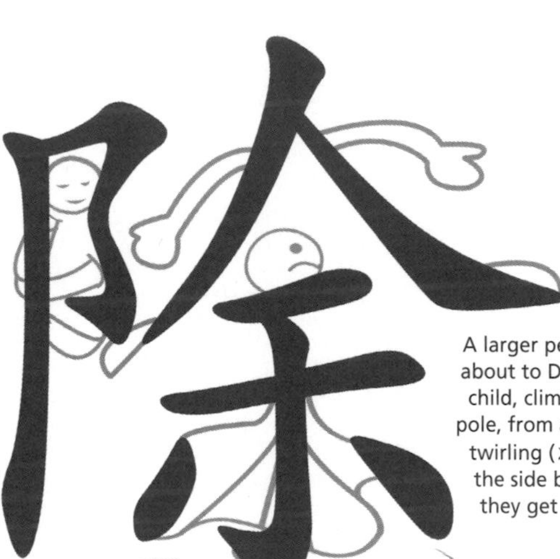

A larger person is about to DIVIDE a child, climbing a pole, from another twirling (朩) on the side before they get hurt.

9 strokes

除 **divide, get rid of, except**

chú

除数 ***chúshù*** divisor

除了 ***chúle*** besides, in addition, except

消除 ***xiāochú*** to eliminate, remove

In the CAPITAL, they often break ground (土) to build skyscrapers with high elevators, reaching for the sun (日).

10 strokes

都 **metropolis, capital**

dū

首都 ***shǒudū*** capital [city]

都市 ***dūshì*** metropolis, city

京都 ***Jīngdū*** Kyoto

10 strokes

部 **section, part, department**

bù

部门 ***bùmén*** department, section, division

部分 ***bùfèn*** section, part

部长 ***bùzhǎng*** department head, section leader

SECTION leaders keep track of the children who are present in each PART of the room.

A child slides down a pole before FOLLOWING another down a path and then jumping over the moon.

11 strokes

Traditional

随 follow, comply with, adapt to 隨

suí

跟随 ***gēnsuí*** to follow

随时 ***suíshí*** at any time

随便 ***suíbiàn*** casual, random

7 strokes

Traditional

陆 land 陸

lù

大陆 ***dàlù*** continent, mainland

陆地 ***lùdì*** land, dry land

The LAND on the mountain (山) is the perfect place for a child to climb and slide down a slope.

7 strokes

兵 soldier, troops, army

bīng

士兵 ***shìbīng*** soldier

兵役 ***bīngyì*** military service

Guns of SOLDIERS point to the top of a hill where the enemy is hiding.

4 strokes

Traditional

队 team, squad, fleet 隊

duì

军队 ***jūnduì*** army, military, troops

乐队 ***yuèduì*** band, orchestra

A child slides down a pole to join a mate from his TEAM standing below.

5 strokes

丘 mound, small hill

qiū

丘陵 ***qiūlíng*** hills

沙丘 ***shāqiū*** sand dune

Unlike a cliff (厂), rolling HILLS undulate in differing directions.

Power 力

2 strokes

力 **force, strength, power, strain**

lì

力量 *lìliàng* **force, might**

权力 *quánlì* **power, authority, jurisdiction**

体力 *tǐlì* **physical/body strength**

The two strokes of this sickle need lots of POWER to wield with FORCE.

5 strokes

加 **add, increase, include**

jiā

参加 *cānjiā* **to participate, take part**

增加 *zēngjiā* **addition, add to, plus**

He would INCREASE his popularity through the power (力) in his voice.

4 strokes

 **method, manage, carry on**

Traditional 

bàn

办法 *bànfǎ* **way, mode, method**

办理 *bànlǐ* **to handle, manage, conduct, carry on**

办公室 *bàngōngshì* **office, bureau**

It is important to MANAGE power (力) when cutting something exactly in half.

5 strokes

 **achievement, success**

gōng

成功 *chénggōng* **success**

功绩 *gōngjī* **achievements, merit**

His highest ACHIEVEMENT led to SUCCESS in the form of more power (力) at work (工).

3 strokes

 **labor, work, construction**

gōng

工作 *gōngzuò* **work, job, task**

工人 *gōngrén* **labor, worker**

工场 *gōngchǎng* **workshop**

Those who WORK in CONSTRUCTION use I–beams.

10 strokes

效 effect, efficiency, imitate

xiào

效法 *xiàofǎ* follow the example of; model oneself upon

效果 *xiàoguo* effect, result

仿效 *fǎngxiào* to imitate, follow the example of

IMITATE the EFFECT of the strength (力) your father (父) has that you felt safe under his roof (亠).

4 strokes

历 experience, undergo, passage of time

Traditional 歷

lì

经历 *jīnglì* to experience, undergo

历史 *lìshǐ* history

学历 *xuélì* academic background

Cliffs (厂) that have EXPERIENCED the PASSAGE OF TIME are symbols of power (力).

7 strokes

努 strive, exert

nǔ

努力 *nǔlì* to work hard, diligent, strive, exertion

The woman (女) works at a table (又) where she STRIVES to EXERT her power (力) and energy for her goals.

7 strokes

助 help, aid, assist

zhù

帮助 *bāngzhù* assistant, aid, help

Keep your eyes open and be ready to use all of your power (力) HELP someone in need of AID.

7 strokes

劳 labor, toil, work

Traditional 勞

láo

劳动 *láodòng* labor, work, manual/physical labor

疲劳 *píláo* fatigue, tired, weariness

Grasses grow tall, after the LABOR of powerful (力) hands WORK to tend them.

8 strokes

势 forces, situation, power

Traditional 勢

shì

形势 *xíngshì* circumstances

势力 *shìlì* power, force, influence

时势 *shíshì* current situation, trends

A wave of the hand (扌) gave the signal for FORCES to show MILITARY STRENGTH and power (力) that circled (丸) the SITUATION.

9 strokes

勇 courage, bravery

yǒng

勇敢 *yǒnggǎn* **bravery, courage**

英勇 *yīngyǒng* **heroic, brave, gallant**

When I have the COURAGE, I put my heart and soul and all of my power (力) into my field (田).

9 strokes

胜 victory, win — Traditional 勝

shèng

优胜 *yōushèng* **better, superior, winning**

胜利 *shènglì* **championship, victory**

It was like a new team was born (生) after our WIN in the competition month (月).

9 strokes

勉 encourage, strive, exertion

miǎn

勉励 *miǎnlì* **to encourage**

勉强 *miǎnqiáng* **reluctantly, forced**

An older brother (兄) will have more power (力) through the EXERTION of his efforts despite possible obstacles.

6 strokes

动 move, motion — Traditional 動

dòng

行动 *xíngdòng* **action, move, operation**

自动 *zìdòng* **automatic, voluntary**

活动 *huódòng* **activity; movable**

To MOVE clouds (云), you don't need much power (力).

13 strokes

勤 diligence, frequent, hard working

qín

勤劳 *qínláo* **diligent, hard working**

勤密 *qínmì* **frequent, regular, constant**

Young HARD WORKING people cut grass for days (日) on end on an extra-long plot of land (土), exhibit DILIGENCE, and exert lots of power (力).

9 strokes

重 heavy, weight, repetition

zhòng/chóng

重量 *zhòngliàng* **weight**

重要 *zhòngyào* **important**

重复 *chóngfù* **to repeat**

A HEAVY cart (车) needed two sets of wheels, but one of these still bent under the weight.

Speech or Words 言/讠

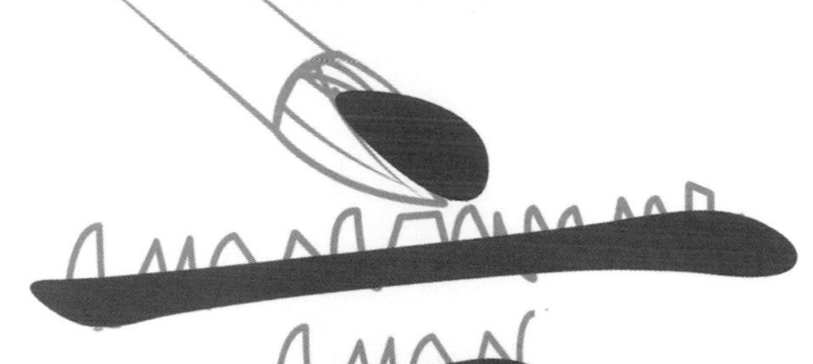

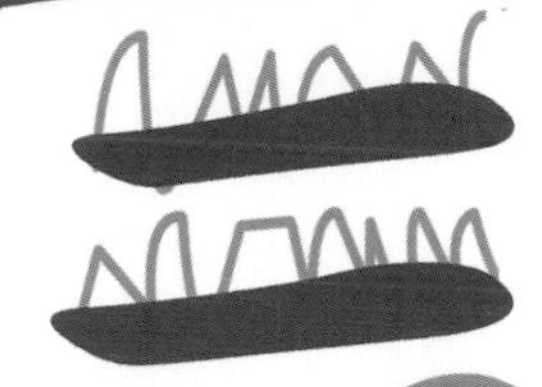

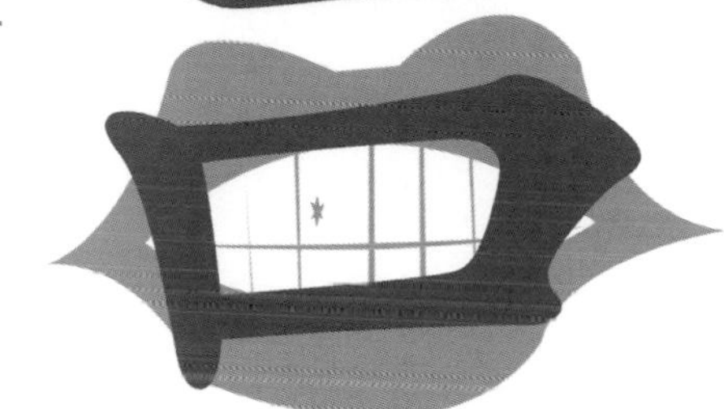

Four lines of a SPEECH were SAID.

7 strokes

言 **say, speech, words**

yán

言语 ***yányǔ*** **speech, talk, language**

言辞 ***yáncí*** **words**

4 strokes

计 **measure, plan, project** Traditional 計

jì

计算 ***jìsuàn*** **to measure**

计划 ***jìhuà*** **plan, project**

设计 ***shèjì*** **design**

He said to go over the PLAN 10 (十) times and implement it before you can MEASURE its success.

5 strokes

训 **train, teach, instruction** Traditional 訓

xùn

训练 ***xùnliàn*** **practice, training**

培训 ***péixùn*** **to train, cultivate**

The teacher's words (讠/言) and INSTRUCTION flowed like a river (川) during her explanation.

6 strokes

许 **allow, promise, permit** Traditional 許

xǔ

允许 ***yǔnxǔ*** **to allow, permit**

也许 ***yěxǔ*** **maybe, perhaps**

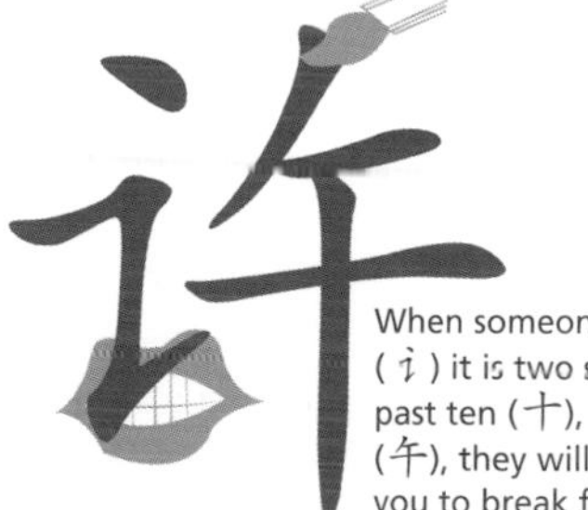

When someone says (讠) it is two strokes past ten (十), or noon (午), they will ALLOW you to break for lunch.

5 strokes

让 let, allow, give way

Traditional 讓

ràng

让步 ***ràngbù*** **to yield, give in**

让路 ***rànglù*** **to give way**

A person said to look up (上) and GIVE WAY to people coming down.

10 strokes

请 please, invite

Traditional 請

qǐng

请问 ***qǐngwèn*** **excuse me, may I ask...**

邀请 ***yāoqǐng*** **to invite**

After I said "PLEASE," they said (讠) that I had the green (青) light to INVITE others.

They say that in THEORY, a person shouldn't put the ladle back in the soup after tasting from it, but we could DISCUSS the practicality of this.

6 strokes

论 theory, discuss, view

Traditional 論

lùn

理论 ***lǐlùn*** **theory**

讨论 ***tǎolùn*** **to discuss**

评论 ***pínglùn*** **commentary, review**

12 strokes

谢 thank

Traditional 謝

xiè

感谢 ***gǎnxiè*** **thanks, gratitude**

谢谢 ***xièxie*** **thank you**

凋谢 ***diāoxiè*** **to wither and fall, die of old age**

It is nice to THANK vocally (讠) those who help you a little (寸) when your body (身) falters.

4 strokes

认 recognize, identify, know

Traditional 認

rèn

认识 ***rènshi*** **understanding, to know**

承认 ***chéngrèn*** **recognition, acknowledgment**

The person said (讠) that he would RECOGNIZE the other person (人).

10 strokes

Traditional

谁 **who, anyone** 誰

shuí/shéi

谁知道 *shéizhīdào* **God knows.../ who would have thought...?**

你是谁 *nǐshì shéi* **Who are you?**

The people in the photo were small birds in a flock and no one could say WHO they were.

6 strokes

Traditional

讲 **speak, discuss, explain** 講

jiǎng

讲话 *jiǎnghuà* **to talk, speak**

讲解 *jiǎngjiě* **to explain, comment**

It is important to DISCUSS where and how a well (井) will be dug for many reasons.

7 strokes

Traditional

证 **prove, certificate** 證

zhèng

证明 *zhèngmíng* **to prove, certify**

证据 *zhèngjù* **evidence**

证书 *zhèngshū* **certificate**

If you can stop and and say that you can PROVE something is correct (正), you should receive a CERTIFICATE.

5 strokes

Traditional

记 **record, scribe, remember** 記

jì

记录 *jìlù* **record, to note**

记忆 *jìyì* **memory, to remember**

日记 *rìjì* **diary**

RECORD personal (己) notes on a long scroll.

8 strokes

Traditional

话 **talk, conversation** 話

huà

说话 *shuōhuà* **chat, to talk**

会话 *huìhuà* **conversation**

电话 *diànhuà* **telephone**

When giving a TALK or having a CONVERSATION, we use lines of words and talk with our mouths, and tongues (舌).

Words (讠) and chants at a temple (寺) were often similar to POETRY.

8 strokes

诗 poetry, poem

Traditional 詩

shī

诗人 ***shīrén*** poet

诗意 ***shīyì*** poetry

9 strokes

说 speak, say, tell of

Traditional 説

shuō

说明 ***shuōmíng*** explanation

小说 ***xiǎoshuō*** novel, (short) story

An older brother (兄) sprouts horns as he likes TO SPEAK about some of the rumors others might TELL OF.

10 strokes

读 read, study, learn

Traditional 讀

dú

阅读 ***yuèdú*** to read

读书 ***dúshū*** reading, study, learning

The teacher said to do two things, READ and STUDY the ten (十) words for a big (大) quiz.

8 strokes

试 test, try, attempt

Traditional 試

shì

试验 ***shìyàn*** test, experiment

尝试 ***chángshì*** to try, attempt

Say that you will ATTEMPT to construct (工) a structure that will TEST your ability to catch (弋) your enemies.

9 strokes

语 word, speech, language — Traditional 語

yǔ

语言 *yǔyán* language

汉语 *Hànyǔ* Chinese language

日语 *Rìyǔ* Japanese language

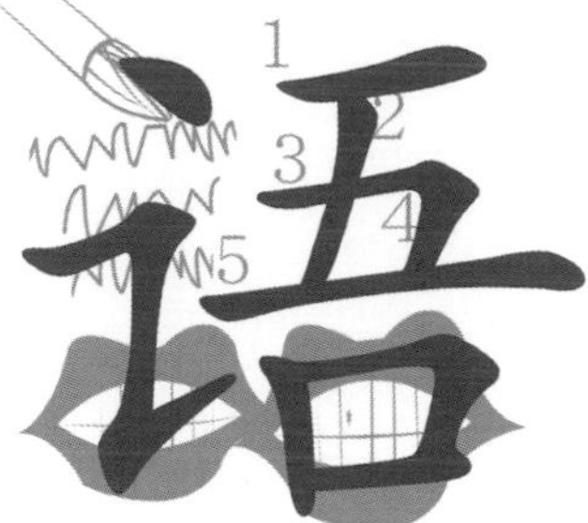

If five (五) people say the same words, they become LANGUAGE.

10 strokes

调 tune, tone, adjust — Traditional 調

diào/tiáo

曲调 *qǔdiào* tune, melody

声调 *shēngdiào* tone, note

调整 *tiáozhěng* adjustment, revision

When writing the words to a TUNE, some are partially confined to saying things about the land (土) and tradition.

10 strokes

谈 discuss, talk — Traditional 談

tán

谈论 *tánlùn* to talk, discuss

谈话 *tánhuà* conversation, talk, chat

When we DISCUSS politics or religion the words often become quite heated and sparks ignite tempers on fire (火).

10 strokes

课 lesson, class, subject — Traditional 課

kè

上课 *shàngkè* to attend class

中文课 *Zhōngwénkè* Chinese language subject/class

教课 *jiāokè* to teach [a class]

In the LESSON, on the SUBJECT of farming, we talked about working in fields (田) and with tree (木) in orchards.

Directions 方向

5 strokes

北 north

běi

北方 *běifāng* north

北京 *Běijīng* Beijing

北海道 *Běihǎidào*
[island of] Hokkaido [*lit.* north sea road]

A table stands on end with a dipper beside it, both pointing upward or NORTH.

4 strokes

方 square, direction

fāng

四方 *sìfāng* square

方向 *fāngxiàng* direction

方法 *fāngfǎ* way, method

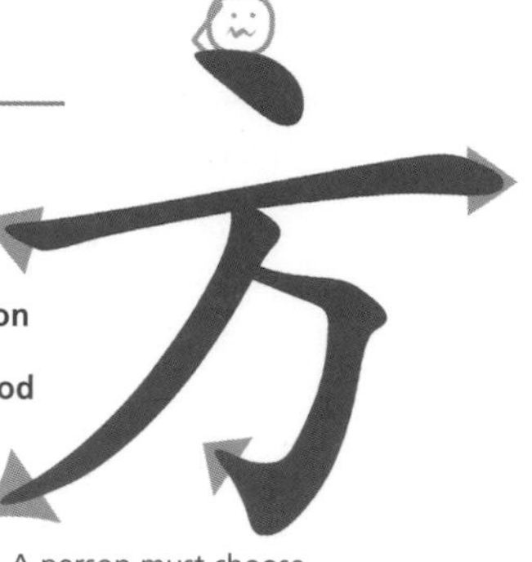

A person must choose which DIRECTION to take all of the time.

9 strokes

 南 south

nán

南方 *nánfāng* south

南美 *Nánměi* South America

The crosshairs of a compass point toward the SOUTH, to New Zealand where lots of sheep (羊) are raised.

8 strokes

放 put, lay, set free, release

fàng

放置 *fàngzhì* placement, to put, lay

释放 *shìfàng* to release, emancipate

放送 *fàngsòng* to broadcast

That person (方) sat at a folding table ready to SET FREE some insects that his child had caught.

5 strokes

 东 east

Traditional  東

dōng

东方 *dōngfāng* orient, east, eastern

东京 *Dōngjīng* Tokyo

If you look at the sun rising behind a tree, you face EAST.

6 strokes

 西 west

xī

西洋 *xīyáng* western

西岸 *xīàn* west coast

With a map hanging from a screen, the last of the four directions are north, south, east, and WEST.

3 strokes

上 on, above, up, on top

shàng

上面 ***shàngmiàn*** **above/up**

上升 ***shàngshēng*** **to rise, go up/ascend**

These two lines or stems point ABOVE the ground and ASCEND upward.

3 strokes

下 below, under

xià

下面 ***xiàmiàn*** **below, under**

下午 ***xiàwǔ*** **afternoon**

Two lines or roots point BELOW the horizon line.

6 strokes

song, melody, bend, twist

qǔ/qū

乐曲 ***yuèqǔ*** **music [composition]**

弯曲 ***wānqū*** **bending, curve**

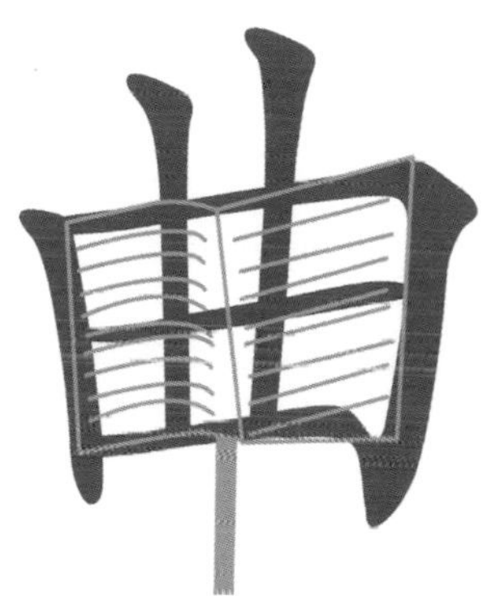

The SONG sheet at the top the stand is ready for someone to BEND or turn the page as the MELODY progresses.

5 strokes

左 left

zuǒ

左边 ***zuǒbiān*** **left**

The scale is on the LEFT of this I-beam (工) and is less heavy than the block on right (右).

5 strokes

right

yòu

右边 ***yòubiān*** **right**

On a scale, the half with the solid block is heavier on the RIGHT side.

Coming and Going 来去

5 strokes

归 **return, go back**

Traditional 歸

guī

回归 ***huíguī*** **to return, regression**

归家 ***guījiā*** **to return home**

RETURN the knife to its place next to the shelf.

10 strokes

 **depart, leave**

Traditional 離

lí

离开 ***líkāi*** **to depart**

分离 ***fēnlí*** **to separate, detach**

距离 ***jùlí*** **distance**

I (厶) wanted to LEAVE my box, but was afraid that bad (凶) things might happen and the lid would be blown off of every situation.

10 strokes

 **trip, travel**

lǚ

旅游 ***lǚyóu*** **trip, travel, tourism, tour**

旅行 ***lǚxíng*** **travel, journey**

旅客 ***lǚkè*** **passenger, traveler**

For a TRIP, a person chooses a direction (方), and goes, waving his arms back and forth as he goes forward.

To CLIMB a mountain by sunset, take plenty of beans (豆) to fill your stomach for energy on the ASCENT.

12 strokes

登 **ascend, climb up**

dēng

登山 ***dēngshān*** **mountain climbing**

登陆 ***dēnglù*** **to land, come ashore**

登记 ***dēngjì*** **to register, check in, entry**

5 strokes

 **issue, departure, discover**

Traditional 

fā

发出 ***fāchū*** **to issue, send out**

出发 ***chūfā*** **departure**

发现 ***fāxiàn*** **discovery, detection**

Before your DEPARTURE to DISCOVER the mountain beyond, have a seat at the table and plan your route.

CHAPTER 5

PLANTS and TREES

We PLANT trees in hopes that they grow straight (直) as you look at them from end to end.

12 strokes

植 plant, grow

zhí

植物 ***zhíwù*** **plants**

种植 ***zhòngzhí*** **to plant, crop**

6 strokes

米 uncooked rice, meter

mǐ

米饭 ***mǐfàn*** **cooked rice**

厘米 ***límǐ*** **centimeter**

The RICE is ready for harvest when the leaves begin to bend down like branches of a tree (木).

Rice 米 and Tree 木

10 strokes

 **flour, powder**

fěn

面粉 ***miànfěn*** **flour, wheat flour**

粉末 ***fěnmò*** **powder, very small pieces**

花粉 ***huāfěn*** **pollen**

Rice (米) broken into smaller components (分) is usually made into FLOUR or POWDER.

4 strokes

 **tree, wood**

mù

木材 ***mùcái*** **wood, timber**

树木 ***shùmù*** **tree[s]**

The branches of this TREE stretch big and tall.

A key MATERIAL in cooking is rice (米) that is stirred with a flattened spoon (斗).

10 strokes

 **feed, materials, expect, guess**

liào

材料 ***cáiliào*** **materials, ingredients**

预料 ***yùliào*** **to expect, anticipate**

8 strokes

 **woods, grove**

lín

树林 ***shùlín*** **woods**

农林 ***nónglín*** **agriculture and forestry**

A small GROVE or WOODS has only a couple of trees.

Three trees overlap on the edge of a FORREST.

12 strokes

 **forest**

sēn

森林 ***sēnlín*** **forest**

5 strokes

本 book, basis, origin, foundation

běn

本子 ***běnzi*** **notebook, book**

根本 ***gēnběn*** **fundamental; key, basis**

The ORIGIN of a tree can be discovered in its roots.

8 strokes

果 fruit, nut

guǒ

果实 ***guǒshí*** **fruit**

结果 ***jiéguǒ*** **result, outcome**

The FRUIT and NUT trees (木) are like individual fields (田) of deliciousness.

10 strokes

根 root, radical

gēn

树根 ***shùgēn*** **tree root**

根源 ***gēnyuán*** **source, root, origin**

The ROOT of a tree (木) is similar to the RADICAL good (良).

8 strokes

松 pine tree

sōng

松树 ***sōngshù*** **pine [tree]**

松鼠 ***sōngshǔ*** **squirrel**

A tree (木) that is green more than eight (八) months that I (厶) can frequently see is a PINE TREE.

11 strokes

检 inspect, examination, investigate

Traditional

檢

jiǎn

检查 ***jiǎnchá*** **inspection, examination**

检验 ***jiǎnyàn*** **to test, examine, inspect**

To be a person (人) who can successfully grow bonsai trees (木), you must INSPECT seedlings carefully as they grow.

9 strokes

树 timber tree, set up, establish

Traditional

樹

shù

树木 ***shùmù*** **trees and shrubs, arbor**

树立 ***shùlì*** **to establish, forming**

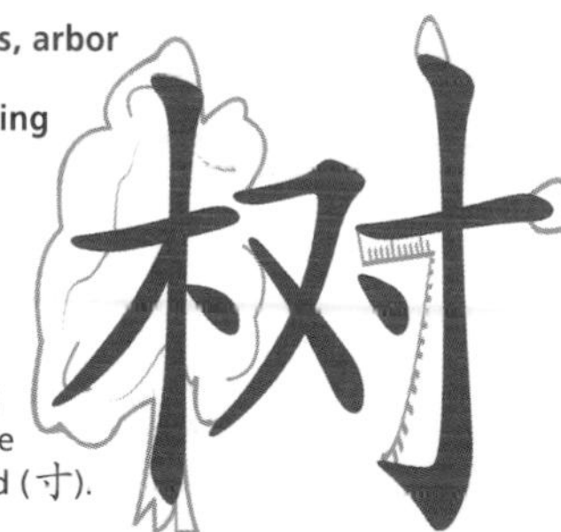

Timber is cut using a table saw and the WOOD is measured (寸).

It is EXTREMELY dangerous to place a chair on a table (又) to climb to the top of a tree (木) to pick fruit, rather than knocking it down with POLES.

7 strokes

Traditional

极 pole, extremely 極

jí

极端 ***jíduān*** **exceedingly, extremely**

南极 ***nánjí*** **South Pole, Antarctica**

8 strokes

Traditional

构 posture, build, pretend 構

gòu

构造 ***gòuzào*** **to build, construct, composition**

架构 ***jiàgòu*** **architecture**

结构 ***jiégòu*** **structure, framework**

Beside the tall tree (木), I (厶) will BUILD hooks (勹) to pull things up after I climb it.

6 strokes

Traditional

 authority, power, rights 權

quán

权力 ***quánlì*** **[political] power, authority**

特权 ***tèquán*** **privilege, special right**

A person spoke about RIGHTS and the POWER exhibited by those with AUTHORITY at a sturdy table by a tree (木).

14 strokes

模 imitate, copy, pattern

mó

模仿 ***mófǎng*** **to imitate, copy, mock**

规模 ***guīmó*** **scale, extent, dimension**

模式 ***móshì*** **model, pattern**

You can COPY the shape of a bonsai tree (木), but like blades of grass, on sunny days (日), they can grow big (大) and out of control quickly.

The wooden (木) SIGNPOST was meant to show (示) others a SYMBOL that would be easily recognized.

9 strokes

Traditional

 signpost, symbol trademark, 標

biāo

标志 ***biāozhì*** **mark, sign, symbol**

目标 ***mùbiāo*** **target, objective, goal**

6 strokes

机 machine, opportunity

Traditional 機

jī

飞机 *fēijī* airplane

机械 *jīxiè* machine, mechanism

时机 *shíjī* opportunity, occasion

When using wood (木), take the OPPORTUNITY to use tools and MACHINES to help with a project.

5 strokes

not yet, have not

wèi

未来 *wèilái* future

This is the tree house dad built that my little sister (妹) has NOT YET seen.

7 strokes

bundle, ream

shù

约束 *yueshù* restraint, to restrict, bind

结束 *jiéshù* ending, conclusion

This tree is in a BUNDLE, with a tie around it, ready to be moved to a new garden.

7 strokes

article, item, strike

Traditional 

tiáo

条款 *tiáokuǎn* article, clause, provision

条件 *tiáojiàn* condition, term, requirement

Our folding table (夂) is a well-made ITEM that seemed to spin around as it was opened.

7 strokes

lumber, timber, talent

cái

木材 *mùcái* wood, timber

材料 *cáiliào* ingredients, materials

人材 *réncái* talented person

This talented (才) person can balance on a wooden (木) TIMBER to show off his TALENT.

5 strokes

end, last, final stage

mò

周末 *zhōumò* weekend

The longest new branch is the LAST grown from the top END of the tree.

8 strokes

枝 **branch, limb**

zhī

树枝 ***shùzhī*** **tree branch, limb**

枝节 ***zhījié*** **minor matters, detail**

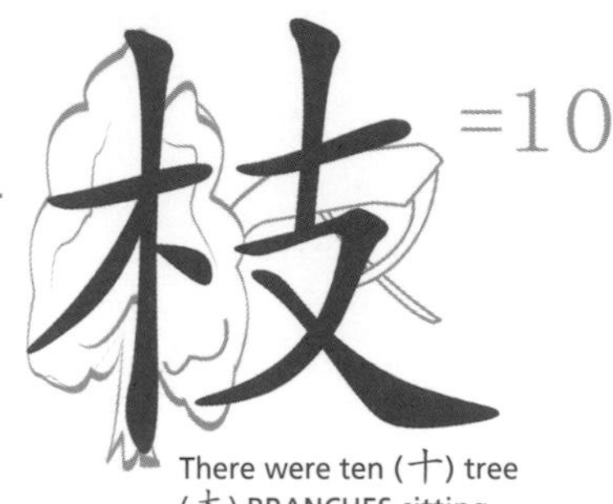

There were ten (十) tree (木) BRANCHES sitting on the table (又).

5 strokes

乐 **happy, music, comfort**

Traditional 樂

lè/yuè

快乐 ***kuàilè*** **happy, joyful, cheerful**

欢乐 ***huānlè*** **joy, pleasure, glee, mirth**

音乐 ***yīnyuè*** **music**

A small (小) person is HAPPY and CHEERFUL as he stretches out his arms to dance to the MUSIC in front of the cliff.

8 strokes

板 **plank, board, stage**

bǎn

木板 ***mùbǎn*** **board, plank**

黑板 ***hēibǎn*** **blackboard, chalkboard**

老板 ***lǎobǎn*** **boss, proprietor, shopkeeper**

A BOARD beside the tree (木) at the base of the cliff (厂) marked where the STAGE would be in front of the tables (又).

10 strokes

桥 **bridge**

Traditional 橋

qiáo

桥梁 ***qiáoliáng*** **bridge**

The stately (乔) BRIDGE stands tall by the tree (木).

5 strokes

 **business, industry**

Traditional 業

yè

工业 ***gōngyè*** **industry**

行业 ***hángyè*** **enterprise, business**

With more construction, BUSINESS and INDUSTRY in Asia (亚) has been booming.

10 strokes

格 grid, lattice, style

gé

格子 *gézi* lattice, grid

性格 *xìnggé* character, personality

资格 *zīgé* qualifications

Through the LATTICE next to the tree (木), we could hear voices (口).

9 strokes

荣 flourish, prosperity, glory

Traditional 榮

róng

繁荣 *fánróng* prosperity, to bloom, flourish

荣耀 *róngyào* glory, honor

Grass and trees (木) will FLOURISH if well cared for.

10 strokes

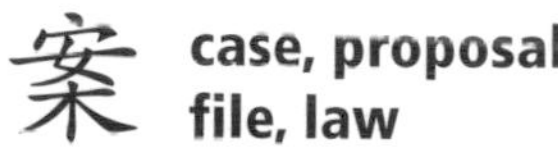

案 case, proposal, file, law

àn

档案 *dǎng'àn* file, record, archives

法案 *fǎ'àn* bill, proposed law, act

The woman (女) enjoyed the peaceful (安) nature of the wood structure and sturdy roof (宀) as she made a PROPOSAL to purchase it.

7 strokes

村 village

cūn

村莊 *cūnzhuāng* village, hamlet

乡村 *xiāngcūn* country, rural

On the edges of a VILLAGE, small (寸) trees (木) both help protect it and supply wood for cooking fires.

9 strokes

查 investigate, search, inspect

chá

检查 *jiǎnchá* inspection, to examine, check

调查 *diàochá* survey, investigation

搜查 *sōuchá* to search

If you want to raise small bonsai trees (木), carefully INVESTIGATE how much sunlight to have each day and INSPECT them daily.

10 strokes

校 school, exam

xiào/jiào

学校 *xuéxiào* school

校长 *xiàozhǎng* school principal

校对 *jiàoduì* to proof, proofread

Long ago, your father might "SCHOOL" you under a roof by a tree, or teach you that 8–2=6.

Fancy Tree, Rice Plant 禾

Rice plants (禾) seem to change few (少) a shades of color every few SECONDS with the sunset.

9 strokes

 **second(s)**

miǎo

一秒 ***yīmiǎo*** **one second**

For your science COURSE, measure (斗) the recent rainfall in the soil of the fancy trees and the rice plants.

9 strokes

科 **branch, department, course**

kē

科学 ***kēxué*** **science**

教科书 ***jiàokēshū*** **textbook**

科目 ***kēmù*** **subject [school]**

7 strokes

 **private, personal, secret**

sī

私人 ***sīrén*** **private, personal**

自私 ***zìsī*** **selfish**

My favorite fancy tree is on PRIVATE property and its location is SECRET.

What is the NAME of that little (小) dancer that would twirl around as gracefully as the leaves fall from a fancy tree (禾)?

10 strokes

称 **weigh, name**

Traditional 稱

chēng

称量 ***chēngliáng*** **to weigh**

称呼 ***chēnghu*** **call, address**

4 strokes

 **Big Dipper, dipper**

dǒu

北斗星 ***běidǒuxīng*** **the Big Dipper**

斗 ***dǒu*** **liquid measure unit (one dipper = 10 liters)**

Two splashes of water spill from this rain guage.

11 strokes

移 shift, move

yí

移动 *yídòng* to move, shift, transfer

移民 *yímín* immigrant, migration, immigration

Fancy trees (禾) frequently (多) SHIFT colors and MOVE our minds with their beauty.

9 strokes

种 plant, species, seed, kind

Traditional 種

zhǒng/zhòng

种子 *zhǒngzǐ* seed

种类 *zhǒnglèi* kind, species

种植 *zhòngzhí* to plant, cultivate, crop

In the middle (中) of the fruit from fancy trees (禾) are SEEDS.

12 strokes

程 distance, journey, degree

chéng

路程 *lùchéng* distance, journey

程度 *chéngdù* degree, level, extent

行程 *xíngchéng* distance traveled, itinerary, route

The king (王) said (口) that he liked the fancy trees (禾) distance traveled, he had seen on a JOURNEY quite some DISTANCE from home.

10 strokes

积 volume, accumulate, contents, pile up

Traditional 積

jī

体积 *tǐjī* volume, bulk

累积 *lěijī* to accumulate

积极 *jījí* positive, active

Leaves from fancy trees (禾) ACCUMULATE and simply (只) need to be picked up.

12 strokes

税 tax, duty

shuì

税收 *shuìshōu* tax, duty

关税 *guānshuì* duty, customs, tariff

My older brother (兄) was so mean that he had horns on his head and charged me a TAX to climb the fancy tree (禾) in the backyard!

Bamboo 竹 / ⺮

Two sections of BAMBOO with young leaves grow fast.

6 strokes

竹 bamboo

zhú

竹竿 ***zhúgān*** **bamboo pole**

爆竹 ***bàozhú*** **firecracker**

11 strokes

第 section, No.

dì

第三课 ***dìsānkè*** **Lesson/ Chapter 3**

My younger brother (弟) used SECTIONS of bamboo rather than normal arrows with his bow to show that he was the NUMBER 1 archer.

The performer balances bamboo (⺮) overhead while the crowd begins to LAUGH.

10 strokes

笑 laugh

xiào

微笑 ***wéixiào*** **to smile**

嘲笑 ***cháoxiào*** **to sneer, laugh at**

12 strokes

答 solution, answer

dá

回答 ***huídá*** **to answer, reply, response**

答案 ***dá'àn*** **answer, solution**

报答 ***bàodá*** **to repay, requite**

These two bamboo shoots match (合) and studying them helped the botanist find a correct SOLUTION to a problem that needed an ANSWER.

12 strokes

策 scheme, plan

cè

策略 ***cèlüè*** **scheme, tactic**

失策 ***shīcè*** **lapse, unwise, inexpedient**

The PLAN to protect the bamboo shoots was to plant trees (木) with thorns, but since thorns hurt, it might not have been the best SCHEME.

12 strokes

等 wait, grade, class, equality

děng

等待 ***děngdài*** **to wait, await**

等级 ***děngjí*** **grade, rank**

平等 ***píngděng*** **equality, evenness**

Like the evenness of stalks of bamboo, meditation at a temple (寺) should bring EQUALITY of mind and spirit to all participants regardless of CLASS.

14 strokes

算 calculate, divining, estimate

suàn

计算 ***jìsuàn*** **to calculate, count**

算术 ***suànshù*** **arithmetic**

预算 ***yùsuàn*** **to estimate, budget**

To CALCULATE how much bamboo will grow, focus your eyes (目) on the young shoots and make an ESTIMATE.

12 strokes

筋 muscle, tendon

jīn

脑筋 ***nǎojīn*** **brain, mind**

抽筋 ***chōujīn*** **cramp**

Like bamboo, every month (月) my MUSCLE power (力) becomes greater.

10 strokes

笔 pen, brush

Traditional 筆

bǐ

圆珠笔 ***yuánzhūbǐ*** **pen (ballpoint pen)**

铅笔 ***qiānbǐ*** **pencil**

毛笔 ***máobǐ*** **Chinese calligraphy writing brush**

14 strokes

 管 pipe, tube, wind instrument, manage

guǎn

管子 ***guǎnzi*** **tube, pipe**

气管 ***qìguǎn*** **trachea, windpipe**

管理 ***guǎnlǐ*** **to manage, administration [of business, etc.]**

Bamboo has caps (冖) between segments, but they grow end to end and can be used as PIPES, or WIND INSTRUMENTS.

The writing BRUSH is made of bamboo.

Grass 草/艹

5 strokes

节 season, period, occasion Traditional 節

jié

季节 *jìjié* **season, period**

节日 *jiérì* **festival, holidays, gala**

节目 *jiémù* **program, show, item**

When a new SEASON begins, fresh grass (艹) can be cut and used.

15 strokes

箱 box, chest, bin, trunk.

xiāng

箱子 *xiāngzi* **box, case, container**

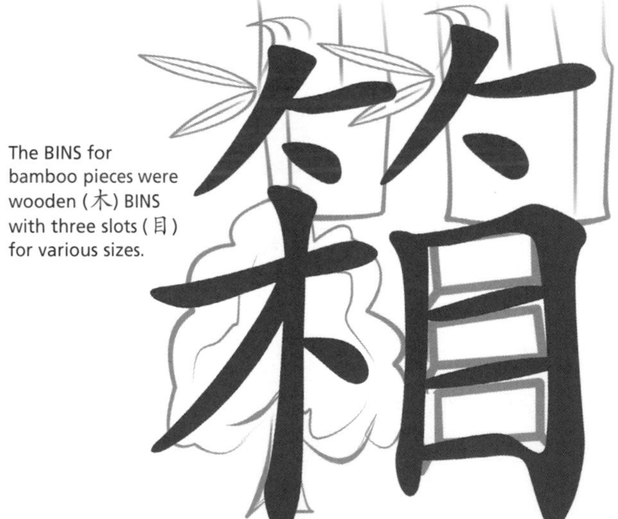

The BINS for bamboo pieces were wooden (木) BINS with three slots (目) for various sizes.

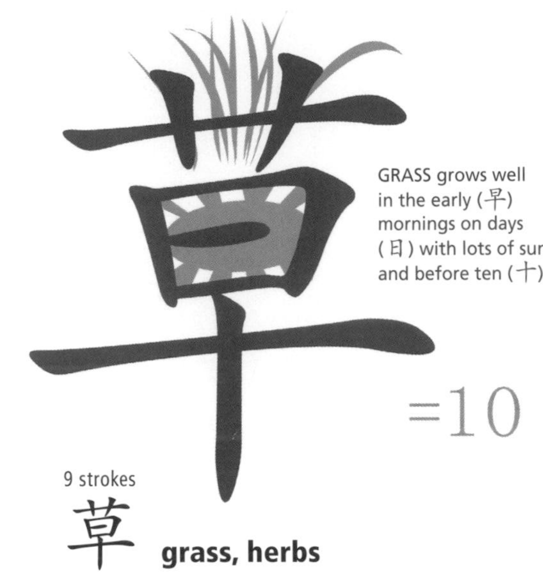

GRASS grows well in the early (早) mornings on days (日) with lots of sun and before ten (十).

9 strokes

草 grass, herbs

cǎo

绿草 *lǜcǎo* **green grass**

草原 *cǎoyuán* **prairie, grassland**

草药 *cǎoyào* **herbs**

8 strokes

若 as if, like

ruò

倘若 *tǎngruò* **as if, supposing, in case**

若干 *ruògān* **several**

The grasses (艹) here look AS IF they grow to the right (右) due to the wind.

7 strokes

花 flower

huā

花瓶 *huāpíng* flower vase

花园 *huāyuán* garden

Through the grass, wild FLOWERS pop up.

10 strokes

荷 lotus, load

hé

荷花 *héhuā* lotus

负荷 *fùhè* load, burden

What a person sees through the grass in the pond is a beautiful LOTUS flower.

8 strokes

英 Britain, outstanding

yīng

英国 *Yīngguó* traditional name for England

英语 *Yīngyǔ* English

英雄 *yīngxióng* hero, heroic

In front of the grassy hill, a gardener in BRITIAN holds a box of seedlings ready to plant.

11 strokes

菜 vegetables, greens, side dish

cài

蔬菜 *shūcài* vegetable

配菜 *pèicài* side dish

Despite the shade of a tree and tall grass, the VEGETABLES grew.

8 strokes

苦 suffering, bitter

kǔ

痛苦 *tòngkǔ* pain, suffering

辛苦 *xīnkǔ* hard, strenuous, laborious

苦味 *kǔwèi* bitterness, bitter taste

Old (古) grass might taste really BITTER and will make you feel like you are SUFFERING if you eat much of it.

4 strokes

艺 art, skill, technique, craft

Traditional 藝

yì

艺术 *yìshù* [fine] art, the arts

技艺 *jìyì* skill, artistry

Making ART with only two (二) blades of grass by myself (厶) could be an interesting performance.

5 strokes

叶 leaf

Traditional 葉

yè

树叶 *shùyè* leaf

落叶 *luòyè* fallen leaves, to lose leaves (of a plant)

The LEAVES of a tree (木) are an entire world (世) of their own for the creatures who live among them.

16 strokes

薄 thin, weak, shallow

bó

单薄 *dānbó* thin, flimsy

薄弱 *bóruò* weak, frail

浅薄 *qiǎnbó* shallow, meager

With too much water, the grasses in all ten (十) SHALLOW fields (田) are now THIN and WEAK with little (寸) strength to stand up against the wind.

12 strokes

落 fall, drop, go down

luò

降落 *jiàngluò* to land, descend

落后 *luòhòu* backward, behind

Grassy herbs sitting on a garden table need DROPS of water to FALL regularly so they grow into delicious accents of flavor.

A person (人) collects TEA leaves from plants by hand.

9 strokes

药 medicine, chemical

Traditional 藥

yào

中药 *Zhōngyào* Chinese medicine

药房 *yàofáng* pharmacy, drugstore

The grasses that make herbal MEDICINE are gathered in a ladle (勺) woven from silk (丝) threads.

9 strokes

茶 tea

chá

茶叶 *cháyè* tea, tea leaf

茶具 *chájù* tea set

CHAPTER 6

ANIMALS

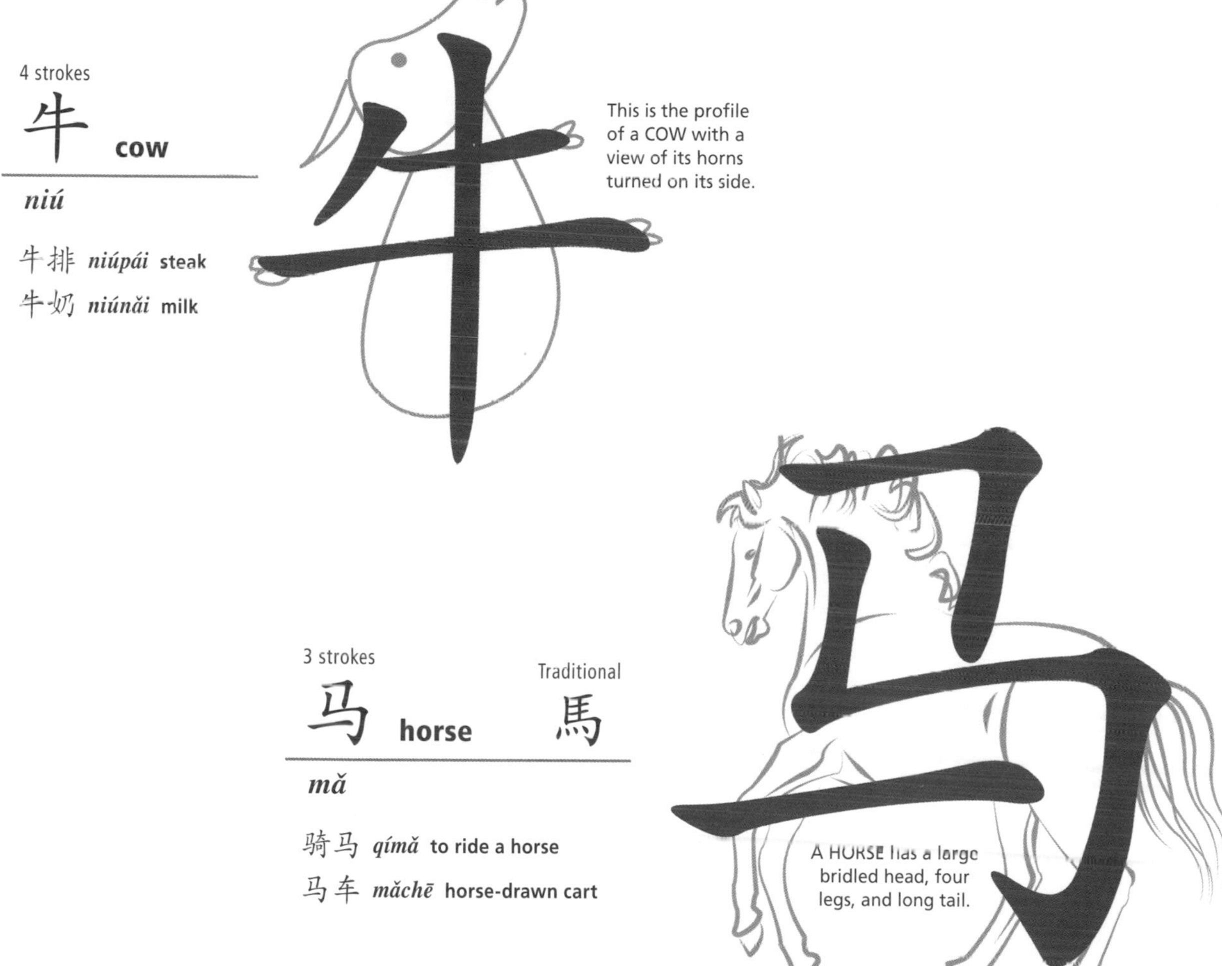

This is the profile of a COW with a view of its horns turned on its side.
A HORSE has a large bridled head, four legs, and long tail.

4 strokes

牛 **cow**

niú

牛排 ***niúpái*** **steak**

牛奶 ***niúnǎi*** **milk**

3 strokes

马 **horse** Traditional 馬

mǎ

骑马 ***qímǎ*** **to ride a horse**

马车 ***mǎchē*** **horse-drawn cart**

Animals 动物

8 strokes

物 thing, object, matter

wù

食物 *shíwù* food

动物 *dòngwù* animal

It's not a cow (牛), but it is a THING that you can never (勿) do without.

This ELEPHANT leans back with its long curved tusk and trunk in the air.

12 strokes

象 elephant, shape

xiàng

大象 *dàxiàng* elephant

印象 *yìnxiàng* impression

8 strokes

牧 care for, shepherd, govern

mù

牧羊 *mùyáng* shepherd

牧师 *mùshī* pastor, [religious] minister

牧场 *mùchǎng* farm [livestock], ranch

Cows (牛) that are well CARED FOR will eventuatlly make good meat to the table (夂).

10 strokes

验 verification, effect, testing

Traditional 驗

yàn

试验 *shìyàn* examination, test

经验 *jīngyàn* experience

10 strokes

特 special

tè

特别 *tèbié* special, unusual

特色 *tèsè* characteristic, distinguishing feature

A cow (牛) at a temple is a SPECIAL thing according to the Hindu religion.

A thoroughbred horse undergoes TESTING by a man who looks for VERIFICATION of the EFFECTS of its food and environment.

14 strokes

像 statue, portrait, likeness

xiàng

影像 *yǐngxiàng* image, portrait

像似 *xiàngsì* to be like, resemble

佛像 *fóxiàng* Buddhist image [statue]

A person stands still as a STATUE next to an elephant (象) to get his PICTURE taken.

9 strokes

差 poor, distinction, difference

chā

差异 *chāyì* difference

差错 *chācuò* error, mistake

A POOR farmer took his sheep (羊) to the newly constructed (工) stockyards so everyone could see the fine DIFFERENCE between his sheep and others.

6 strokes

羊 sheep

yáng

绵羊 *miányáng* sheep

山羊 *shānyáng* goat

A SHEEP has two ears, a tail, two sets of legs, and a wide belly in the middle.

5 strokes

议 discuss, talk, confer

Traditional 議

yì

会议 *huìyì* meeting, conference

议论 *yìlùn* discussion, argument, debate

We can DISCUSS what to do and say (讠) where to mark choices with an "X".

9 strokes

美 beauty, beautiful

měi

美丽 *měilì* beautiful, pretty

美国 *Měiguó* United States

美国人 *Měiguórén* American (people)

Long ago, sheep were prized and a big one was considered very BEAUTIFUL.

7 strokes

迟 slow, late

Traditional 遲

chí

迟到 *chídào* late, tardy

延迟 *yánchí* to delay, postpone

Go SLOW along the path and measure (尺) it until LATE in the day.

10 strokes

appearance, model, pattern Traditional 樣

yàng

样子 *yàngzi* **appearance, looks, pattern**

榜样 *bǎngyàng* **example, model**

There is a MANNER in which you should keep sheep (羊) around trees (木) for shade and be sure to have water (水) nearby.

A big (大) DOG is going to eat a treat.

4 strokes

犬 **dog**

quǎn

警犬 *jǐngquǎn* **canine, police dog**

8 strokes

fortune, lucky, happiness

xìng

幸福 *xìngfú* **fortunate, happiness**

幸好 *xìnghǎo* **luckily, fortunately**

幸会 *xìnghuì* **very pleased to meet you**

When a little sheep (羊) sees fertile soil (土) with lush grass it feels HAPPINESS in its good FORTUNE.

5 strokes

dragon Traditional 龍

lóng

长龙 *chánglóng* **a long queue**

恐龙 *kǒnglóng* **dinosaur**

The DRAGON grabs a pearl that has come out of the cauldron.

The furry tail of a CAT is just there, in the grass by the field (田).

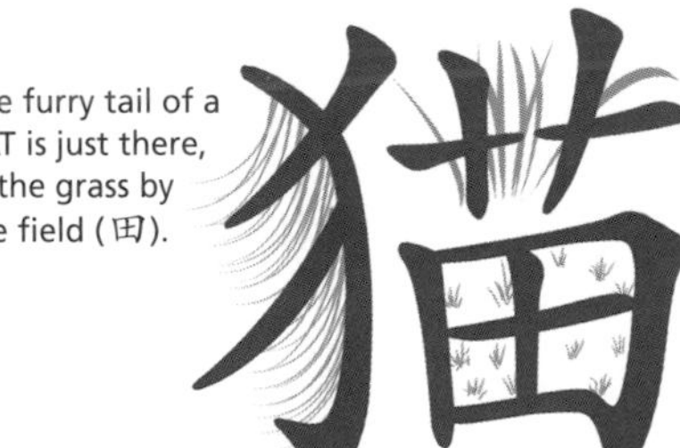

11 strokes

猫 **cat** Traditional 貓

māo

小猫 *xiǎomāo* **kitten**

10 strokes

狸 **raccoon**

lí

狸猫 ***límāo*** leopard cat

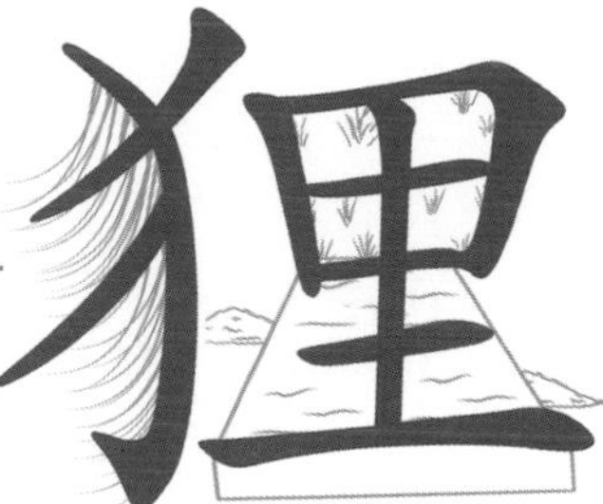

The racoon's tail sticks out as he enters his burrow in the ground (土) just beside the field (田).

8 strokes

狐 **fox**

hú

狐狸 ***húlí*** fox

银狐 ***yínhú*** silver fox

I saw the long hairs of a FOX (犭) and its paw (爪) prints myself (厶).

9 strokes

独 **single, spontaneously**

Traditional

獨

dú

独身 ***dúshēn*** bachelor, unmarried

孤独 ***gūdú*** solitude, loneliness

独立 ***dúlì*** independent

A SINGLE insect might jump SPONTANEOUSLY from the hair of a dog (犭) to you.

5 strokes

犯 **crime, offense**

fàn

犯人 ***fànrén*** offender, convict

犯罪 ***fànzuì*** crime

冒犯 ***màofàn*** to offend, violate

Long hairs were found at the scene of the CRIME when police searched around the area.

4 strokes

毛 **fur, hair**

máo

毛发 ***máofà*** hair

羊毛 ***yángmáo*** wool, fleece

This pig has a lot of scruffy FUR as compared to normal hair.

7 strokes

状 **status, conditions, circumstances**

Traditional

狀

zhuàng

状态 ***zhuàngtài*** current status, condition

状况 ***zhuàngkuàng*** situation, circumstance

CIRCUMSTANCES were right for the dog (犬) to catch the bone though he was backed into a corner.

9 strokes

将 future, lead, commander

Traditional 將

jiāng

将来 *jiānglái* future

将军 *jiāngjūn* general, checkmate (in chess game)

将领 *jiànglǐng* commander–in–chief

The COMMANDER flipped the table up on end that evening (夕) when he made the decision TO LEAD the others on a small (寸) detour.

14 strokes

熊 bear

xióng

熊 *xióng* bear

熊猫 *xióngmāo* panda (bear cat)

If I (厶) saw a BEAR by the light of a flickering moon (月), its paws might look like big spoons in the air.

10 strokes

能 can, may, ability, talent, skill

néng

可能 *kěnéng* likelihood, possibility

才能 *cáinéng* talent, ability

When I (厶) spent a month (月) stirring the soup, my TALENT and SKILL with a dipper (匕) improved.

5 strokes

鸟 bird

Traditional 鳥

niǎo

雀鸟 *quèniǎo* birds

This BIRD with a little feather on its head rests on a perch, its tail feather hanging low.

4 strokes

为 act as, do, become, make

Traditional 為

wéi/wèi

作为 *zuòwéi* to act as, action

行为 *xíngwéi* behavior

因为 *yīnwèi* because

ACT AS powerful (力) as possible so as to MAKE a big mark become two.

12 strokes

集 **gather, meet, flock**

jí

集合 *jíhé* **assembly, set, to gather, meet**

集体 *jítǐ* **group [of living things], crowd**

A FLOCK of birds (隹) will GATHER in a tree (木).

6 strokes

羽 **feather**

yǔ

羽毛 *yǔmáo* **feather, plume**

羽毛球 *yǔmáoqiú* **badminton**

These two wing FEATHERS are both split.

6 strokes

杂 **miscellaneous, mixed, various**

Traditional 雜

zá

杂志 *zázhì* **magazine**

复杂 *fùzá* **complex, complicated**

There are VARIOUS ideas of how to rank (朩) MISCELLANEOUS trees for their beauty and strength (力)

3 strokes

习 **study, practice, exercise, learn**

Traditional 習

xí

学习 *xuéxí* **to learn, study**

练习 *liànxí* **practice, exercise, drill**

习惯 *xíguàn* **habit, custom**

This feather dropped from a bird that was LEARNING to fly.

10 strokes

 **difficult, trouble, impossible**

Traditional 難

nán

困难 *kùnnán* **hard, difficult**

苦难 *kǔnàn* **suffering, distress**

灾难 *zāinàn* **disaster, catastrophe**

A bird in TROUBLE lands next to the table.

8 strokes

 **fish**

Traditional 

yú

金鱼 *jīnyú* **goldfish**

钓鱼 *diàoyú* **fishing, to fish**

The head of a FISH dives deep into the bottom of a field (田) as its tail flips up.

Shellfish 贝

4 strokes

贝 **shell, shellfish** Traditional 

bèi

贝壳 ***bèiké*** shell

宝贝 ***bǎobèi*** treasure, darling, baby [term of endearment]

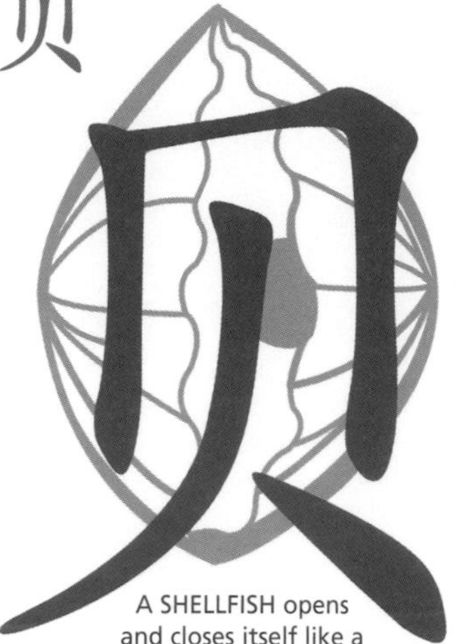

A SHELLFISH opens and closes itself like a blinking eye (目).

8 strokes

败 **failure, defeat** Traditional 

bài

打败 ***dǎbài*** to defeat, beat

失败 ***shībài*** failure, blunder

He suffered DEFEAT, as would a shellfish on a picnic table (夊).

6 strokes

则 **then, otherwise, principle** Traditional 則

zé

否则 ***fǒuzé*** otherwise, else

原则 ***yuánzé*** principle

You must use a knife (刂) to open a shellfish, OTHERWISE you might not be able to crack it.

8 strokes

 **goods, freight, property** Traditional 貨

huò

货物 ***huòwù*** goods, cargo, freight

货币 ***huòbì*** currency

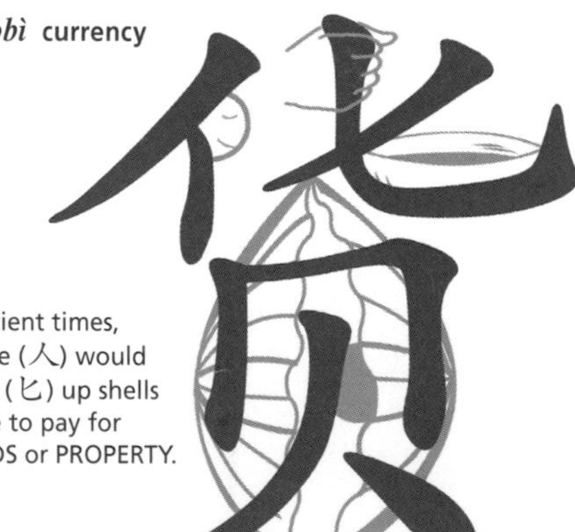

In ancient times, people (人) would scoop (匕) up shells to use to pay for GOODS or PROPERTY.

6 strokes

 **negative, bear, owe, defeat** Traditional 

fù

负面 ***fùmiàn*** negative [side]

背负 ***bēifù*** to bear

负伤 ***fùshāng*** to be wounded/injured

A shellfish will suffer DEFEAT when a sharp object pries it open.

8 strokes

质 **substance, quality** Traditional 質

zhí

品质 ***pǐnzhí*** quality [material]

性质 ***xìngzhì*** nature, property, character

As a matter of QUALITY control, ten (十) of the shells split by axes (斤) were checked for valuable pearls.

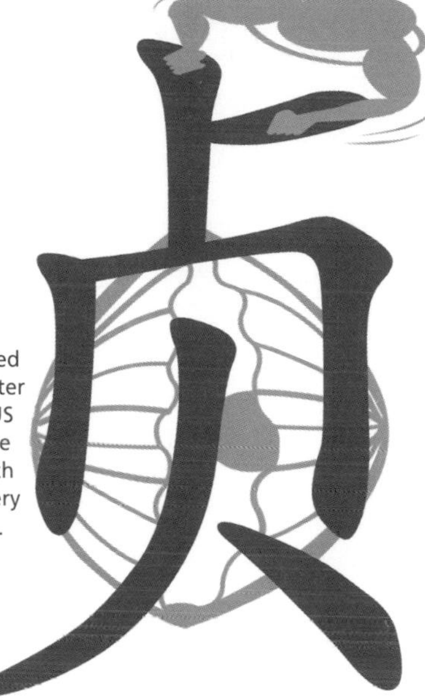

The fortune teller predicted that if the sitter was VIRTUOUS they would be rewarded with a pearl in every shellfish (贝).

8 strokes

贮 **savings, store** Traditional 貯

zhù

贮存 ***zhùcún*** storage

贮藏 ***zhùcáng*** to store up, lay in

STORE your SAVINGS of shellfish in a building with the roof and a chimney (宀) and spend them one (一) at a time.

6 strokes

贞 **chaste, virtuous, upright** Traditional 貞

zhēn

贞节 ***zhēnjié*** chastity

贞操 ***zhēncāo*** virginity

9 strokes

费 **cost, fee** Traditional 費

fèi

费用 ***fèiyòng*** cost, fee, expense

经费 ***jīngfèi*** fund, expenditure

会费 ***huìfèi*** meeting/event expense

The COST of goods could be paid for in shellfish in the past but the price on the spreadsheet grid always went up and down.

6 strokes

买 **buy** Traditional 買

mǎi

购买 ***gòumǎi*** to buy, purchase

买卖 ***mǎimài*** business, trade, buying and selling, transaction

The shelves here are fully stocked with items to BUY.

7 strokes

员 **member, person** Traditional 員

yuán

成员 ***chéngyuán*** member

员工 ***yuángōng*** staff, personnel

店员 ***diànyuán*** clerk, store employee

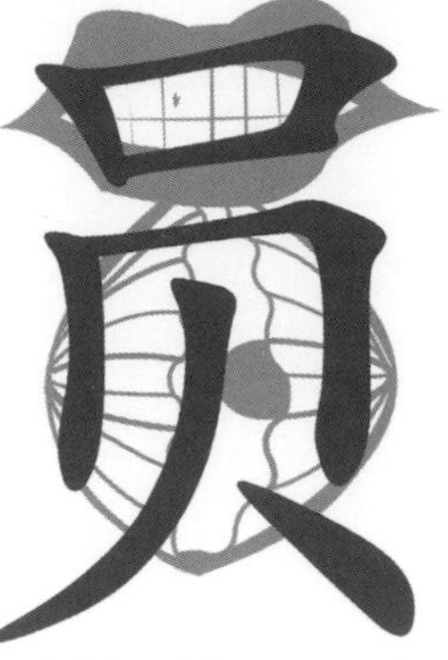

A MEMBER of the supermarket staff found shellfish so a PERSON who looked for them could buy them to feed hungry mouths (口).

11 strokes

惯 **get used to, become experienced** Traditional 慣

guàn

习惯 ***xíguàn*** habit, custom, practice

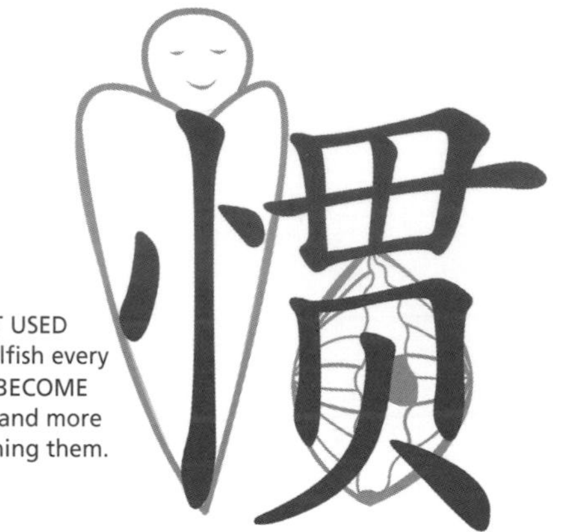

When you GET USED TO eating shellfish every (每) day, you BECOME EXPERIENCED and more skillful at opening them.

Your eyes (目) look over the COUNTY in which you yourself (厶) live.

7 strokes

县 **county** Traditional 縣

xiàn

县长 ***xiànzhǎng*** county head

9 strokes

测 **measure, survey, examine** Traditional 測

cè

测量 ***cèliáng*** measure, survey

猜测 ***cāicè*** to guess, conjecture

The picnic PLAN was to find shellfish in the water (氵), use a knife to open them, and eat them while they were fresh.

12 strokes

赏 **prize, reward, appreciate** Traditional 賞

shǎng

赏赐 ***shǎngcì*** to reward, award

欣赏 ***xīnshǎng*** to appreciate, admire, enjoy

When bits of knowledge are handled right, and you are told how to open shellfish (贝) correctly, your REWARD is a delicious treat with maybe a pearl as a PRIZE.

Insect 昆虫 and Bugs 臭虫

INSECTS can be found inside (中) every ecosystem and often have segmented legs.

6 strokes

虫 **insect, bug** Traditional 蟲

chóng

昆虫 ***kūnchóng*** **insect, bug**

小虫 ***xiǎochóng*** **small insect, small bug**

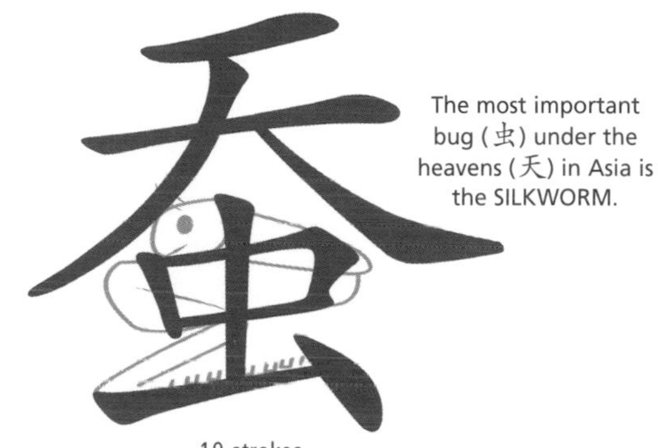

The most important bug (虫) under the heavens (天) in Asia is the SILKWORM.

10 strokes

蚕 **silkworm** Traditional 蠶

cán

蚕丝 ***cánsī*** **silk thread**

蚕虫 ***cánchóng*** **silkworm**

4 strokes

 **wind, air, style** Traditional 

fēng

刮风 ***guāfēng*** **windy**

风气 ***fēngqì*** **atmosphere, trend, style**

A bug's house walls are bowed from the forces of a strong WIND.

9 strokes

 **although, even if** Traditional 雖

suī

虽然 ***suīrán*** **although, despite**

虽则 ***suīzé*** **though, even if**

ALTHOUGH bugs (虫) may be small, their mouths (口) may sing loudly.

Skin 皮 and Meat 肉

5 strokes

皮 **skin, leather**

pí

皮肤 ***pífū*** **skin**

顽皮 ***wánpí*** **naughty, mischievous, disobedient**

Below a cliff, a table is set up to sell LEATHER handbags.

10 strokes

被 **quilt, passive**

bèi

棉被 ***miánbèi*** **quilt, comforter**

被动 ***bèidòng*** **passive**

被迫 ***bèipò*** **be forced**

The clothing was warm as a QUILT though it looks very PASSIVE as it hangs next to the table and the stand.

4 strokes

爪 **claw, talon**

zhǎo (zhuǎ)

爪印 ***zhǎoyìn*** **paw print**

爪牙 ***zhǎoyá*** **collaborator, accomplice (in crime)**

Three TALONS are visible on this CLAW.

6 strokes

肉 **meat**

ròu

牛肉 ***niúròu*** **beef**

肌肉 ***jīròu*** **muscle**

The carcass of an animal hangs in this enclosure where the MEAT is for sale in a market, ribs showing.

9 strokes

革 **reform, revolution**

gé

改革 ***gǎigé*** **to reform**

革命 ***gémìng*** **revolution**

In the middle (中) of a ten-year period of REFORM, people got together to move things forward without starting a REVOLUTION.

Eating 食 and Drinking 饮

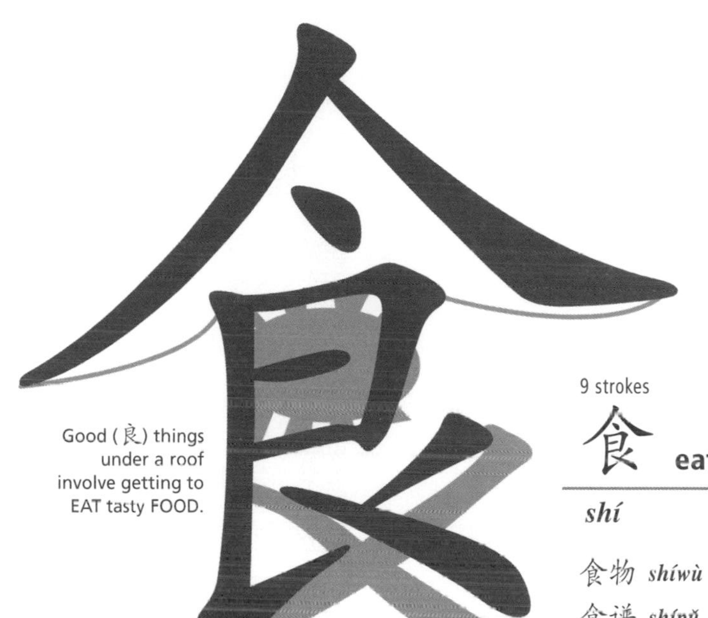

Good (良) things under a roof involve getting to EAT tasty FOOD.

7 strokes

良 **good, pleasing**

liáng

良好 ***liánghǎo*** **good**

优良 ***yōuliáng*** **excellent, the best**

The GOOD thing on a sunny day (日) is marked by an X.

9 strokes

食 **eat, food**

shí

食物 ***shíwù*** **food**

食谱 ***shípǔ*** **recipe, cookbook**

7 strokes

饭 **meal, cooked rice** Traditional 飯

fàn

米饭 ***mǐfàn*** **cooked rice**

炒饭 ***chǎofàn*** **fried rice**

7 strokes

饮 **to drink** Traditional 飲

yǐn

饮水 ***yǐnshuǐ*** **drinking water**

饮料 ***yǐnliào*** **beverage, drinks**

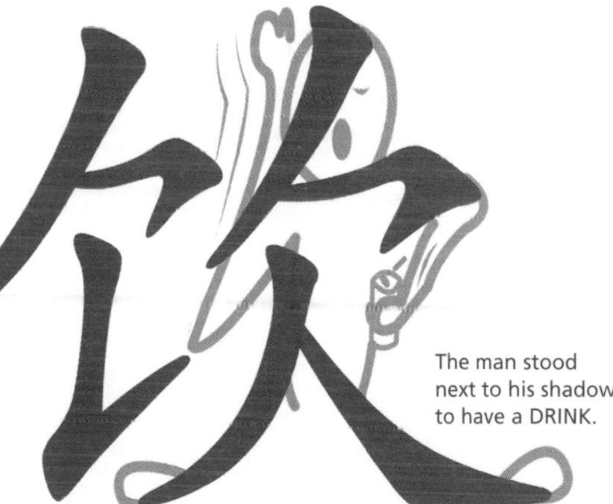

The man stood next to his shadow to have a DRINK.

Eat a MEAL with COOKED RICE by a cliff on a picnic table.

LARGE BUILDINGS have food to eat and bureaucrats (官) [office workers] who run things.

11 strokes

馆 **building, large building (facility)** Traditional 館

guǎn

图书馆 ***túshūguǎn*** **library**

体育馆 ***tǐyùguǎn*** **gymnasium**

旅馆 ***lǚguǎn*** **hotel**

4 strokes

 **warehouse, cellar, cabin** Traditional 

cāng

仓库 ***cāngkù*** **storehouse, warehouse**

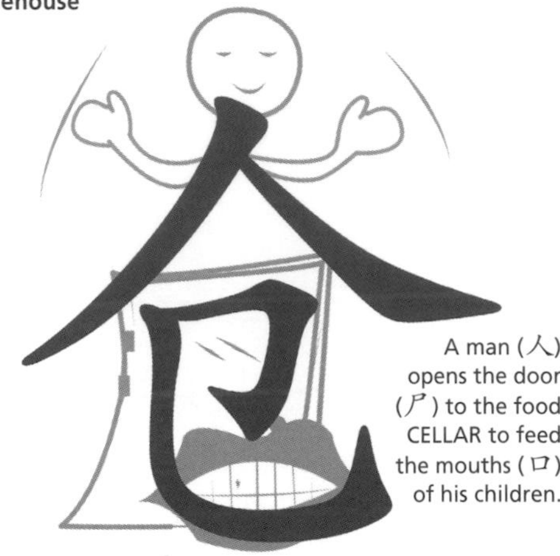

A man (人) opens the door (尸) to the food CELLAR to feed the mouths (口) of his children.

6 strokes

 **start, create, hurt, begin** Traditional 創

chuàng

创立 ***chuànglì*** **establishment, founding**

创造 ***chuàngzào*** **creation**

创伤 ***chuàngshāng*** **trauma, wound**

START in the granary (仓) to pick the ingredients to BEGIN making fresh bread, then cut it with a knife (刂).

9 strokes

 **foster, bring up** Traditional 養

yǎng

养育 ***yǎngyù*** **to raise, bring up, foster**

营养 ***yíngyǎng*** **nutrition, nourishment**

保养 ***bǎoyǎng*** **maintenance, to maintain**

养

Often, we BRING UP sheep (羊) and develop farms to produce wool, and mutton for food (食).

CHAPTER 7

THE WORLD

Lines echo as they zoom out to view the WORLD from space and how it might be seen after a few more GENERATIONS.

5 strokes

世 life, lifetime, generation, world

shì

世纪 ***shìjì*** **century**

世代 ***shìdài*** **generations**

世界 ***shìjiè*** **world**

Day, Sun 日

4 strokes

日 **day, sun**

rì

日期 ***rìqí*** **date**

星期日 ***xīngqírì*** **Sunday**

日本 ***Rìběn*** **Japan**

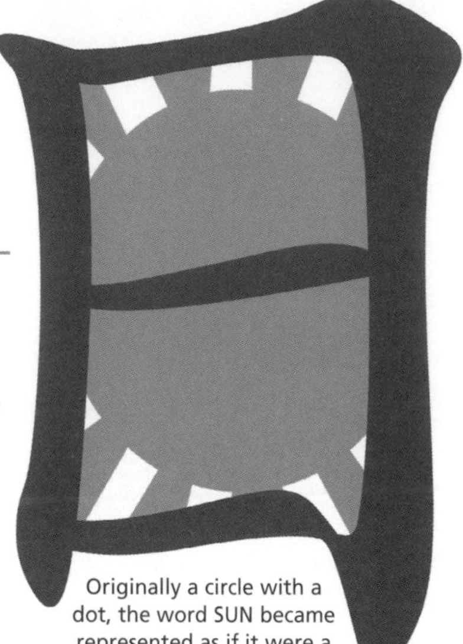

Originally a circle with a dot, the word SUN became represented as if it were a window from which to see the brightest light.

7 strokes

时 **time, hour** Traditional 時

shí

时间 ***shíjiān*** **time, period**

小时 ***xiǎoshí*** **hour**

People knew what TIME it was because the temple bell was struck on the HOUR.

12 strokes

晴 **clear up, fine**

qíng

晴天 ***qíngtiān*** **fine/ clear weather**

On a FINE sunny day there are CLEAR, blue (青) skies.

8 strokes

明 **bright, light**

míng

明日 ***míngrì*** **tomorrow**

明白 ***míngbái*** **to understand, realize**

说明 ***shuōmíng*** **explanation, caption**

The BRIGHTEST time of night is when the sun reflects off the moon.

9 strokes

昨 **yesterday, previous**

zuó

昨天 ***zuótiān*** **yesterday**

昨晚 ***zuówǎn*** **last night**

This was made (作) a day earlier—YESTERDAY.

11 strokes

晚 nightfall, night

wǎn

晚上 *wǎnshàng* at night, in the evening

晚安 *wǎn'ān* good night

The time when my older brother practices weightlifting is at NIGHT when the sun (日) has gone.

9 strokes

冒 adventure, risk

mào

冒险 *màoxiǎn* adventure, risk

冒失 *màoshī* presumptuous, boldness

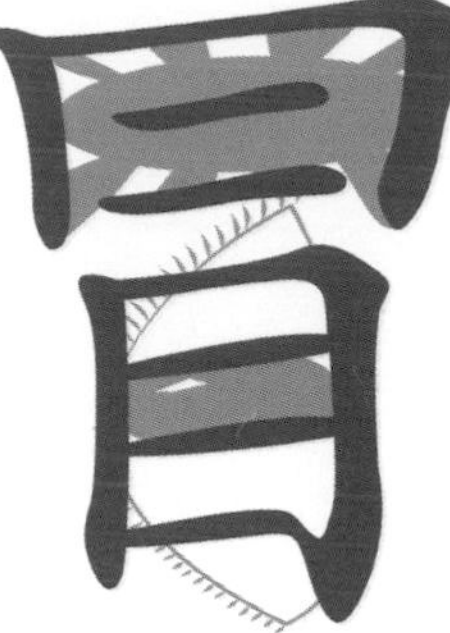

You RISK getting bad sunburn when the sun is high in the sky.

13 strokes

暖 warm

nuǎn

温暖 *wēnnuǎn* warm

暖气 *nuǎnqì* warm air, heating

The WARMTH of the air on a hot day caused one (一) of my friends (友) to break into a heavy sweat.

13 strokes

暗 dark, dim

àn

阴暗 *yīn'àn* dark, gloomy

昏暗 *hūn'àn* dusky, dim

Standing between two suns, it may seem DARK because you're blinded by the light.

12 strokes

晶 sparkle, crystal

jīng

水晶 *shuǐjīng* crystal, quartz

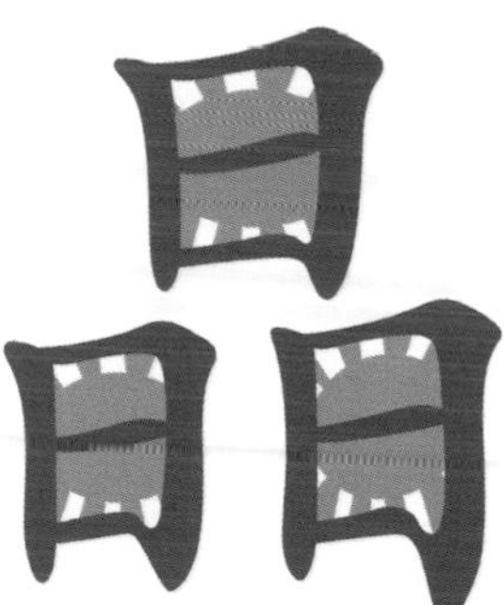

CRYSTAL will SPARKLE when the sun (日) is reflected repeatedly.

6 strokes

早 morning, early

zǎo

早上 *zǎoshang* morning

早餐 *zǎocān* breakfast

For young people, seeing the sun (日) before ten (十) o'clock in the MORNING is EARLY.

8 strokes

易 easy, simple

yì

容易 *róngyì* easy

贸易 *màoyì* [foreign] trade, commerce

交易 *jiāoyì* transaction, business deal

Some days, SIMPLE things are not (勿) always EASY to accomplish.

9 strokes

星 star, spot

xīng

明星 *míngxīng* movie star, celebrity

火星 *huǒxīng* Mars [planet]

星期 *xīngqí* week

A new STAR is born (生) when a new sun (日) begins to burn brightly.

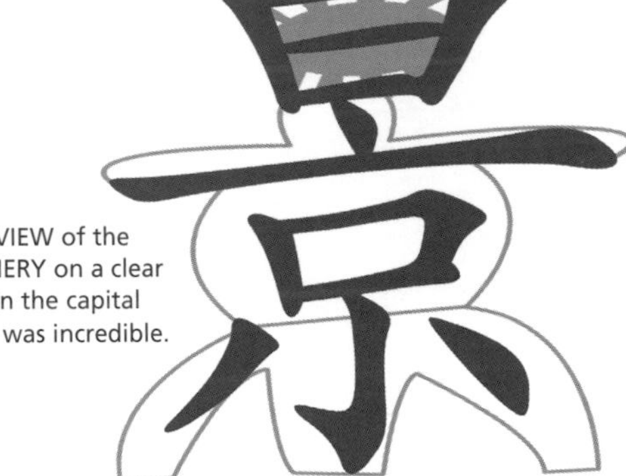

The VIEW of the SCENERY on a clear day in the capital (京) was incredible.

12 strokes

景 scenery, view

jǐng

景色 *jǐngsè* scenery, landscape

背景 *bèijǐng* background

9 strokes

是 is/am/are, right, yes

shì

还是 *háishì* or, still, nevertheless

是非 *shìfēi* right and wrong, dispute

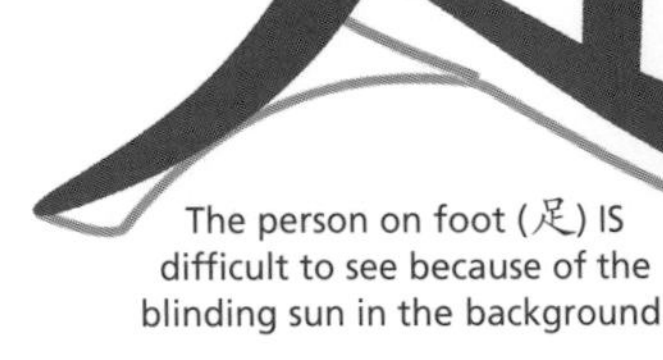

The person on foot (足) IS difficult to see because of the blinding sun in the background.

15 strokes

暴 violent, fierce, cruel, outburst

bào

暴力 *bàolì* violent, force

暴乱 *bàoluàn* riot, rebellion, revolt

On a day when we were with common (共), friends, an OUTBURST of noise came when water (水) was spilled on one of them.

3 strokes

干 able, stem, tree trunk

Traditional 幹

gàn

能干 *nénggàn* competent, capable

树干 *shùgàn* trunk [tree]

干部 *gànbù* cadres, officials

This TREE TRUNK is tall and ABLE to support the branches above.

12 strokes

朝 dynasty, towards, facing

cháo/zhāo

王朝 *wángcháo* dynasty

朝着 *cháozhe* towards, facing

朝阳 *zhāoyáng* sunny

With tens of years before and after the glory days of the last DYNASTY, it would still eventually be FACING its end just as the moon (月) is eclipsed by new morning light.

9 strokes

昼 daytime, daylight

Traditional 晝

zhòu

白昼 *báizhòu* daytime, daylight

昼夜 *zhòuyè* day and night

The DAYLIGHT entered through the doorway (尸) in the height of the day.

9 strokes

厚 thick, deep, profound

hòu

厚度 *hòudù* thickness

深厚 *shēnhòu* deep, profound, solid

The DEEP shadow of a cliff (厂) provided shade from the sun in the middle of the day for children (子) as they played.

8 strokes

 **dark, evening**

hūn

黄昏 ***huánghūn*** **evening**

昏迷 ***hūnmí*** **to be in a coma, unconscious**

Layers of clouds made the sky DARK in the EVENING as the sun was setting.

9 strokes

 **incense, smell**

xiāng

香味 ***xiāngwèi*** **aroma, fragrance**

香水 ***xiāngshuǐ*** **perfume**

香港 ***Xiānggǎng*** **Hong Kong**

A fancy tree (禾) has a strong SMELL in the heat of the sun (日).

12 strokes

 **universal, wide(ly), generally**

pǔ

普及 ***pǔjí*** **universal, popular, widespread**

普通 ***pǔtōng*** **ordinary, common, average, usual**

The grasses GENERALLY received equal (並) amounts of sunlight to give them a UNIVERSAL appearance.

5 strokes

 **old, former, used**

Traditional 

jiù

旧日 ***jiùrì*** **olden times**

旧约 ***jiùyuē*** **Old Testament**

The man thinks about a day when they USED to do things in an OLD-fashioned way.

12 strokes

 **temporarily, a while**

Traditional 

zàn

暂时 ***zànshí*** **temporary**

暂定 ***zàndìng*** **tentative, temporary**

A logger with an axe (斤) and his cart (车) TEMPORARILY halted one day to look at the sun.

12 strokes

 **hot, heat**

shǔ

暑气 ***shǔqì*** **heat, summer heat**

暑假 ***shǔjià*** **summer vacation**

When the HOT sun HEATS the soil from top to bottom, it can cause cracks to form in the earth.

Time 时

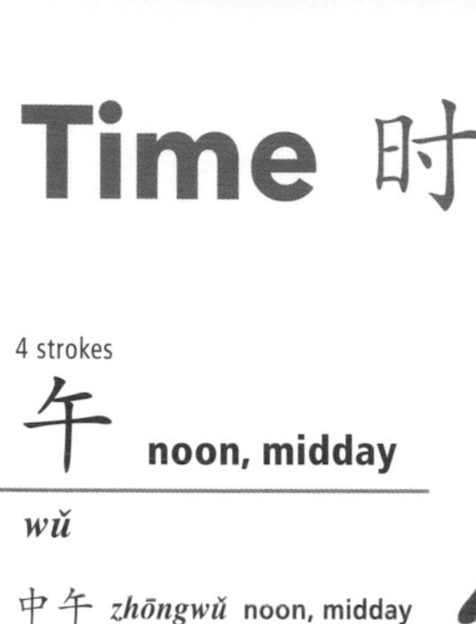

4 strokes

午 noon, midday

wǔ

中午 ***zhōngwǔ*** noon, midday

MIDDAY begins when two strokes of the little hand pass ten (十) and it becomes 12:00 NOON.

A person laying down for sleep should think about his mother (母) EVERY day.

7 strokes

每 every

měi

每天 ***měitiān*** every day

6 strokes

年 year, age

nián

年龄 ***niánlíng*** age

新年 ***xīnnián*** New Year

Every YEAR I get a birthday cake with many parts representing the past twelve months.

8 strokes

周 week Traditional 週

zhōu

下周 ***xiàzhōu*** next week

周末 ***zhōumò*** weekend

It takes a WEEK to walk around the soil (土) of a field to plant food for hungry mouths (口).

9 strokes

毒 poison, toxic

dú

毒药 ***dúyào*** **poison, toxic**

有毒 ***yǒudú*** **poisonous**

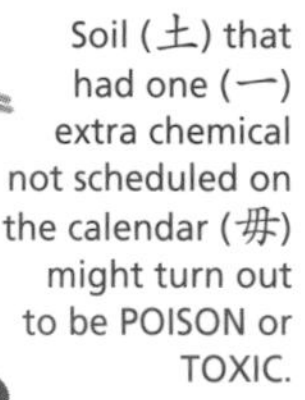

Soil (土) that had one (一) extra chemical not scheduled on the calendar (毋) might turn out to be POISON or TOXIC.

A LONG–TIME AGO, people had long hair tied in topknots.

3 strokes

久 long, long time

jiǔ

永久 ***yǒngjiǔ*** **permanent, everlasting**

长久 ***chángjiǔ*** **long, for a long time**

4 strokes

及 and, come up to, reach, as well as

jí

以及 ***yǐjí*** **and, as well as**

及时 ***jíshí*** **timely, promptly**

及格 ***jígé*** **to pass, qualify**

Stack that table AS WELL AS this one on top of the other so you can REACH what you need.

8 strokes

刻 time, moment, engrave, carving

kè

时刻 ***shíkè*** **moment**

雕刻 ***diāokè*** **craving, engraving**

After taking TIME to cook a big meal, he or she takes the lid (亠) off of the pot to begin CARVING.

Moon 月

4 strokes

月 **month, moon**

yuè

一月 ***yīyuè*** **January**

月亮 ***yuèliàng*** **moon**

It is easy to see the crescent MOON with part of an eye (目) visible.

On a blue moon, things are QUIET as a plant sprouts another set of young (青) leaves.

14 strokes

静 **quiet** Traditional 靜

jìng

安静 ***ānjìng*** **quiet, peaceful**

冷静 ***lěngjìng*** **calm, composed**

12 strokes

最 **utmost, most, extreme**

zuì

最多 ***zuìduō*** **most, the largest**

最近 ***zuìjìn*** **recently, lately**

最初 ***zuìchū*** **initial, primary, beginning**

The MOST interesting story is one that I heard one day from a table an EXTREMELY long distance away.

Though she did not HAVE name recognition yet, she made her debut as if she were a star peaking out from behind the moon.

12 strokes

期 **period, time, term**

qī

时期 ***shíqī*** **period, phrase, time**

学期 ***xuéqī*** **semester, term**

The SEMESTER calendar in China was written on the hanging scroll and was based on the lunar calendar.

6 strokes

有 **possess, have, exist**

yǒu

拥有 ***yǒngyǒu*** **to have, own, possess**

有名 ***yǒumíng*** **famous, well-known**

8 strokes

育 educate, raise

yù

培育 *péiyù* to foster, cultivate, train

教育 *jiàoyù* to educate, education

养育 *yǎngyù* to be raised/ brought up [child]

I (厶) GREW UP over many moons (月), RAISED under my parents' roof.

8 strokes

服 clothing

fú

服装 *fúzhuāng* clothing, garment

制服 *zhìfú* uniform

A month's (月) clothing had been hung on a hook above the table, waiting to be folded and put away.

8 strokes

夜 night, evening

yè

今夜 *jīnyè* tonight, this evening

半夜 *bànyè* midnight

5 strokes

用 use

yòng

使用 *shǐyòng* to use, employ, apply

作用 *zuòyòng* action, effect, function

To USE your salary efficiently, divide the month (月) in half to make sure that you have enough money at the end.

A person is home for the NIGHT with a roof over his head, sitting at a folding table.

In the evening (夕), my DREAM began in front of a small woods (林).

11 strokes

梦 dream

Traditional 夢

mèng

做梦 *zuòmèng* dreaming, to daydream

梦想 *mèngxiǎng* to dream of, fantasize

5 strokes

外 outside, external, foreign

wài

外面 ***wàimiàn*** outside, outdoors, external

外国人 ***wàiguórén*** foreigner

In the evening (夕), you might step OUTSIDE of your routine and seek out a fortune teller (卜).

6 strokes

多 many, frequent, much

duō

许多 ***xǔduō*** many, much, numerous

多少 ***duōshǎo*** how much

On MANY nice evenings (夕) there is MUCH to do.

I HOPE to fix or replace the broken container by next full moon (月) before the king (王) notices it.

6 strokes

死 death, die

sǐ

死亡 ***sǐwáng*** to die, deceased

死板 ***sǐbǎn*** rigid, stiff, inflexible

A line (一) is drawn at DEATH where many cultures need to bury their dead by evening (夕) after washing them with ladles (匕) of water.

11 strokes

望 hope, desire, look

wàng

希望 ***xīwàng*** to hope, wish for

张望 ***zhāngwàng*** to look around, peep

失望 ***shīwàng*** disappointment, despair

Fire 火 / 灬

Two logs leaning against each other are on FIRE and have flying sparks.

4 strokes

火 **fire**

huǒ

火把 ***huǒbǎ*** **torch**

军火 ***jūnhuǒ*** **firearms, ammunition**

At the foot of a mountain, by a cliff, we used CHARCOAL to grill burgers.

9 strokes

炭 **charcoal, coal, carbon**

tàn

煤炭 ***méitàn*** **coal**

6 strokes

灯 **lamp, light** Traditional 燈

dēng

电灯 ***diàndēng*** **electric light**

灯具 ***dēngjù*** **lighting fixtures**

Like a spark of fire (火), the LAMP post was a very bright LIGHT.

10 strokes

烧 **bake, burning** Traditional 燒

shāo

焚烧 ***fénshāo*** **to burn, incineration**

焙烧 ***bèishāo*** **to bake, broil, grill**

发烧 ***fāshāo*** **to have a fever**

The stack of ribs sits on a table next to a fire (火) that is BURNING well.

The wood will BURN on a campfire fire (火) in the evening (夕) as the old dog (犬) sits nearby.

16 strokes

燃 **burn, blaze, ignite**

rán

燃烧 ***ránshāo*** **to burn, combustion**

燃油 ***rányóu*** **fuel**

15 strokes

熟 ripen, acquire skill

shú

成熟 *chéngshú* mature, ripe

熟练 *shúliàn* skilled, proficient

Children (子) will ACQUIRE SKILLS as if they were on fire when a lid is removed and they will become very well rounded (丸).

9 strokes

点 mark, point, decimal point

Traditional 點

diǎn

重点 *zhòngdiǎn* emphasis, stress, focal point

要点 *yàodiǎn* main point, essential

九点钟 *jiǔdiǎnzhōng* nine o'clock

Being on fire (灬) might be a MARK of having a good fortune and that you will have luck in earning all of the POINTS possible on a test.

10 strokes

热 hot, heat

Traditional 熱

rè

炎热 *yánrè* hot, heat

热情 *rèqíng* passionate, enthusiasm, zeal

Keep your hand (手) away from some circles (丸) to avoid being in the line of fire (灬) and to avoid the HEAT and HOT tempers.

4 strokes

无 nothingness, none, not

Traditional 無

wú

虚无 *xūwú* nothingness, non-existence

无奈 *wúnài* helpless

A person does NOT lie face down on a bed of nails over flames of a fire with NOTHING happening.

12 strokes

然 correct, so, if so, well

rán

当然 *dāngrán* of course, certainly

然而 *rán'ér* however, but, yet

自然 *zìrán* nature, spontaneously

In evenings (夕) dogs (犬) are the SORT OF THINGS with 4 legs that sleep at the foot of a bed to make sure everything is WELL.

13 strokes

照 illuminate, shine

zhào

照亮 *zhàoliàng* to illuminate, shine

参照 *cānzhào* to refer, consult, reference

照耀 *zhàoyào* to shine on

On a day when the sun is SHINING, cutting like a knife (刀), someone will say it's hot as blazes.

Water 水 / 氵

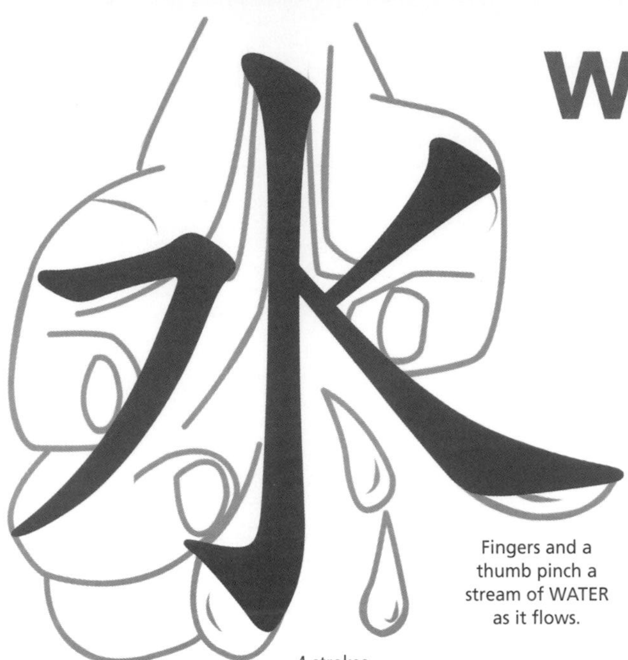

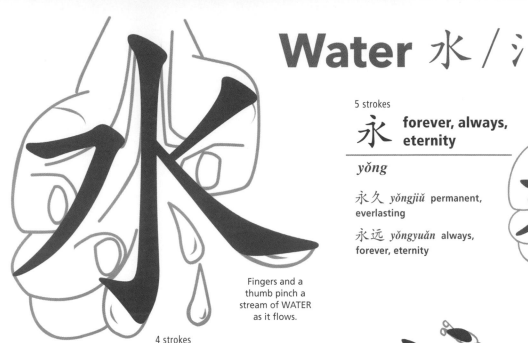

Fingers and a thumb pinch a stream of WATER as it flows.

5 strokes

永 forever, always, eternity

yǒng

永久 ***yǒngjiǔ*** **permanent, everlasting**

永远 ***yǒngyuǎn*** **always, forever, eternity**

Droplets of water evaporate over a LONG period for what may seem like an ETERNITY.

4 strokes

水 water

shuǐ

喝水 ***hēshuǐ*** **to drink water**

汽水 ***qìshuǐ*** **soft drink, soda water**

Water splashes as someone dives off of a board to SWIM.

8 strokes

泳 swim

yǒng

游泳 ***yóuyǒng*** **swimming**

游泳池 ***yóuyǒngchí*** **swimming pool**

When water is FROZEN into ICE, it can crack the top of a container.

6 strokes

冰 ice, frozen, icicle

bīng

冰茶 ***bīngchá*** **iced tea**

冰冻 ***bīngdòng*** **to freeze, frost**

8 strokes

录 record

Traditional 錄

lù

记录 ***jìlù*** **record, minutes, notes**

录音 ***lùyīn*** **[audio] recording**

RECORD the deep layers (彐) of snow to see its effect on water (水) levels.

10 strokes

海 ocean, sea

hǎi

海洋 *hǎiyáng* ocean, sea

Water falling every calendar day, month, and year eventually creates an OCEAN.

10 strokes

流 flow, current

liú

流动 *liúdòng* to flow, to be mobile

河流 *héliú* river, stream

潮流 *cháoliú* trend, tide, current

When I (厶) wash in a river, it feels good as the water FLOWS by.

12 strokes

湖 lake

hú

湖泊 *húbó* lake

湖南 *Húnán* Hunan province (China)

湖畔 *húpàn* lakefront

The water from the old (古) LAKE shimmered in the moon's (月) light.

3 strokes

也 also, as well

yě

也是 *yěshì* also

也许 *yěxǔ* maybe, perhaps

If we fish in this apparently dry pond AS WELL, we might ALSO catch fish here.

6 strokes

池 pond, reservoir

chí

水池 *shuǐchí* pond, pool

电池 *diànchí* battery [think "reservoir of energy"]

The water level rises as it collects and is found in a POND where we fish.

8 strokes

波 waves

bō

波浪 *bōlàng* wave, surge, billow

波动 *bōdòng* fluctuation

脑波 *nǎobō* brain waves

Water splashes in WAVES against a dotted cliff where a table (又) has to be tied down.

12 strokes

港 harbor

gǎng

港 *hǎigǎng* harbor

港口 *gǎngkǒu* port

Tens of people meet together at the HARBOR to say goodbye.

11 strokes

混 mix, blend

hùn

混合 *hùnhé* to be mixed, to be blended with

混乱 *hǔnluàn* confusion, chaos

MIX equal parts of water and sunlight before making the comparison (比).

9 strokes

洗 to wash

xǐ

清洗 *qīngxǐ* to clean, wash clean

洗澡 *xǐzǎo* to bathe, bath

洗衣店 *xǐyīdiàn* laundry

Water is used TO WASH seedlings planted previously.

8 strokes

注 pour, irrigate

zhù

注入 *zhùrù* injection, infusion, to pour

注意 *zhùyì* caution, to note, notice

关注 *guānzhù* attention, to follow closely

The lord of the estate allowed one to IRRIGATE fields or POUR water.

6 strokes

冲 rinse, wash

Traditional

沖

chōng

冲洗 *chōngxǐ* to rinse, wash

冲淡 *chōngdàn* to dilute, water down, weaken

冲刷 *chōngshuā* to scour, wash away

Cut through the middle of stains like an arrow as you WASH and then RINSE.

8 strokes

油 grease, oil, fat

yóu

油脂 *yóuzhī* grease, oil, fat

石油 *shíyóu* oil, petroleum, kerosene

Draining the water from a field (田) and drilling down, they found OIL!

16 strokes

激 stimulate, excite

jī

刺激 *cìjī* to stimulate, excited

感激 *gǎnjī* grateful, to appreciate, gratitude

The water washed white (白) in different directions (方) in a VIOLENT rain on the picnic table (夊).

12 strokes

温 warm, temperature

wēn

温暖 *wēnnuǎn* warm [water, etc.]

温度 *wēndù* temperature

温泉 *wēnquán* hot spring [spa]

Use WARM water every day to wash the dishes.

The morning (朝) TIDE came in as the moon faded.

15 strokes

潮 tide, moist, humid

cháo

潮湿 *cháoshī* damp, moist, humid

潮流 *cháoliú* trend, current

10 strokes

凉 refreshing, nice and cool

Traditional 涼

liáng

凉快 *liángkuài* cool, refreshing

荒凉 *huāngliáng* desolate, wild, barren

A REFRESHING rain fell on the lanterns in the capital (京).

6 strokes

汤 soup

Traditional 湯

tāng

汤匙 *tāngchí* soup spoon

Water (氵) is heated to make SOUP.

11 strokes

减 subtract, reduce, decrease, cut

Traditional 減

jiǎn

减少 *jiǎnshǎo* to reduce, cut down, lessen

减肥 *jiǎnféi* to lose weight, slim down

The water level against the cliff began to DECREASE as one (一) soldier told (口) another to put down their halberds (戈).

8 strokes

沿 run alongside, follow along

yán

边沿 *biānyán* edge, rim

沿线 *yánxiàn* along the railway line

A man wanted to sit at a table ALONG THE RIVER bank to talk (口).

13 strokes

源 source, origin

yuán

来源 *láiyuán* souce, origin

资源 *zīyuán* resources, natural resources

Water at the base of the cliff (厂) has its ORIGIN in a little (小) white (白) spring.

9 strokes

派 group, clique, school (of)

pài

派别 *pàibié* faction, school, group

分派 *fēnpài* to assign, apportion

Water splashes repeatedly against a GROUP of pillars supporting a dock.

10 strokes

准 standard, accurate

Traditional 準

zhǔn

标准 *biāozhǔn* standard, norm

水准 *shuǐzhǔn* level, standard

准备 *zhǔnbèi* to be ready, planned, preparation

A STANDARD measure of water depth could be determined by how high it is on the legs of a tall bird (隹), but it would hardly be ACCURATE.

5 strokes

汉 Chinese, Han dynasty, man

Traditional 漢

hàn

汉语 *Hànyǔ* Chinese language

汉字 *Hànzì* Chinese characters

汉子 *hànzi* man

At the waterside table the MAN told us about the HAN DYNASTY.

9 strokes

洋 ocean, western style

yáng

海洋 *hǎiyáng* ocean, sea

大西洋 *Dàxīyáng* Alantic Ocean

Water splashes on the WEST side of this sheep.

7 strokes

求 request, beg, want, require

qiú

要求 *yāoqiú* to claim, demand, require, requisition

If you have only one (一) drop of water, you will REQUIRE more.

9 strokes

活 life, living, lively

huó

生活 *shēnghuó* lively, living

活动 *huódòng* action, activity, movable

干活 *gànhuó* to work

A huge tongue pokes out of a mouth to taste the flavors of LIFE.

The METHODS and LAWS governing water use on my (厶) land are important.

8 strokes

法 method, rule, law

fǎ

方法 *fāngfǎ* method, way

法律 *fǎlǜ* legal, juridical, law

5 strokes

去 go to, past, remove, leave

qù

过去 *guòqù* the past, bygone days

去年 *qùnián* last year

When I (厶) dug into the soil, I found a relic of the PAST that I didn't want to REMOVE.

11 strokes

清 pure, cleanse

qīng

清洁 ***qīngjié*** **clean, hygienic**

血清 ***xuèqīng*** **serum**

CLEANSE your body and mind with water to feel fresh as new blue-green (青) leaf bud.

6 strokes

决 decide, fix, agree upon

Traditional 決

jué

决定 ***juédìng*** **to decide, determine**

处决 ***chǔjué*** **executed, put to death**

After the water damage, the person needed to DECIDE how to FIX the broken side of this box.

Bathing with water helped my older brother's (兄) smelly CONDITION improve.

7 strokes

况 condition, situation

Traditional 況

kuàng

情况 ***qíngkuàng*** **situation, circumstances**

状况 ***zhuàngkuàng*** **condition, status**

现况 ***xiànkuàng*** **present condition**

11 strokes

深 deep, dark, profound

shēn

深切 ***shēnqiè*** **deep, profound, heartfelt**

深沉 ***shēnchén*** **deep, dark, concealing real feelings**

The water below the tree was DARK because of the shade from the cover of the tree and how DEEP the water was.

10 strokes

消 eliminate, disappear, extinguish

xiāo

消除 ***xiāochú*** **to eliminate, remove, clear up**

消失 ***xiāoshī*** **to disappear, vanish**

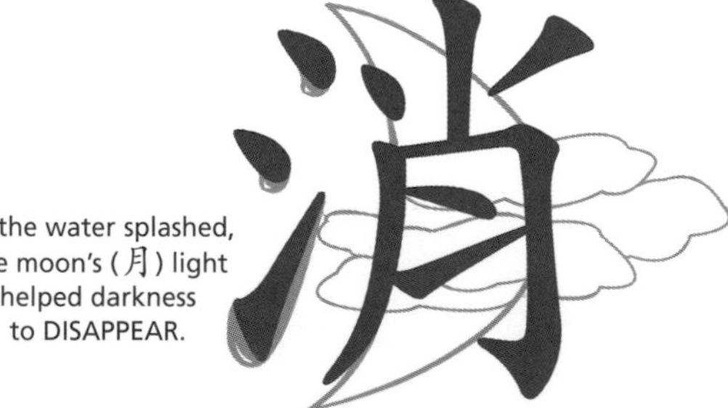

As the water splashed, the moon's (月) light helped darkness to DISAPPEAR.

8 strokes

治 cure, heal, be at peace

zhì

医治 *yīzhì* to cure, heal, treat

统治 *tǒngzhì* to rule, govern

政治 *zhèngzhì* politics, political

I said that the water can CURE/HEAL anything.

9 strokes

济 aid, help, assistant

Traditional 濟

jì

救济 *jiùjì* relief, to relieve

经济 *jīngjì* economy, economics, finance

If the water splashes higher and higher, don't be the person who stops to read the instructional writing (文) showing how to climb a ladder safely.

7 strokes

汽 vapor, steam

qì

蒸汽 *zhēngqì* steam

汽车 *qìchē* car, automobile

When water is added to hot air, it might make VAPOR or STEAM.

11 strokes

液 fluid, liquid, juice

yè

液体 *yètǐ* liquid, fluid

血液 *xuèyè* blood

Snails SECRETE a lot of FLUID and can be seen often in the evening (夜) and in dark wet places.

4 strokes

气 gas, air, breath

Traditional 氣

qì

空气 *kōngqì* air, atmosphere, breath

气体 *qìtǐ* gas

气味 *qìwèi* odor, smell, flavor

As a person lies down to sleep, his BREATH weaves in and out of layers of sheets and blankets and warms the AIR.

13 strokes

满 full, enough, pride

Traditional 滿

mǎn

满足 *mǎnzú* to satisfy, to be sufficient

自满 *zìmǎn* complacency, self-satisfied

ENOUGH water had fallen to make the grass tall and to make the workers within (冂) in the fields happy.

14 strokes

performance, act, play

yǎn

演奏 *yǎnzòu* musical performance

表演 *biǎoyǎn* to perform [a play], show, exhibition

The PLAY was held under a roof (宀) with a small stage elevated above a field (田) next to the water.

10 strokes

wine, alcohol

jiǔ

酒精 *jiǔjīng* alcohol

啤酒 *píjiǔ* beer

Water splashes on the side of a WINE bottle with a little left in the bottom and a stopper on top.

10 strokes

distribute, spouse, exile

pèi

分配 *fēnpèi* allocation, to distribute

配偶 *pèi'ǒu* spouse, mate

When you DISTRIBUTE some of the wine yourself (己) ensure that everyone gets a taste.

9 strokes

洲 **continent, sandbar, island**

zhōu

亚洲 *yàzhōu* Asia

非洲 *fēizhōu* Africa

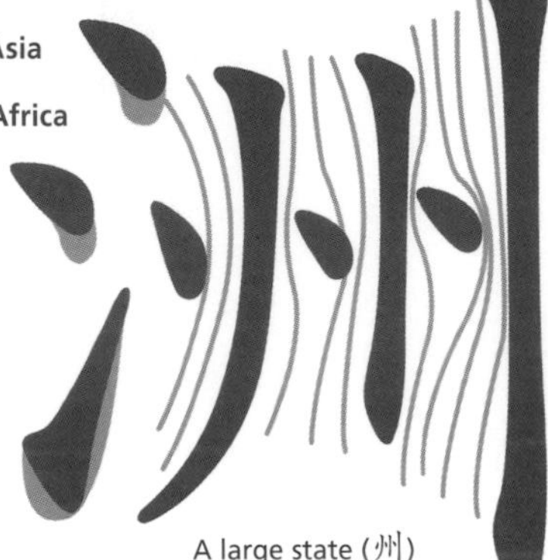

A large state (州) surrounded by lots of water might be a CONTINENT.

3 strokes

川 **river, stream, creek**

chuān

四川 *Sìchuān* Szechuan province [China]

Three strokes of a large RIVER flow smoothly.

6 strokes

州 **state, province**

zhōu

加州 *Jiāzhōu* California [US]

神州 *shénzhōu* China

Within the river, several independent island STATES exist.

8 strokes

 **river, stream**

hé

河流 ***héliú*** **river, stream**

黄河 ***Huánghé*** **Yellow River**

That STREAM will possibly (可) flow into a larger RIVER.

6 strokes

江 **river**

jiāng

江河 ***jiānghé*** **rivers**

江山 ***jiāngshān*** **country, landscape**

长江 ***Chángjiāng*** **Yangtze River**

This RIVER will flow through a set of locks that are being constructed (工).

8 strokes

 **pond, swamp** Traditional 澤

zé

沼泽 ***zhǎozé*** **swamp, marsh**

色泽 ***sèzé*** **color**

A table sitting near a SWAMP needs extra foundational supports to keep it from sinking in water.

12 strokes

 **bay, gulf, fleet** Traditional 

wān

海湾 ***hǎiwān*** **bay, gulf, harbor**

台湾 ***Táiwān*** **Taiwan**

Water bends like a bow (弓), eventually faning out toward the GULF.

7 strokes

 **not, disappear, sink**

méi/mò

没有 ***méiyǒu*** **no; not having**

没事 ***méishì*** **nothing**

沉没 ***chénmò*** **to sink**

The tables should NOT be dirty, so take water from the SINK and make the dirt DISAPPEAR.

7 strokes

 **sand**

shā

沙漠 ***shāmò*** **desert**

沙滩 ***shātān*** **sandy beach**

SAND is material that can be washed away with only a little (少) water.

Springs 泉

9 strokes

spring, fountain

quán

喷泉 ***pēnquán*** fountain

泉水 ***quánshuǐ*** spring water

温泉 ***wēnquán*** hot spring, spa

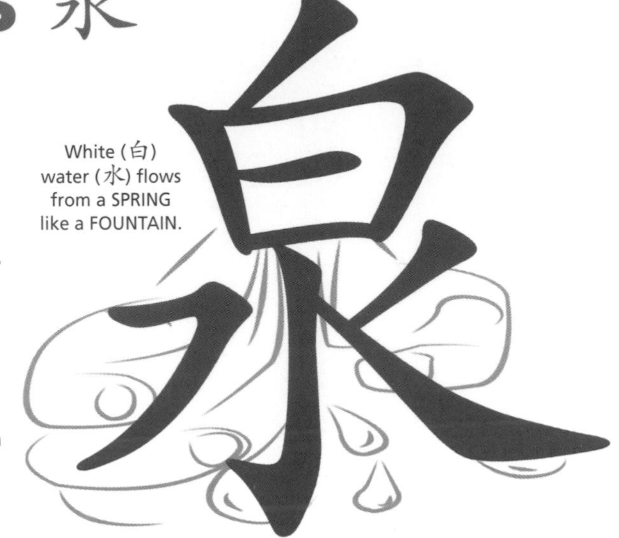

White (白) water (水) flows from a SPRING like a FOUNTAIN.

10 strokes

original, primary, raw, wilderness

yuán

原因 ***yuányīn*** reason, cause, origin

原野 ***yuányě*** open country, champaign, field

The MEADOW below the cliff (厂) has a small white stream (泉) and seems to be very PRIMITIVE WILDERNESS.

8 strokes

thread, string, line, route

Traditional

xiàn

路线 ***lùxiàn*** route, itinerary, line

线索 ***xiànsuǒ*** clue, trail

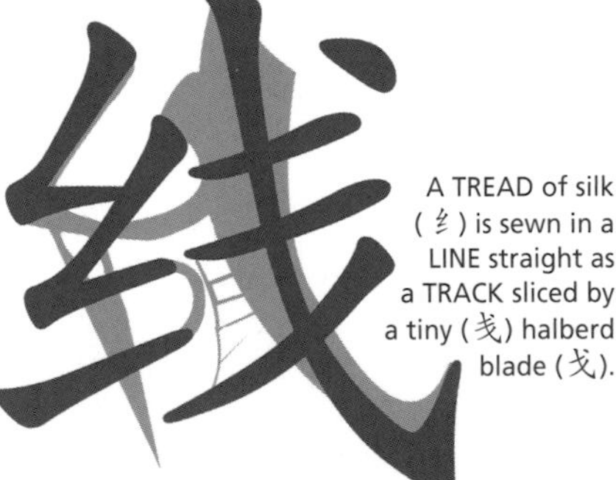

A TREAD of silk (纟) is sewn in a LINE straight as a TRACK sliced by a tiny (戋) halberd blade (戈).

A needle sewing pieces of silk together makes a CONNECTION.

7 strokes

系 **relate, connection**

Traditional 係

xì

系数 ***xìshù*** coefficient, modulus

关系 ***guānxì*** relation, connection

Gold (Metal)

8 strokes

金 **gold**

jīn

黄金 ***huángjīn*** **gold**

现金 ***xiànjīn*** **cash**

The king (王) wore lots of shiny GOLD and jewels.

11 strokes

银 **silver** Traditional 銀

yín

银色 ***yínsè*** **silver (color)**

银行 ***yínháng*** **bank [finance]**

Of all of the metals under the sun (日), SILVER is almost as good (良) as the king's gold.

16 strokes

镜 **mirror, lens** Traditional 鏡

jìng

镜子 ***jìngzǐ*** **mirror**

眼镜 ***yǎnjìng*** **spectacles, glasses**

The king stood (立) in front of the MIRROR to look (见) at his gold.

10 strokes

铁 **iron** Traditional 鐵

tiě

铁路 ***tiělù*** **railroad**

地下铁 ***dìxiàtiě*** **subway**

The king's gold is too weak to be used for a warrior's halberd (戈) blade so the lord had it made from IRON.

13 strokes

错 **wrong, mistake** Traditional 錯

cuò

错误 ***cuòwù*** **error, mistake**

错过 ***cuòguò*** **to miss (an opportunity, etc.)**

It might be WRONG for the king to assume that there was more gold in ancient times and days (日) gone by.

Soil, Earth, Ground 土/⼟

3 strokes

土 **soil, earth, ground, dirt**

tǔ

泥土 ***nítǔ*** soil, ground

土地 ***tǔdì*** plot of land, territory

The SOIL of fields in China looks like it is divided into squares with all of the GROUND used efficiently.

5 strokes

圣 **holy, saint, master** Traditional 聖

shèng

神圣 ***shénshèng*** sacred, holy

圣人 ***shèngrén*** saint, sage, wisemen

圣经 ***shèngjīng*** bible, scripture

The MASTER used the altar table on the land to perform a HOLY sacrifice.

6 strokes

场 **field, location, place, scene** Traditional 場

chǎng

现场 ***xiànchǎng*** site, scene, spot

运动场 ***yùndòngchǎng*** sports field, exercise yard

工场 ***gōngchǎng*** workshop

The PLACE where the soil (土) has deep rows is the LOCATION of the FIELD.

6 strokes

地 **ground, earth, land**

dì

地理 ***dìlǐ*** geography

地图 ***dìtú*** map

A man had lots of GROUND, and dug a pond (池) in the EARTH so he could fish and draw water for his crops.

7 strokes

址 **site, location**

zhǐ

地址 ***dìzhǐ*** address (of location)

This is the LOCATION where you should stop and examine the soil.

14 strokes

境 boundary, border, territory

jìng

边境 *biānjìng* border, frontier, boundary

环境 *huánjìng* environment, circumstance

At the borders of the land (土), centurions would stand (立) guard, looking (见) for intruders.

11 strokes

域 region, area, district, range

yù

区域 *qūyù* district, area, region

Defending his land (土) with sharp halberds (戈) successfully, the warrior declared (口) this REGION his.

10 strokes

埋 to be buried, to be hidden, cover

mái

埋葬 *máizàng* to bury [in ground/tomb]

埋藏 *máicáng* hidden in the earth, bury

With high ground (土) on two sides, the field is mostly HIDDEN or BURIED from sunlight.

15 strokes

增 increase, add, strengthen

zēng

增加 *zēngjiā* to increase, multiply

增强 *zēngqiáng* to strengthen, increase

Across the land (土) where there was enough sunlight (日), fields (田) began having an INCREASED yield.

7 strokes

均 equal, even, level, average

jūn

平均 *píngjūn* average, level

均等 *jūnděng* equal, fair

Soil (土) broken with a plow and plants will provide only an AVERAGE harvest without fertilizer.

6 strokes

在 exist, in, at, be

zài

存在 *cúnzài* to exist, presence, existence

实在 *shízài* really, in reality, honestly

现在 *xiànzài* now, current, present time

AT a post, there EXISTS a person who is jumping all over the land (土).

11 strokes

public chamber, hall, court

táng

食堂 ***shítáng*** dining hall, canteen

礼堂 ***lǐtáng*** hall, auditorium, assembly hall

The HALL where COURT was held on the ground (土) was where the judgments were said (口) and sunlight was shed on dark situations.

5 strokes

甘 sweet, willingly

gān

甘甜 ***gāntián*** sweet

甘薯 ***gānshǔ*** sweet potato

甘心 ***gānxīn*** willingly

Freshly baked TASTY, SWEET treats sit waiting in a traditional basket.

11 strokes

basic, fundamental, foundation

jī

基本 ***jīběn*** basic, fundamental

基金 ***jījīn*** fund, foundation (money)

基因 ***jīyīn*** gene

The FUNDAMENTAL facts of what sweet (甘) foods in the basket do to your diet are as plain as the soil (土) upon which we walk.

8 strokes

its, that, such, they

qí

其他 ***qítā*** other, else

其实 ***qíshí*** in fact, as a matter of fact

THEY suggest that having a basket of SUCH sweet (甘) foods at the table could make you fat, but I disagree.

12 strokes

this, such

sī

斯文 ***sīwén*** cultured, decent

莫斯科 ***Mòsīkē*** Moscow

SUCH sweet (甘) pastries as those in THIS basket should be cut (斤) equally to be fair.

7 strokes

报 report, news

Traditional 報

bào

报告 *bàogào* to report, inform

情报 *qíngbào* intelligence, information

报纸 *bàozhǐ* newspaper

Listen to the NEWS and sit down at your table under the light to put your hand (扌) to writing your REPORT about it.

6 strokes

老 old, old age, ancient

lǎo

老人 *lǎorén* the aged, old person

古老 *gǔlǎo* ancient, age-old

老师 *lǎoshī* teacher

If you use only an ANCIENT ladle (匕) to till the soil (土) you will reach OLD AGE quickly and not yield much food.

6 strokes

压 pressure, oppress, push, overwhelm

Traditional 壓

yā

压力 *yālì* pressure, overwhelming force

血压 *xuèyā* blood pressure

When a farmer's land (土) is under the shade of a cliff (厂), there is PRESSURE to try to prevent the shade OVERWHELMING crops.

6 strokes

考 test, exam, consider, think over

kǎo

考试 *kǎoshì* examination, test

考虑 *kǎolǜ* to consider, think about

思考 *sīkǎo* to think, reflect, thought

CONSIDER how dry soil (土) splits in the heat or when broken by a sword.

9 strokes

型 type, model, pattern, mould

xíng

模型 *móxíng* model, mould, pattern

小型 *xiǎoxíng* small size, small scale

To MOULD or shape a MODEL in mud, a knife (刂) can be used to open (开) holes in the soil (土).

8 strokes

者 someone, person (who does something)

zhě

作者 *zuòzhě* author, writer

记者 *jìzhě* reporter, journalist

SOMEONE who farms cuts through the soil and tends it day by day.

Mountain 山 and Dotted Cliff 广

The outline of a MOUNTAIN can be implied here.

3 strokes

山 mountain

shān

高山 *gāoshān* alpine, high mountains

泰山 *Tàishān* Taishan Mountain (China)

山顶 *shāndǐng* mountain top, hilltop

8 strokes

岸 shore, coast, beach

àn

岸边 *ànbiān* shore, coast, beach

海岸 *hǎi'àn* coast, seashore

At the base of a mountain cliff is a SHORE where BEACH towels hang to dry.

7 strokes

谷 valley

gǔ

山谷 *shāngǔ* valley

峡谷 *xiágǔ* gorge, canyon

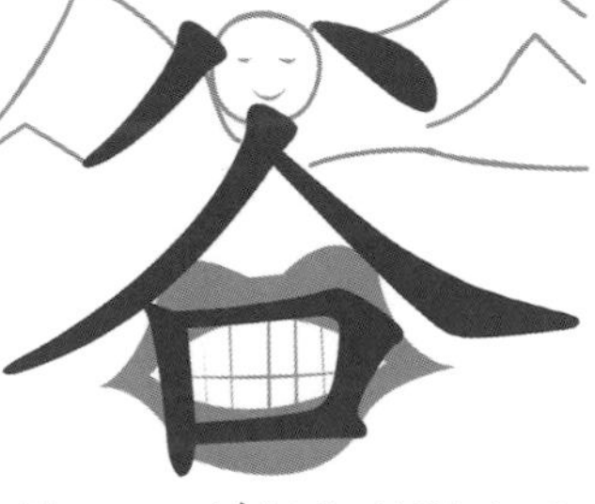

The person (人) talked (口) about how much he loved living between mountain peaks in a VALLEY.

6 strokes

岁 year, year (of age)

Traditional 歲

suì

岁月 *suìyuè* years

几岁 *jǐsuì* how old?

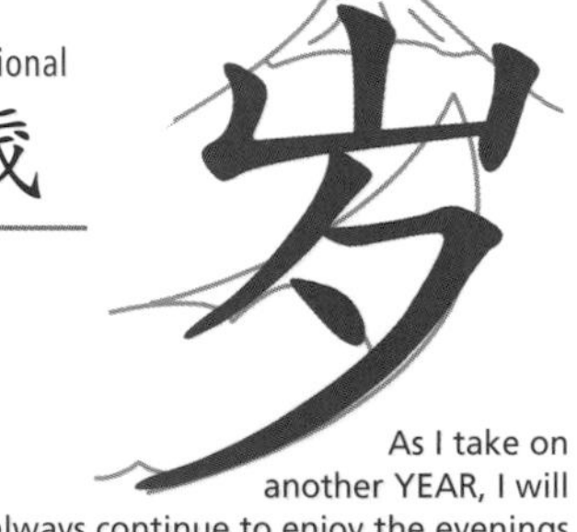

As I take on another YEAR, I will always continue to enjoy the evenings (夕) and climb many mountains.

8 strokes

岩 boulder, rock, cliff

yán

岩石 *yánshí* rock

溶岩 *róngyán* lava

A large ROCK (石) lies at the base of the CLIFF of a mountain.

7 strokes

Traditional

 **island** 

dǎo

岛屿 ***dǎoyǔ*** **islands**

A large bird sits on an ISLAND, the top of an undersea mountain.

5 strokes

 **out, exit, leave**

chū

出口 ***chūkǒu*** **to exit, exporting**

出现 ***chūxiàn*** **to appear, arise**

出发 ***chūfā*** **departure**

When you can see the low foothill of the mountain (山), you are about to EXIT the plains and LEAVE flatlands behind.

7 strokes

Traditional

 **two, both (used before measure words)** 

liǎng

两边 ***liǎngbiān*** **two pieces**

两样 ***liǎngyàng*** **different**

The people (人) were BOTH hiding in the pot with the lid on it along with their untold taels of gold.

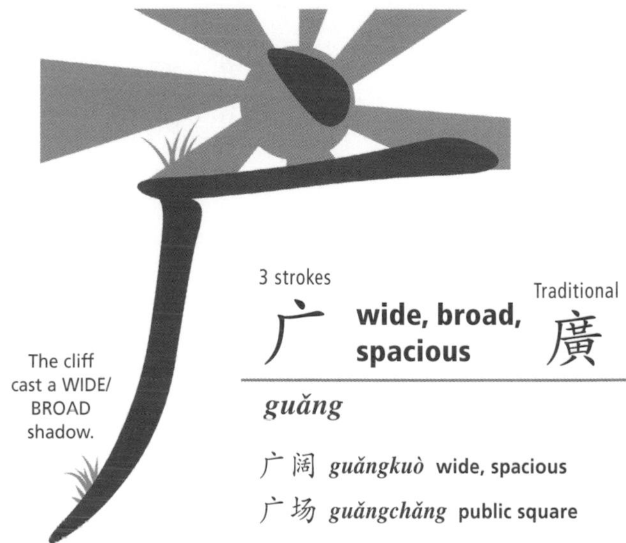

The cliff cast a WIDE/ BROAD shadow.

3 strokes

Traditional

广 **wide, broad, spacious** 廣

guǎng

广阔 ***guǎngkuò*** **wide, spacious**

广场 ***guǎngchǎng*** **public square**

7 strokes

 **sequence, order, preface, beginning**

xù

次序 ***cìxù*** **order, sequence**

程序 ***chéngxù*** **procedure, order, sequence**

I (厶) will start at the BEGINNING, but first I should PREFACE with an explanation of why the cliff is dotted.

At the base of the dotted cliff is a tree (木) below which I will make my BED and camp.

7 strokes

 **bed**

chuáng

起床 ***qǐchuáng*** **getting out of bed**

8 strokes

底 **bottom, base**

dǐ

海底 *hǎidǐ* bottom of the ocean, seabed

彻底 *chèdǐ* thorough, complete

The absolute BOTTOM of the cliff is the lowest or shortest (低) point of the BASE.

9 strokes

度 **degrees, occurrence, time**

dù

程度 *chéngdù* degree, level, extent

温度 *wēndù* temperature

再度 *zàidù* once again, one more time

Each TIME we picnic under the dotted cliff, we play on the swing next to the table (又).

8 strokes

府 **residence, mansion, official residence**

fǔ

政府 *zhèngfǔ* government

府邸 *fǔdǐ* mansion

At the base of the dotted cliff is where I will build my tiny (寸) RESIDENCE.

7 strokes

库 **warehouse, storehouse**

Traditional 庫

kù

仓库 *cāngkù* warehouse, depot, storehouse

国库 *guókù* national treasure, exchequer

The carts (车) of goods are in the WAREHOUSE at the base of the dotted cliff.

8 strokes

店 **store, shop**

diàn

商店 *shāngdiàn* shop, store

饭店 *fàndiàn* restaurant, hotel, diner

酒店 *jiǔdiàn* hotel

Below a dotted cliff sits a STORE where a fortune teller (占) works.

7 strokes

应 **promise, answer, should**

Traditional

應

yìng/yīng

答应 *dāyìng* to promise, agree

应对 *yìngduì* response, answer

应该 *yīnggāi* should, ought to

When someone makes a PROMISE that he saw something in the grass by the cliff, you SHOULD check it out.

4 strokes

厅 hall, government office

Traditional 廳

tīng

餐厅 *cāntīng* restaurant, dining hall

市政厅 *shìzhèngtīng* city hall

The pin is stuck on the spot where the GOVERNMENT OFFICE can be found at the base of the cliff.

10 strokes

座 seat, place, base

zuò

座位 *zuòwèi* seat, place

座子 *zuòzi* base, stand

At the base of the cliff is a PLACE where two people (人) find a SEAT on the ground (土) to relax in the shade.

4 strokes

气 spirit, atmosphere

Traditional 氣

qì

气概 *qìgài* spirit, mettle

天气 *tiānqì* weather

A person's (人) SPIRIT can be quite enthusiastic in an ATMOSPHERE that is supportive of his or her cliff-climbing hobby.

12 strokes

痛 pain, hurt, sorrow

tòng

疼痛 *téngtòng* painful, sore, ache

悲痛 *bēitòng* grieved, sorrow

牙痛 *yátòng* toothache

The thorns on the side of the dotted cliff at night can HURT and I (マ) will have to make use (用) of the first aid kit.

9 strokes

庭 courtyard, garden, yard

tíng

家庭 *jiātíng* household, family

法庭 *fǎtíng* court, court room

庭园 *tíngyuán* flower garden

At the base of the dotted cliff is a GARDEN where warriors took long strides (廴) while they showed off and posed with their fancy helmets (壬).

7 strokes

延 prolong, delay, extent

yán

延长 *yáncháng* extent, to prolong, lengthen

延期 *yánqí* to postpone, delay, extension

To PROLONG life, you must stop (止) and take a minute before you continue on the path.

Stone 石

5 strokes

石 stone, rock

shí

石头 ***shítóu*** **stone, rock**

石油 ***shíyóu*** **petroleum**

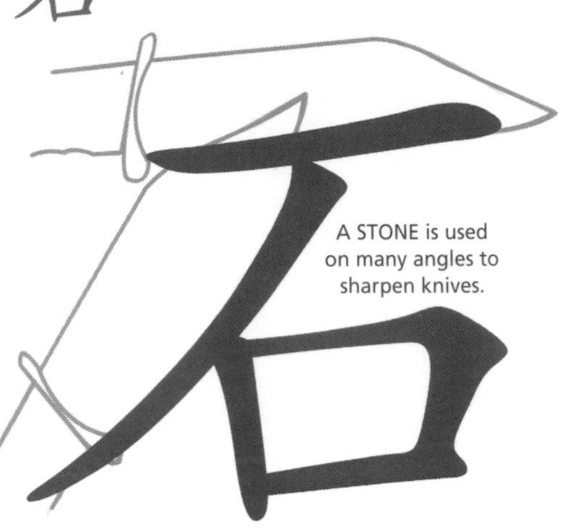

A STONE is used on many angles to sharpen knives.

10 strokes

破 rip, tear, destroy

pò

破坏 ***pòhuài*** **to damage, destroy, destruction**

破碎 ***pòsuì*** **broken, crushed, tattered**

We thought the stones that fell from the cliff would DESTROY the table (又) where the leather (皮) had been drying.

9 strokes

研 research, polish, study

yán

研究 ***yánjiū*** **research, study**

研磨 ***yánmó*** **to polish, grind**

To build a gate for a temple, STUDY your tools for cutting and carving and after finishing constructions. Later POLISH the result.

14 strokes

磁 magnet

cí

磁石 ***císhí*** **magnet**

磁性 ***cíxìng*** **magnetic, magnetism**

MAGNETS stick together like immovable stones (石) sown together with silk (糸) threads.

9 strokes

砂 sand, gravel

shā

砂砾 ***shālì*** **gravel**

砂糖 ***shātáng*** **granulated sugar**

As if cut by a blade, stones are broken down over time into a few (少) particles until they eventually become SAND.

12 strokes

确 correct, true

Traditional 確

què

确实 ***quèshí*** **indeed, true**

正确 ***zhèngquè*** **correct**

It is TRUE that a stone (石) sits at the corner (角) where the CORRECT path turns.

Rain 雨

8 strokes

雨 **rain**

yǔ

下雨 *xiàyǔ* to rain

雨天 *yǔtiān* rainy weather

Through a window, you can see drops of RAIN tapping against the glass.

It can be an ELECTRIC experience to fly a kite in the rain.

5 strokes

 **electricity** Traditional 

电 **electricity** Traditional 電

diàn

电气 *diànqì* electric, electricity

电动 *diàndòng* electrical

电话 *diànhuà* telephone

11 strokes

雪 **snow**

xuě

雪花 *xuěhua* snowflakes

下雪 *xiàxuě* snowfall

Through the window the SNOW is essentially frozen rain that piles up in layers.

4 strokes

云 **cloud** Traditional 雲

yún

白云 *báiyún* white cloud

云霞 *yúnxiá* clouds

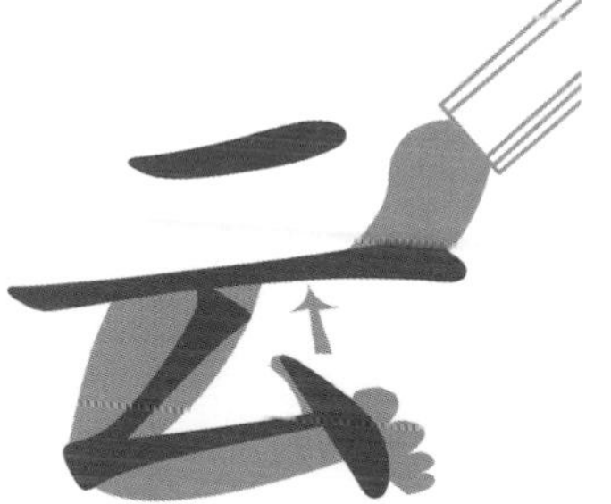

I (厶) say is one CLOUD (云) is nice, but with two (二) CLOUDS comes rain.

13 strokes

雷 **thunder, lightning bolt**

léi

打雷 *dǎléi* thunder

雷雨 *léiyǔ* thunderstorm

When rain (雨) falls on rice fields (田), THUNDER rolls and LIGHTNING can light up the fields.

Four Seasons 四季

9 strokes

春 springtime, spring

chūn

春天 ***chūntiān*** **spring**

春节 ***chūnjié*** **Chinese New Year, Spring Festival**

Three months into a year brings SPRING, and people and plants flourish in extended sunlight.

We sat on the folding table (夂) in the yard wishing SUMMER was more than one hundred (百) days long.

10 strokes

夏 summer

xià

夏天 ***xiàtiān*** **summer**

炎夏 ***yánxià*** **hot summer**

In AUTUMN, the colors of fancy trees resemble fire as their leaves turn.

9 strokes

秋 autumn, fall (season)

qiū

秋天 ***qiūtiān*** **fall, autumn**

5 strokes

冬 winter

dōng

冬天 ***dōngtiān*** **winter**

冬眠 ***dōngmián*** **hibernation**

Sometimes an icy WINTER seems to go on and on as snowflakes pile up below and on the folding table.

CHAPTER 8

MEDIEVAL

4 strokes

王 **king, ruler**

wáng

国王 *guówáng* king
女王 *nǚwáng* queen

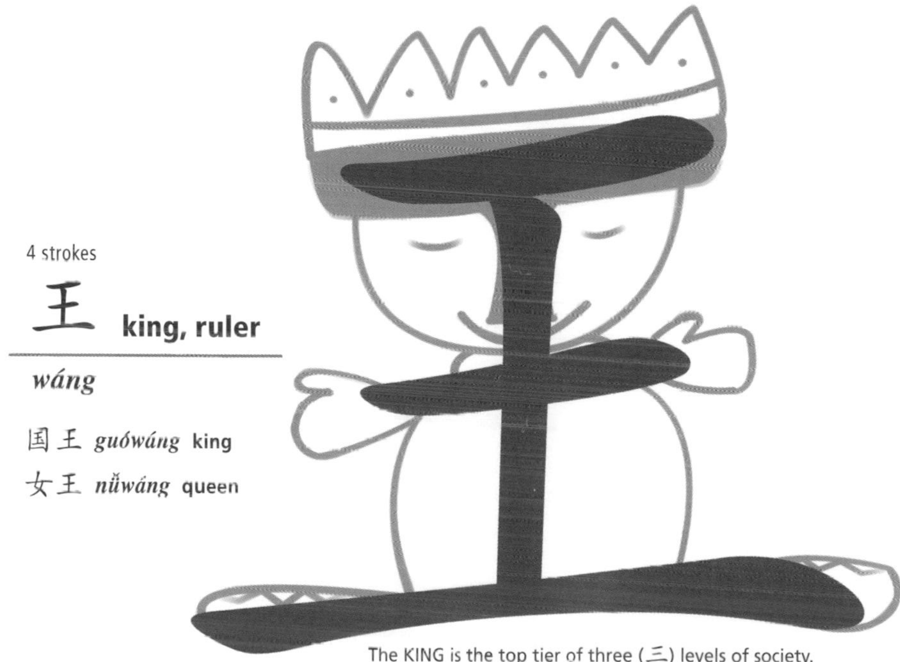

The KING is the top tier of three (三) levels of society.

Medieval 中世纪

5 strokes

主 main, primary, chief, principal

zhǔ

主要 *zhǔyào* main, major, primary

主管 *zhǔguǎn* person in charge, manager

The MAIN person wearing a large feather in his hat is the CHIEF.

5 strokes

玉 jewel, jade

yù

玉石 *yùshí* emerald, jade

碧玉 *bìyù* jasper

The king (王) keeps his ball close, as he eventually will keep track of his JEWELS and JADE.

Under the king (王), trade was FLOURISHING and every day (日) merchants were more PROSPEROUS than the one before.

8 strokes

旺 flourishing, prosperous

wàng

旺盛 *wàngshèng* exuberant, blooming

兴旺 *xīngwàng* prosperous, flourishing

The king was the first to believe that the world was a SPHERE, turning round and round on an axis and that it was made mostly of water.

10 strokes

班 squad, unit, group

bān

班级 *bānjí* class, grade

上班 *shàngbān* go to work

轮班 *lúnbān* [work] shift

Within each GROUP, there is a leader who acts like a king (王).

11 strokes

球 ball, sphere

qiú

地球 *dìqiú* earth, globe, planet

棒球 *bàngqiú* baseball

球赛 *qiúsài* ball game

11 strokes

理 **reason, truth, logic, care**

lǐ

理由 *lǐyóu* **reason**

料理 *liàolǐ* **to arrange, to handle, take care of**

理解 *lǐjiě* **understanding, comprehension**

A good king (王) rules both fields (田) and other lands (土) with REASON and LOGIC.

5 strokes

甲 **shell, 1st place, be better than, armor**

jiǎ

龟甲 *guījiǎ* **tortoise shell**

甲等 *jiǎděng* **class A**

盔甲 *kuījiǎ* **armor**

A shield of ARMOR held up by a spike might BE BETTER THAN one made of paper.

8 strokes

现 **present, current, appear, arise**

Traditional 現

xiàn

出现 *chūxiàn* **to appear, arise, emerge**

现在 *xiànzài* **now, present**

A good king looks at the CURRENT situation and prepares for conditions that may ARISE.

5 strokes

 **from, cause, reason**

yóu

因由 *yīnyóu* **cause, reason**

由于 *yóuyú* **because of, due to**

A signpost on the edge of a field states the REASON why the field is special.

A sign is posted and ready to EXPLAIN a new advertiser's ad and EXPRESS his/her desire.

5 strokes

 **explain, express, state**

shēn

申请 *shēnqǐng* **application, request**

申诉 *shēnsù* **to appeal**

Knight, Warrior, Scholar 士

3 strokes

士 scholar, knight, warrior

shì

学士 *xuéshì* scholar, bachelor degree

武士 *wǔshì* knight, warrior, samurai

士兵 *shìbīng* soldiers

We can see the broad shoulders of a WARRIOR sitting upright with the distinguished look of a SCHOLAR.

7 strokes

 sound, voice, tone

Traditional 聲

shēng

声调 *shēngdiào* tone, note

声音 *shēngyīn* sound, voice

声誉 *shēngyù* reputation, prestige, fame

When a warrior came, people knew it was he when they heard his VOICE through the door (尸).

9 strokes

结 tie, bind, unite, join

Traditional 結

jié

结束 *jiéshù* ending, to finish

结构 *jiégòu* structure, architecture

结果 *jiéguǒ* result, to bear fruit

If you say your string of luck (吉) is good, you can TIE it to various aspects of your life.

8 strokes

 sell, sale

Traditional 

mài

售卖 *shòumài* to sell

出卖 *chūmài* offer to sell, to betray

Ten clerks SELL goods on the floor while the boss (头) below pays them in coin.

Offer to say (口) PROPITIOUS wishes to a faithful KNIGHT before and after a battle and he will be LUCKY.

6 strokes

 lucky, propitious

jí

吉祥 *jíxiáng* lucky, auspicious, propitious

Arrow 矢

5 strokes

 **dart, arrow**

shǐ

飞矢 ***fēishǐ*** **flying arrow**

矢言 ***shǐyán*** **vowed**

This archer, with a feather in his cap, has an ARROW, but no bow.

An SHORT archer needs a SHORT arrow to pierce a bean (豆).

12 strokes

短 **short (length)**

duǎn

短缺 ***duǎnquē*** **shortage**

简短 ***jiǎnduǎn*** **brief, short**

知

The archer KNOWS how to hit a target through experience and WISDOM.

8 strokes

 **know, knowledge, wisdom**

zhī

知识 ***zhīshì*** **knowledge, information**

知道 ***zhīdào*** **to know, be aware of**

7 strokes

 **beans, pea**

dòu

豆子 ***dòuzi*** **beans, bean curd**

豌豆 ***wāndòu*** **pea**

BEAN stalks produce one (一) flower which gives way to a bean to eventually feed hungry mouths (口).

14 strokes

疑 **doubt, distrust, suspect, question**

yí

怀疑 ***huáiyí*** **to suspect, doubt/distrust**

疑问 ***yíwèn*** **doubt, question**

When an archer uses a spoon (匕) to stir DISTRUST in others, he himself must have at least one (一) plan to duck and use his feet (疋) to escape.

Gods 礻

9 strokes

神 **gods, mind, soul**

shén

神 *shén* **gods/God**

精神 *jīngshén* **spirit, vigor**

The GODS put up a signboard to attract more SOULS to come to the temple.

7 strokes

社 **association, society**

shè

会社 *huìshè* **association, alliance**

社会 *shèhuì* **society, community**

A god dedicated to the land gives a blessing to a new ASSOCIATION that has been formed.

9 strokes

祖 **ancestor, founder**

zǔ

祖先 *zǔxiān* **ancestor**

祖父 *zǔfù* **grandfather**

鼻祖 *bízǔ* **founder, originator**

The names of our ANCESTORS are listed on stele in the graveyard.

5 strokes

礼 **ceremony, courtesy**

Traditional 禮

lǐ

典礼 *diǎnlǐ* **ceremony, celebration**

礼貌 *lǐmào* **courtesy, politeness**

For a noble or a god, kneeling as a COURTESY is a form of CEREMONY might be necessary.

13 strokes

福 **fortune, luck**

fú

幸福 *xìngfú* **happiness, blessed**

福利 *fúlì* **welfare, well being**

May the souls speak with one (一) voice (口) and wish you LUCK and FORTUNE for your fields (田).

9 strokes

祝 **pray, celebrate, congratulate**

zhù

祝福 *zhùfú* **blessing, to bless**

庆祝 *qìngzhù* **congratulations, celebration**

My big mouth older brother (兄) would always PRAY to and CELEBRATE the gods of our ancestors.

CHAPTER 9

TOOLS

2 strokes

刀 **knife, blade, sword**

dāo

剪刀 *jiǎndāo* scissors

剃刀 *tìdāo* razor

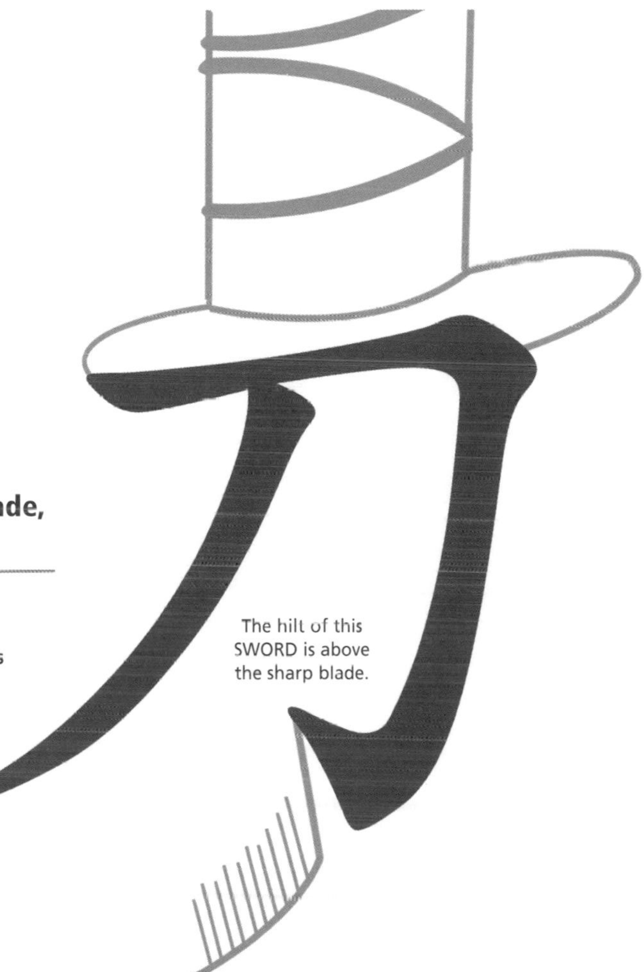

The hilt of this SWORD is above the sharp blade.

Swords 刀 and Blades 刂

4 strokes

切 cut, slice, be close to, correspond to

qiē

切开 *qiēkāi* **to cut, slit**

亲切 *qīnqiè* **kindness, cordial, gentleness**

A sword (刀) was used to SLICE and CUT down all seven (七) enemies.

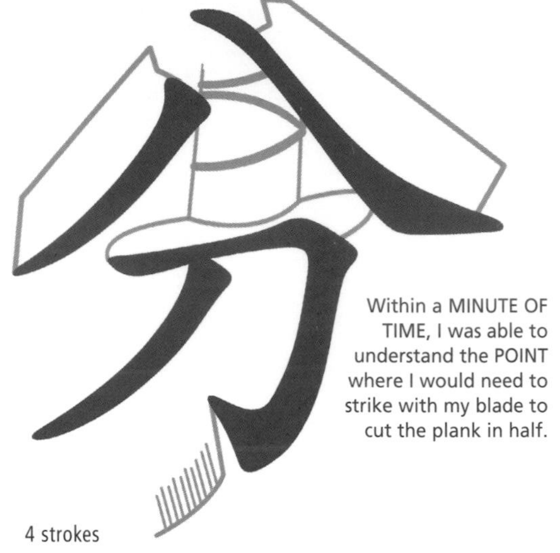

Within a MINUTE OF TIME, I was able to understand the POINT where I would need to strike with my blade to cut the plank in half.

7 strokes

初 first time, beginning

chū

最初 *zuìchū* **initial, first, primary**

初期 *chūqí* **beginning, start, initial stage**

In the dramatic BEGINNING, the movie started with the grim scene of a villain skillfully wielding a blade (刀) like a god.

4 strokes

分 part, point, minute of time

fēn

两分钟 *liǎngfēnzhōng* **two minutes**

分配 *fēnpèi* **distribution, allocation**

This person has the one (一) extra big (大) TICKET, waving his arms with excitement after winning the prize sword (刀).

8 strokes

券 ticket, certificate

quàn

债券 *zhàiquàn* **bonds**

奖券 *jiǎngquàn* **lottery ticket**

入场券 *rùchǎngquàn* **admission tickets**

5 strokes

务 task, duties Traditional 務

wù

任务 *rènwù* **task, duty, mission**

业务 *yèwù* **business, professional affair**

事务所 *shìwùsuǒ* **firm, office**

One TASK was to use my strength (力) to trim the grass around the picnic table (夂).

6 strokes

份 part, portion, share

fèn

部份 ***bùfèn*** **share, part, section**

股份 ***gǔfèn*** **share, stock**

A person uses a sword to cut (刀) something in half to SHARE PORTIONS with others.

7 strokes

别 separate, another

bié

特别 ***tèbié*** **special, particular**

别离 ***biélí*** **parting, farewell**

After talking (口) about how to SEPARATE their possessions, they simply took a sword (刀) of ANOTHER friend and cut things as if with a knife (刂).

6 strokes

列 file, row, column

liè

行列 ***hángliè*** **line, row**

排列 ***páiliè*** **arrangement, to array, put in order**

There were many things stacked up in the COLUMN on this evening's (夕) schedule, but I cut through them like a knife.

7 strokes

判 sentence, judgment

pàn

判决 ***pànjué*** **judgment, decision**

裁判 ***cáipàn*** **trial, referee, judge, umpire**

A JUDGMENT was made to cut possessions in half (半) as if they were twigs severed with a sword.

Through an open door (尸), freshly PRINTED fabric can be seen drying and will soon be ready to be cut into strips with a knife (刂).

8 strokes

刷 brush, scrub

shuā

刷牙 ***shuāyá*** **to brush teeth**

印刷 ***yìnshuā*** **printing**

7 strokes

利 profit, benefit, advantage

lì

利用 ***lìyòng*** **to use, utilization**

有利 ***yǒulì*** **favorable, advantageous, better**

A fancy tree, when cut with a huge knife, can lead to a huge PROFIT, but is of BENEFIT as-is too.

11 strokes

 **vice, deputy, assistant**

fù

副手 *fùshǒu* **assistant**

副词 *fùcí* **adverb**

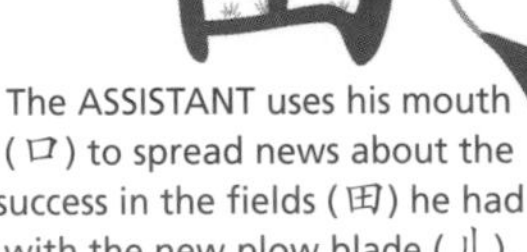

The ASSISTANT uses his mouth (口) to spread news about the success in the fields (田) he had with the new plow blade (刂).

As they touched the bottom of the roof (宀), plants in the fertile soil (土) were CUT OFF with a knife and vegetables were planted to feed hungry mouths (口).

8 strokes

 **make, manufacture** Traditional 

zhì

制造 *zhìzào* **to manufacture, make**

制成品 *zhìchéngpǐn* **finished products**

Grow more cotton to MANUFACTURE fabric to be dried (巾) and cut to MAKE clothes.

12 strokes

 **cut off, mow, divide, break**

gē

割草 *gēcǎo* **to cut/mow the grass**

分割 *fēngē* **segmentation, parting, to cut up, breaking up**

9 strokes

 **in front, before, ago**

qián

前面 *qiánmiàn* **in front**

以前 *yǐqián* **before, previous, formerly**

Some say the blades of grass IN FRONT of the house grow quicker if you cut them with a knife (刂) BEFORE a full moon (月).

10 strokes

 **drama, play** Traditional 

jù

剧场 *jùchǎng* **theater/playhouse**

京剧 *jīngjù* **Beijing/Peking opera**

The PLAY was about a knife (刂) next to an old (古) door (尸).

Writing Brush 聿

4 strokes

书 book, write

Traditional 書

shū

读书 *dúshū* reading, to study

书写 *shūxiě* to write

图书馆 *túshūguǎn* library

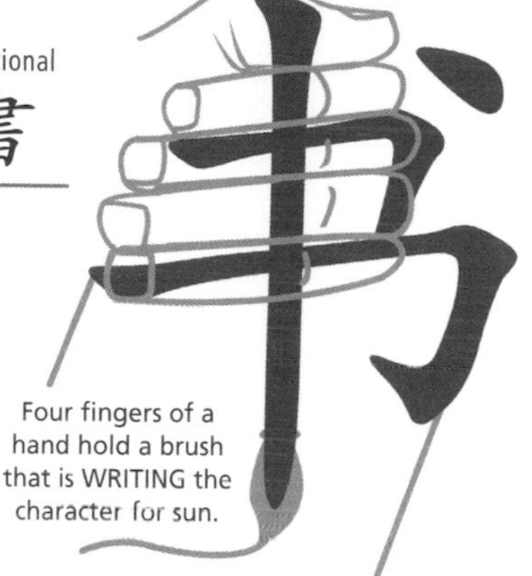

Four fingers of a hand hold a brush that is WRITING the character for sun.

10 strokes

健 healthy, health, strength

jiàn

健康 *jiànkāng* healthy

健全 *jiànquán* strong, perfect, robust

To remain in good HEALTH and STRENGTH, a person should take long strides (廴) and use a brush on his teeth after eating.

8 strokes

 build

jiàn

建立 *jiànlì* to establish, create, set up

建設 *jiànshè* to build, construct

To BUILD something, architects would first use a brush to draw a plan and then take long strides (廴) to complete it correctly.

8 strokes

 matter, thing, business, job

shì

事业 *shìyè* career, enterprise

旧事 *jiù shì* an old matter or affair, a past event

One THING you can eat with your mouth (口) from a handheld skewer is meat.

11 strokes

 healthy, peaceful, abundant

kāng

健康 *jiànkāng* health, healthy

康复 *kāngfù* rehabilitation, to recover from an illness

At the base of a cliff (广) is a PEACEFUL place where water (水) flows and you can relax with ease and use a brush and ink to sketch.

6 strokes

 fight, dispute, struggle, contend

Traditional 爭

zhēng

战争 *zhànzhēng* war

争吵 *zhēngchǎo* to quarrel, dispute

When you ARGUE and someone throws barbs during the DISPUTE, a person with an official rank (尹) can stop it.

Books 书 and Writing 写

5 strokes

册 **counter for bound volumes, (books)**

Traditional 冊

cè

册子 ***cèzi*** pamphlet, booklet

手册 ***shǒucè*** manual, handbook

This is a set of BOUND VOLUMES of.

4 strokes

片 **piece, slice, one-sided**

piàn

一片 ***yīpiàn*** a piece, a slice

片刻 ***piànkè*** moment, instant, short while

唱片 ***chàngpiàn*** record, disc, disk

This ONE–SIDED character is like a SLICE of an orange.

An inkwell sits on a wide table, ready for fancy LANGUAGE to be written down to add to the wealth of LITERATURE in the CULTURE.

8 strokes

版 **printing block/ plate, edition**

bǎn

版本 ***bǎnběn*** edition, version

出版 ***chūbǎn*** publishing, release

出版社 ***chūbǎnshè*** publisher, press

The first PRINTING BLOCK of the EDITION was printed on a sheet at a table (又) under a cliff (厂) that still looked fresh as a slice (片) of orange.

4 strokes

文 **culture, language, literature**

wén

文化 ***wénhuà*** culture, civilization, literacy

文学 ***wénxué*** literature

文字 ***wénzì*** writing, scripture, character, letter [of alphabet]

6 strokes

 **cross, intersect, pay, deliver**

jiāo

交叉 ***jiāochā*** to cross, intersect

交换 ***jiāohuàn*** exchange/ switching, to swap

交通 ***jiāotōng*** transportation, communication

Dad (父) is trying to keep a lid on things between his busy life and all of the COMING AND GOING of the kids.

Show or Indicate 示

11 strokes

票 ticket, ballot

piào

门票 *ménpiào* tickets

投票 *tóupiào* voting, poll

票据 *piàojù* bills, note, receipt

A BALLOT is slipped through the lid of a collection box and later the winner is announced on a signboard (示).

5 strokes

示 show, indicate, point out

shì

显示 *xiǎnshì* to demonstrate, show

表示 *biǎoshì* to represent, express

指示 *zhǐshì* indication, directions

A signpost SHOWS important information, POINTED OUT by the flashing light.

In the evening as the moonrise occurs, a sign (示) can be seen to CELEBRATE the night sky and other RITUAL events.

11 strokes

祭 ritual, celebrate, worship

jì

祭祀 *jìsì* to sacrifice, celebrate

拜祭 *bàijì* to worship

13 strokes

禁 prohibition, ban

jìn

禁止 *jìnzhǐ* prohibition, ban

监禁 *jiānjìn* to jail, imprison

Around the woods (林) in dry conditions, you see signposts (示) for a PROHIBITION of burning or a fire BAN.

Divining Rod 卜

5 strokes

占 occupy, have, get, capture

Traditional 佔

zhàn

占据 *zhànjù* to occupy, hold

占领 *zhànlǐng* to capture

To say what he sees when FORTUNE-TELLING the man uses rods and other tools in DIVINING someone's future.

2 strokes

卜 divine, tell fortunes

bǔ

占卜 *zhānbǔ* to divine

占卜者 *zhānbǔ zhě* prognosticator

People who might also tell the FORTUNES of others use a forked stick to DIVINE the water.

Bow 弓

3 strokes

弓 bow

gōng

弓箭 ***gōngjiàn*** **bow and arrow**

A traditional BOW had a deep bend where the archer would hold it.

7 strokes

张 lengthen, stretch, spread

Traditional 張

zhāng

扩张 ***kuòzhāng*** **expansion, outspread**

主张 ***zhǔzhāng*** **advocacy, to maintain, viewpoint, assertion**

STRETCH a bow's (弓) long (长) string.

4 strokes

引 pull, tug, quote

yǐn

牵引 ***qiānyǐn*** **to draw, drag, tow**

吸引 ***xīyǐn*** **to attract, draw, fascinate**

In archery, you PULL the bow's (弓) string along with an arrow.

12 strokes

强 strong

Traditional 強

qiáng

强壮 ***qiángzhuàng*** **strong, robust, sturdy**

强迫 ***qiángpò*** **to force, compel**

10 strokes

弱 weak, frail

ruò

弱者 ***ruòzhě*** **weak person, the weak**

脆弱 ***cuìruò*** **fragile, weak**

These two bows had WEAK strings that just snapped.

A bow (弓) can sometimes be pulled by a bug (虫) who considers itself STRONG and uses its mouth (口) to eat a lot.

Axe 斤

13 strokes

新 **new**

xīn

新鲜 ***xīnxiān*** fresh, latest

新闻 ***xīnwén*** news

Leaning his axe against a tree and standing on top of the branches, one sees NEW things in the distance.

7 strokes

近 **near, close to**

jìn

附近 ***fùjìn*** nearby, neighboring

最近 ***zuìjìn*** recently, lately

My grandfather kept the axe (斤) NEAR the door so he could grab it as he strode on the path to the woodpile.

7 strokes

折 **fold, break, fracture, bend**

zhé

折断 ***zhéduàn*** to break/fracture

骨折 ***gǔzhé*** bone fracture

打折 ***dǎzhé*** discounts

To FOLD or BREAK hard material with your hands (手), you might need an axe (斤).

Spears 戈

A CITY was built on land (土) next to a cliff and was defended with halberds (戈).

9 strokes

城 **city, town**

chéng

城市 ***chéngshì*** city, town

中国城 ***Zhōngguóchéng*** Chinatown

8 strokes

武 **warrior, military**

wǔ

武术 ***wǔshù*** martial arts

武器 ***wǔqì*** weapons

A WARRIOR might shout "Halt" (止) and stand firm with his halberd.

9 strokes

残 cruel, leftover, remainder

Traditional 殘

cán

残酷 *cánkù* cruel, brutal

残缺 *cánquē* incomplete

残留 *cánliú* to remain, leftover

As the moon (月) rises, the blade (戈) nearby is used to cut the LEFTOVER food from the day's three (三) meals.

7 strokes

我 I, me, myself

wǒ

我们 *wǒmen* we, us

I took my hands (手) and twirled the halberds (戈) MYSELF to show off.

9 strokes

 war, battle, match

Traditional 

zhàn

战争 *zhànzhēng* war

战斗 *zhàndòu* fighting, combat, battle

A divination (占) showed that the use of halberd blades in the WAR would be successful.

6 strokes

成 turn into, become, grow

chéng

成为 *chéngwéi* to become, turn into

完成 *wánchéng* to complete, accomplish, fulfill

组成 *zǔchéng* to form, constitute

A blade was used to cut a notch into the cliff to plant a seed that will GROW to BECOME a healthy plant.

6 strokes

 ceremony, function

shì

仪式 *yíshì* ceremony, rite

方式 *fāngshì* mode, style

公式 *gōngshì* formula

Before construction (工) begins, a CEREMONY is held and a halberd (戈) cuts through a ribbon.

12 strokes

 sanction, judge, decision, tailor

cái

裁判 *cáipàn* referee, judge, trial

裁剪 *cáijiǎn* cutting, to cut out [a pattern]

裁缝 *cáiféng* tailor, dressmaker

A JUDGE can make a DECISION on land (土) rights peacefully rather than using halberds (戈) to settle conflict over it.

Well 井 and Fields 田

4 strokes

井 **well, orderly**

jǐng

天井 *tiānjǐng* small courtyard in the middle of a buidling

井然 *jǐngrán* orderly

A WELL must be built in an ORDERLY manner.

10 strokes

耕 **till, cultivate**

gēng

耕种 *gēngzhòng* to till, cultivate

耕地 *gēngdì* farmland, arable land

A farmer used a plow (耒) with disks of wood to TILL a field and then put the CULTIVATED grain in a storage well (井).

The FARM was made of many small FIELDS (田).

5 strokes

田 **farm, field**

tián

田园 *tiányuán* countryside, rural

麦田 *màitián* wheat field

7 strokes

里 **village, inside**

lǐ

邻里 *línlǐ* neighborhood

乡里 *xiānglǐ* village

里面 *lǐmiàn* inside, interior

The VILLAGE was on land (土) just below the field (田).

12 strokes

量 **quantity, weight, consider**

liàng

数量 *shùliàng* quantity

重量 *zhòngliàng* weight

量度 *liàngdù* measurements

There is always a day (日) when one (一) CONSIDERS the quantity of grain from the fields (田) on their land (土).

9 strokes

界 **boundary, extent, group, circle**

jiè

界限 *jièxiàn* boundary, limit

界定 *jièdìng* definition, resolution

各界 *gèjiè* all walks of life, all circles

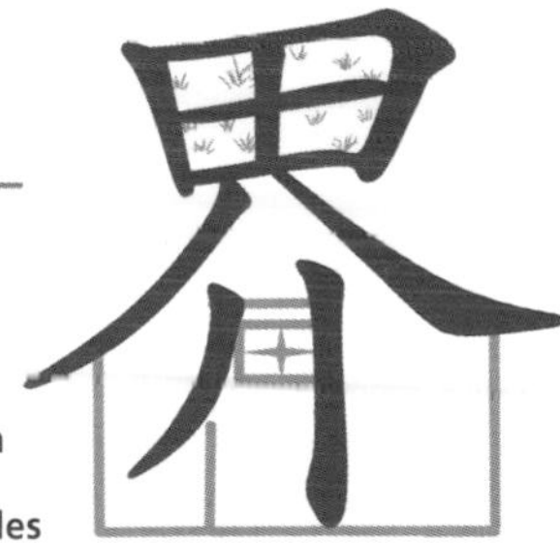

The EXTENT of the property included the field and a house.

9 strokes

俚 vulgar, rustic

lǐ

俚语 *lǐyǔ* slang

俚俗 *lǐsú* vulgar

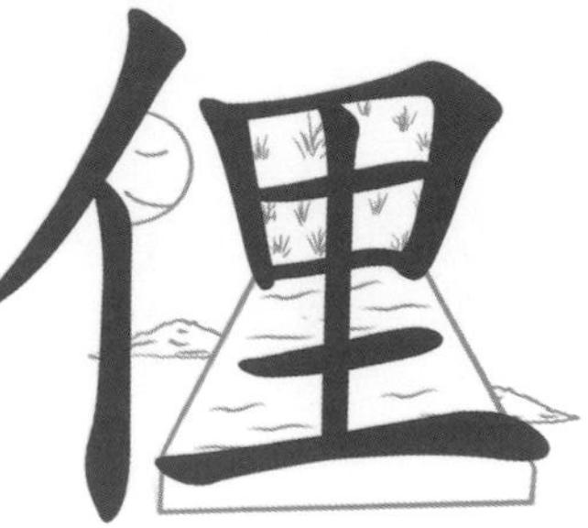

An ILL MANNERED person trailed in soil from the field.

10 strokes

 save, retain, keep, remain

liú

保留 *bǎoliú* to retain, keep, reserve

停留 *tíngliú* to remain, stop

留学生 *liúxuéshēng* student studying aboard

I (厶) turned around and HALTED when I lost my knife (刀) in the field (田).

11 strokes

 slightly, omission, abbreviation

lüè

简略 *jiǎnlüè* brief, simple, to abbreviate

战略 *zhànlüè* strategy

省略 *shěnglüè* omission, abbreviation

Beside the field (田), there is a picnic table (夂) that would be SLIGHTLY better if there was food on it.

This pinpoint marks the ward (丁) where the FIELD of your parent's home (里) was.

11 strokes

野 plains, field, wild

yě

野外 *yěwài* field, plain

原野 *yuányě* champaign, plains, open land

野生 *yěshēng* wild, uncultivated

8 strokes

画 picture

Traditional 畫

huà

画画 *huàhuà* to paint

画家 *huàjiā* painter (artist)

A four–panel manga PICTURE/ program about fields (田) can be seen on the big screen TV.

6 strokes

异 uncommon, unusual

Traditional 異

yì

差异 *chāyì* difference, divergence

异议 *yìyì* objection, opposition, dissent

It is UNCOMMON for me to finish work between the hours of 9 to 11 (巳) and finally wash my two hands (廾) off tasks for the day.

CHAPTER 10

TRANSPORTATION and BUILDINGS

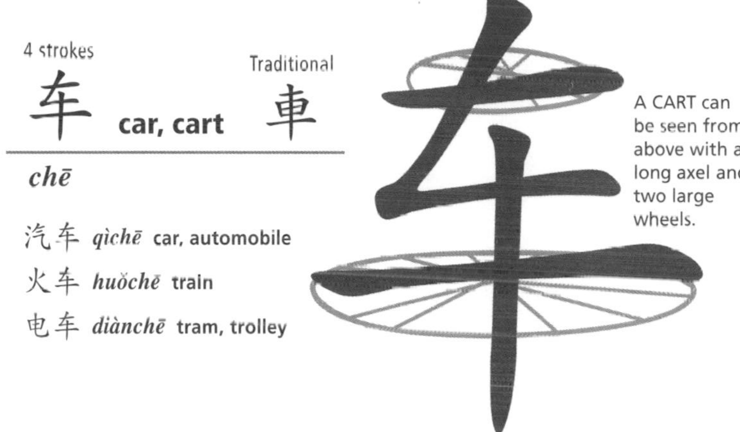

A CART can be seen from above with a long axel and two large wheels.

4 strokes

车 **car, cart** Traditional 車

chē

汽车 *qìchē* car, automobile

火车 *huǒchē* train

电车 *diànchē* tram, trolley

My HOUSE and my ROOM is through the door on my (厶) land.

9 strokes

屋 **house, room**

wū

房屋 *fángwū* houses, buildings

Vehicles 车

10 strokes

 **ride, board, multiplication**

chéng

乘客 *chéngkè* passenger

乘数 *chéngshù* multiplier

People would RIDE in palanquins in East Asia past trees.

8 strokes

 **revolve, change, turn around** Traditional 轉

zhuǎn

转动 *zhuǎndòng* to turn, spin

回转 *huízhuǎn* rotation, to revolve

转变 *zhuǎnbiàn* to change, transform

A big cart (车) cannot TURN AROUND in a field as easily as a little (寸) one.

8 strokes

 **wheel, ring, circle** Traditional 輪

lún

车轮 *chēlún* wheel

轮船 *lúnchuán* ship, steamboat

The man had volumes (冊) of instruction manuals about fixing the WHEELS and parts of cars (车).

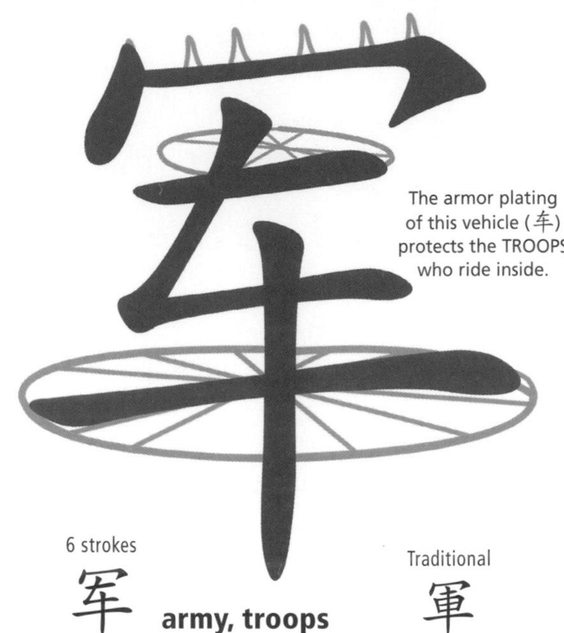

The armor plating of this vehicle (车) protects the TROOPS who ride inside.

6 strokes

军 **army, troops** Traditional 軍

jūn

军队 *jūnduì* army, troops

将军 *jiāngjūn* general, army general, shogun

9 strokes

轻 **light, lax** Traditional 輕

qīng

轻微 *qīngwéi* light, slight

轻松 *qīngsōng* relaxed

Use a light cart (车) when traveling over flowing water (巠) in a construction zone.

10 strokes

航 navigate, cruise

háng

航海 *hánghǎi* **to sail, navigate, sea voyage**

航空 *hángkōng* **aviation**

航线 *hángxiàn* **route, shipping line**

Before you try to NAVIGATE a boat (舟), sit at your little table (几) under the awning to plan your route.

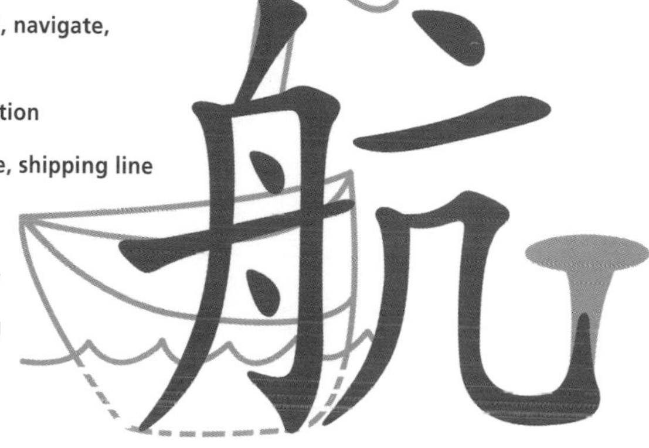

10 strokes

般 sort, kind

bān

一般 *yībān* **general, ordinary**

百般 *bǎibān* **by all means**

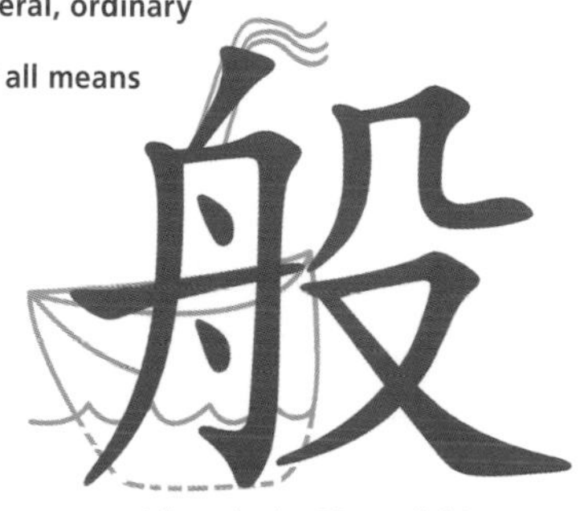

A boat is the SORT of thing that is too big to be built on a desk or a table, but that is the KIND of object that one dreams of constructing.

11 strokes

船 ship, boat, vessel

chuán

轮船 *lúnchuán* **ship**

帆船 *fānchuán* **sailboat, yacht, junk**

A BOAT has a pointy bow, and happy passengers talk as they step off.

FLY off cliff after cliff, flapping your hands as you go.

3 strokes

飞 fly, scatter

Traditional 飛

fēi

飞行 *fēixíng* **to fly**

飞机 *fēijī* **airplane**

Tables 又/夂/几

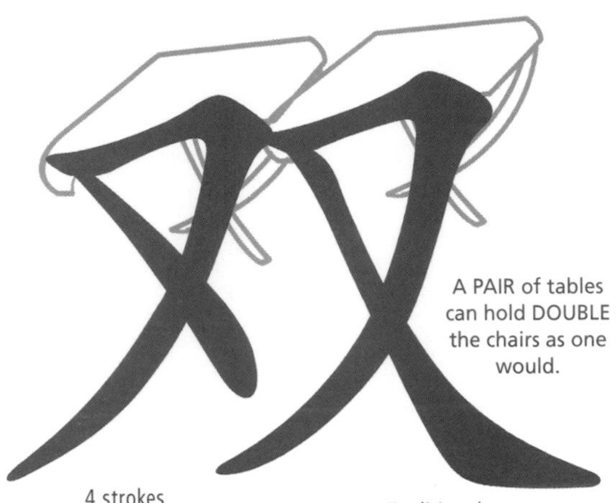

A PAIR of tables can hold DOUBLE the chairs as one would.

4 strokes

双 **double, pair** Traditional 雙

shuāng

双重 ***shuāngchóng*** **double, dual**

双方 ***shuāngfāng*** **both sides**

一双 ***yīshuāng*** **one pair**

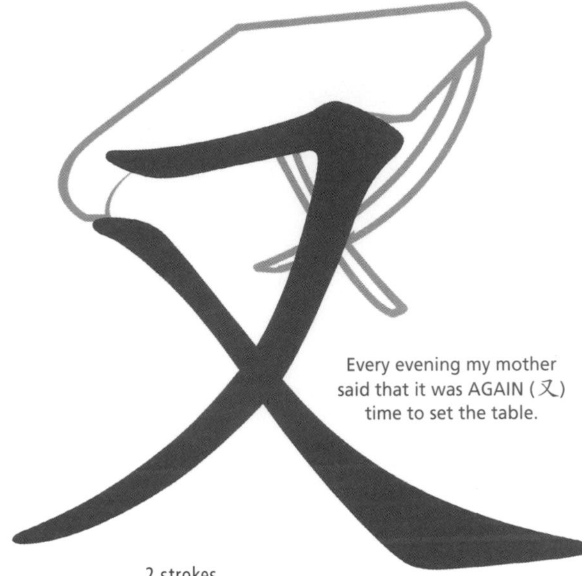

Every evening my mother said that it was AGAIN (又) time to set the table.

2 strokes

又 **furthermore, also, on the other hand, again**

yòu

又是 ***yòushì*** **also is**

4 strokes

友 **friend**

yǒu

朋友 ***péngyǒu*** **friend, partner, pal**

友善 ***yǒushàn*** **friendly**

A FRIEND leans across a table to shake your hand.

10 strokes

爱 **love, affection** Traditional 愛

ài

爱情 ***àiqíng*** **love**

爱人 ***àirén*** **lover**

A cap is put on this roof with sprinkles of knowledge about the friend (友) below, and LOVE is in the air.

4 strokes

 **anti, on the contrary**

fǎn

反叛 ***fǎnpàn*** **to rebel, revolt**

反对 ***fǎnduì*** **opposition, to reverse, oppose**

I expected the table below the cliff (厂) to be ready for our picnic, but the OPPOSITE was true and we had to wait for others to finish.

4 strokes

 **branch, support, sustain**

zhī

支付 ***zhīfù*** **to pay, payment**

支持 ***zhīchí*** **to support, sustain in, stand-by**

At each BRANCH of the school, there are ten (十) tables where students practice writing, SUPPORTED by a teacher.

9 strokes

 **politics, government**

zhèng

政府 ***zhèngfǔ*** **government**

政治 ***zhèngzhì*** **politics, political**

财政 ***cáizhèng*** **financial, finance**

One hopes that politicians will stop and do the correct (正) thing when they sit around folding tables (夊) and negotiate laws.

11 strokes

救 **salvation, save, reclaim**

jiù

挽救 ***wǎnjiù*** **to save, rescue, remedy**

急救 ***jíjiù*** **first aid, emergency treatment**

People didn't believe that the world was round, but now most think that our only SALVATION will be to sit down at a table and make a plan to SAVE the planet.

Seeing the tall bamboo (⺮) bent and broken near a folding table, all that I could do was to cover my mouth (口) in RESPECT for nature's power.

12 strokes

 **respect, honor**

jìng

尊敬 ***zūnjìng*** **to respect, honor**

致敬 ***zhìjìng*** **to salute, pay tribute, greet**

12 strokes

散 scatter, disperse, spend

sàn

分散 ***fēnsàn*** **to disperse, scatter**

散布 ***sànbù*** **to spread, distribute**

Tens (十) of meteors SCATTER in the moonlight as we sit, stargazing at the folding table.

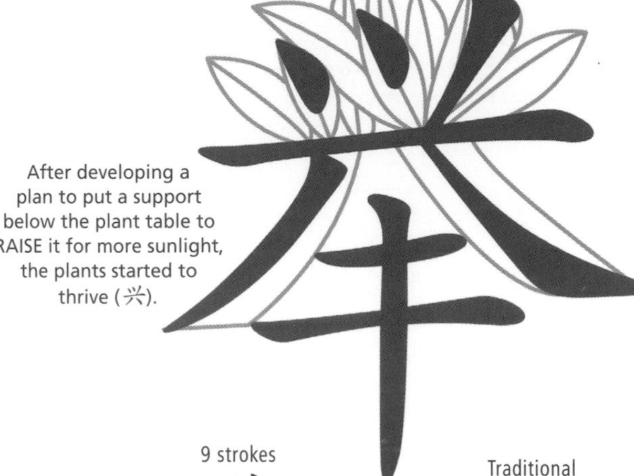

After developing a plan to put a support below the plant table to RAISE it for more sunlight, the plants started to thrive (兴).

9 strokes

举 raise, lift up Traditional 舉

jǔ

举起 ***jǔqǐ*** **to lift, uphold, raise**

选举 ***xuǎnjǔ*** **election**

举行 ***jǔxíng*** **to hold, in process**

5 strokes

处 deal with, condemn, place Traditional 處

chù

处理 ***chǔlǐ*** **to handle, process, treat, dealing with**

办事处 ***bànshìchù*** **office, agency**

A person sits down at a table (夊) in a PLACE with his favorite fortune teller (卜) to DEAL WITH an issue.

10 strokes

敌 enemy, opponent Traditional 敵

dí

敌人 ***dírén*** **enemy, foe**

敌意 ***díyì*** **hostility, enmity, animosity**

The ENEMY started the fight by sticking his tongue (舌) out at me as we sat at the folding table.

6 strokes

兴 interest, prosper, desire, glad Traditional  興

xìng/xīng

兴趣 ***xìngqù*** **interest, liking**

高兴 ***gāoxìng*** **happy, glad**

兴盛 ***xīngshèng*** **to flourish, prosper, thrive**

I am GLAD that the plants on this table are able to flourish and PROSPER.

7 strokes

reformation, change, modify, renew

gǎi

改变 ***gǎibiàn*** **to change, alter, amend**

改正 ***gǎizhèng*** **correction, revision, amendment**

To CHANGE the broken parts on the left to make a new folding table you might have to MODIFY some pieces.

16 strokes

整 whole, entire, complete

zhěng

完整 ***wánzhěng*** **complete, whole, entire**

整理 ***zhěnglǐ*** **to put in order, arrange**

整齐 ***zhěngqí*** **neat, tidy**

6 strokes

receive, obtain

shōu

收入 ***shōurù*** **income, revenue**

收集 ***shōují*** **to collect, gather**

收成 ***shōuchéng*** **harvest, crop**

OBTAIN a sign with which to connect (丩) with people and a table from where you can sit with others at event.

BE READY to bundle (束) up tree saplings on a picnic table correctly (正) so they will BE PREPARED to ship on time to customers.

8 strokes

take, fetch

qǔ

采取 ***cǎiqǔ*** **to take, adopt, choose**

取消 ***qǔxiāo*** **to cancel, abolishment**

Use your ears (耳) to listen for signs from your opponent carefully to know when to TAKE an opportunity to win when gambling at a table.

8 strokes

accept, receive, undergo

shòu

接受 ***jiēshòu*** **to receive, accept**

忍受 ***rěnshòu*** **to endure, bear, stand**

ACCEPT a challenge to take a swipe at UNDERGOING a test on the three subjects or bits of knowledge you studied at the table.

Roofs 宀 / 宀

5 strokes

写 write, describe, compose

Traditional 

xiě

描写 *miáoxiě* **to describe**

写字 *xiězì* **writing**

写意 *xiěyì* **freehand**

The author would DESCRIBE and WRITE down every detail about the contortionist's emergence from the vessel.

12 strokes

 wealth, enrich, abundant

fù

富有 *fùyǒu* **rich, wealthy, abundant**

富豪 *fùháo* **rich and powerful with status**

富士山 *Fùshìshān* **Mt. Fuji**

Under a roof (宀), one (一) the mouth (口) of a man with WEALTH tells others what happened with his fields (田) and his ABUNDANT yield.

They say they ALLOW eight (八) people to stay (宀) in cottages in the valley (谷).

10 strokes

 allow, permit, contain, looks

róng

容许 *róngxǔ* **to allow, permit, tolerate**

容貌 *róngmào* **looks, appearance**

内容 *nèiróng* **subject, contents**

A GUEST under a roof in an inn with a chimney at a folding table uses his mouth (口) to speak to the person behind the table for a reservation.

9 strokes

 guest, visitor, customer

kè

客人 *kèrén* **guest, visitor**

旅客 *lǚkè* **traveler, passenger [transport]**

客气 *kèqi* **polite, modest, courteous**

10 strokes

 palace

gōng

宫殿 *gōngdiàn* **palace**

故宫 *Gùgōng* **Imperial Palace**

白宫 *Báigōng* **The White House**

Under the roof (宀) of a SHINTO SHRINE or a PALACE, a network of mouths of people joined together [吕] to support the gods or royals.

10 strokes

 harm, injury

hài

伤害 *shānghài* **to harm, hurt, injure**

灾害 *zāihài* **calamity, disaster**

When a roof (宀) is pushed up by plants that keep growing extra tall limbs, one should use his mouth to yell before someone gets HARMED or sustains INJURY.

8 strokes

宜 fitting, appropriate, suitable, good

yí

适宜 ***shìyí*** suitable, appropriate, fit

便宜 ***piányi*** cheap

Under a roof (宀), when an eye (目) is more grounded, things are most SUITABLE.

12 strokes

寒 cold

hán

寒冷 ***hánlěng*** cold, chill, frigid

寒风 ***hánfēng*** cold wind

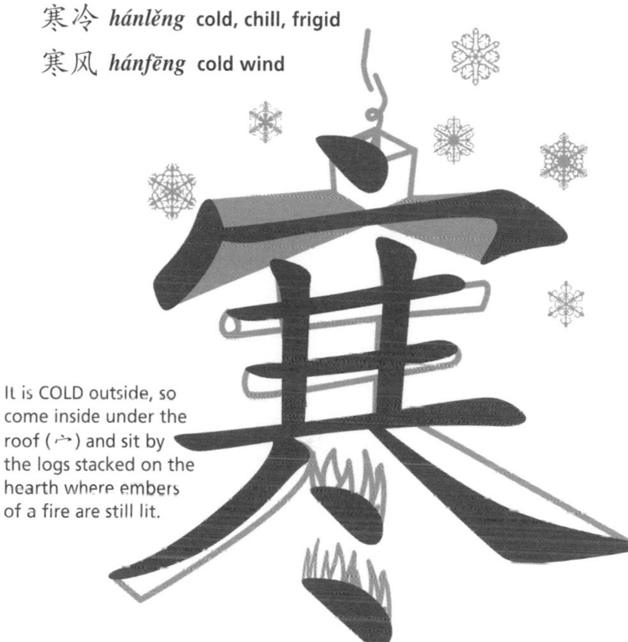

It is COLD outside, so come inside under the roof (宀) and sit by the logs stacked on the hearth where embers of a fire are still lit.

When at home under a roof (宀), if I cross my heart (心) and swear to SECRECY, I would fall off a mountain (山) before I divulge the SECRET.

11 strokes

密 secrecy, density

mì

稠密 ***chóumì*** dense

秘密 ***mìmì*** secret, confidential

11 strokes

宿 constellation, inn, lodging

sù

宿舍 ***sùshè*** dormitory, living quarters

寄宿 ***jìsù*** to lodge, board

For LODGING under a roof in an INN, you often pay one hundred dollars for one night.

7 strokes

冷 cold, frosty, chill

lěng

冰冷 ***bīnglěng*** ice-cold

冷漠 ***lěngmò*** indifferent, unconcerned

It was COLD and ice (冫) was forming as we received our orders (令) to jump into action before the CHILL set in too hard.

14 strokes

察 observe, inspect, examine

chá

监察 *jiānchá* **to inspect, supervise, control**

警察 *jǐngchá* **police**

观察 *guānchá* **observation**

Under a large roof (宀), spectators EXAMINE how others celebrate (祭) an event.

7 strokes

完 completion, perfect, end

wán

完全 *wánquán* **entire, whole**

完成 *wánchéng* **to complete, accomplish, fulfill**

The primary (元) goal of the children under the roof (宀) was to get PERFECT straight "A" scores.

6 strokes

守 guard, protect, defend

shǒu

守卫 *shǒuwèi* **guard, to defend, protect**

保守 *bǎoshǒu* **conservative, prudent**

To PROTECT your new roof and chimney (宀), measure (寸) it and GUARD from the weather by being sure it is sealed well.

8 strokes

宝 treasure, wealth, valuables

Traditional

寶

bǎo

宝石 *bǎoshí* **gem, jewel**

宝贝 *bǎobèi* **treasure, darling, baby**

Many children seem to have a WEALTH of TREASURE under the roof (宀), playing like kings with all of their jewels (玉).

6 strokes

安 safe, secure, peaceful

ān

平安 *píngān* **peaceful, safe**

安静 *ānjìng* **quiet, calm, stillness**

安全 *ānquán* **safe**

It is sometimes CHEAPER and SAFER for a woman (女) to be home under her own roof and do online shopping.

8 strokes

宗 religion, main point, origin

zōng

宗教 *zōngjiào* **religion**

宗旨 *zōngzhǐ* **aim, purpose**

The MAIN POINT of the RELIGION practiced under the roof (宀) should be easy to show (示) and explain.

8 strokes

官 official

guān

官员 ***guānyuán*** **official, officer**

In front of the OFFICIAL building, there was a guardhouse with a small roof and chimney (宀).

9 strokes

室 room

shì

教室 ***jiàoshì*** **classroom**

A ROOM for myself (厶) would have a nice roof (宀), but even a dirt floor (土) would do.

8 strokes

定 determine, fix, decide

dìng

决定 ***juédìng*** **to decide, determine**

预定 ***yùdìng*** **to reserve, make a reservation**

Under a roof, someone filling big shoes will FIX the way we DETERMINE how far to walk.

6 strokes

至 arrive, until

zhì

至 ***zhì*** **to arrive**

直至 ***zhízhì*** **until**

I will continue working the lands UNTIL I am about to pass them on to my heirs.

8 strokes

实 reality, truth

Traditional

實

shí

真实 ***zhēnshí*** **real, truth, truthful**

现实 ***xiànshí*** **reality, actual, tangible**

实验 ***shíyàn*** **experiment**

Under a roof (宀), the chief (头) with two bars on his shoulder laid out the REALITY of the situation ahead.

8 strokes

到 arrive, reach, until

dào

到达 ***dàodá*** **to reach, get to, arrive**

直到 ***zhídào*** **until, into, while**

UNTIL (到) you get to the mark where the finish line was cut in the sand with a blade, continue to try.

9 strokes

宣 declare, proclaim, say, announce

xuān

宣布 ***xuānbù*** **declaration, proclamation**

宣传 ***xuānchuán*** **publicity, to advertise**

Under a roof with a chimney, they will ANNOUNCE plans for the day.

9 strokes

突 suddenly, dash, charge

tú

突然 ***túrán*** **abruptly, suddenly**

冲突 ***chōngtú*** **conflict, clash**

Under a roof a person kicked a big (大) surprise that SUDDENLY jumped upward from below.

7 strokes

究 investigate, research, study

jiū

研究 ***yánjiū*** **to study, research**

究竟 ***jiūjìng*** **exactly, actually**

After he spent time on RESEARCH under the roof, he poked at nine holes through theories and beliefs about the STUDY and its findings.

8 strokes

空 empty, sky

kōng

空虚 ***kōngxū*** **emptiness, hollowness**

天空 ***tiānkōng*** **sky**

空气 ***kōngqì*** **air, atmosphere, breath**

In the EMPTY space below the roof (宀) is a hole (穴) with a window from which you can see the SKY.

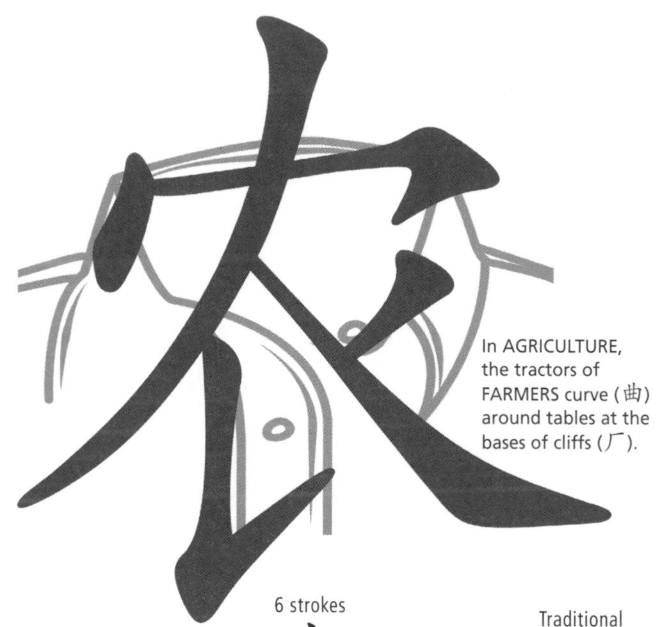

In AGRICULTURE, the tractors of FARMERS curve (曲) around tables at the bases of cliffs (厂).

6 strokes

农 agriculture, farmers

Traditional 農

nóng

农业 ***nóngyè*** **agriculture, farming**

农场 ***nóngchǎng*** **farm (noun)**

农民 ***nóngmín*** **farmer, peasant**

Door 户 and Gate 门

4 strokes

door, household

hù

户外 *hùwài* **open air, outdoors**

户口 *hùkǒu* **population**

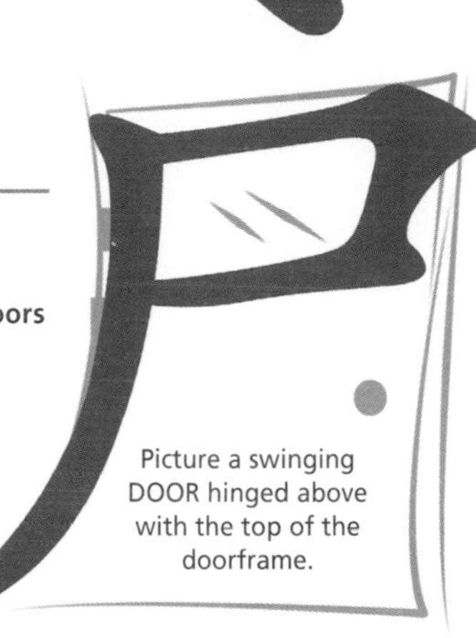

Picture a swinging DOOR hinged above with the top of the doorframe.

8 strokes

place

suǒ

场所 *chǎngsuǒ* **place, arena**

厕所 *cèsuǒ* **toilet, lavatory**

Beside the door (户) is the PLACE where my grandfather left the axe (斤) for protection and for when he went out to cut wood.

7 strokes

bureau, board, office, conclusion

jú

邮局 *yóujú* **post office**

结局 *jiéjú* **ending, conclusion, final**

People often take huge steps to bypass mouthy officials at a government BUREAU or OFFICE.

8 strokes

session, period

jiè

届时 *jièshí* **then**

第一届 *dìyījiè* **first term/session**

A reason is delivered through an open door.

A reason (由) is delivered through an open door.

8 strokes

居 **reside, exist, live with**

jū

居住 *jūzhù* **to live, reside, occupancy**

寄居 *jìjū* **sojourner, to live away from home**

10 strokes

展 unfold, expand

zhǎn

展开 ***zhǎnkāi*** **to unfold, expansion, development**

展览 ***zhǎnlǎn*** **exhibition, to show, display**

Coming through an open door with grass stains, mom UNFOLDS clean clothes for me.

7 strokes

Traditional

 layer, floor, social class 層

céng

层次 ***céngcì*** **level, stage, phase**

大气层 ***dàqìcéng*** **atmosphere**

They say (云) that a SOCIAL CLASS is just one part of how we divide each other though I (厶) think we are equal when we walk through the door to the next FLOOR.

12 strokes

Traditional

 belong, subordinate official 

shǔ

属于 ***shǔyú*** **to belong, be classified**

家属 ***jiāshǔ*** **family member/ dependent**

下属 ***xiàshǔ*** **subordinate**

Through an open door is a bug (虫) jumping over a little table.

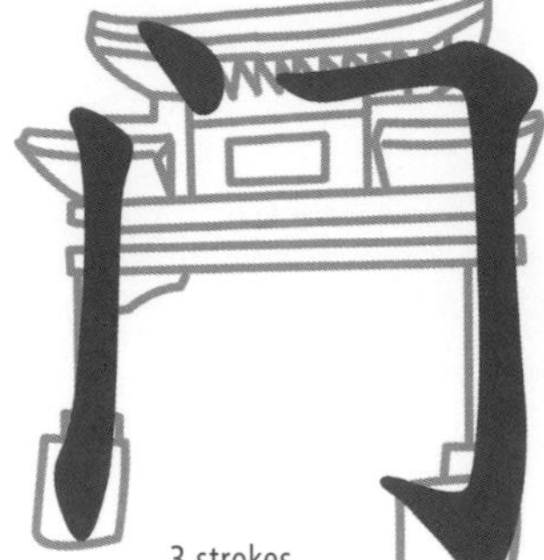

This GATE has a space at the top for a sign.

3 strokes

Traditional

门 door, gate 

mén

门口 ***ménkǒu*** **doorway, gate**

部门 ***bùmén*** **department, division**

6 strokes

Traditional

 question, ask, problem 

wèn

质问 ***zhìwèn*** **to interrogate, question, inquiry**

问题 ***wèntí*** **problem, trouble, question**

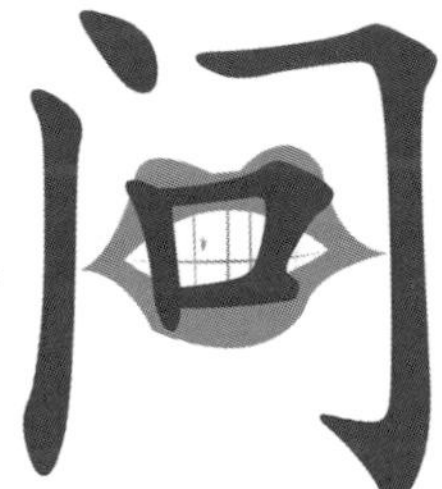

If a PROBLEM exists and a QUESTION needs to be asked, put your mouth (口) to the gate (门) and ASK it.

7 strokes

Traditional

 interval, space 

jiān

时间 ***shíjiān*** **time, period**

瞬间 ***shùnjiān*** **instant, jiffy, immediately**

The sun (日) is only visible from the enclosure for a short INTERVAL of time.

4 strokes

开 **open, unfold, unseal** Traditional 開

kāi

公开 ***gōngkāi*** **public, open to the public**

开始 ***kāishǐ*** **to start, begin, commence**

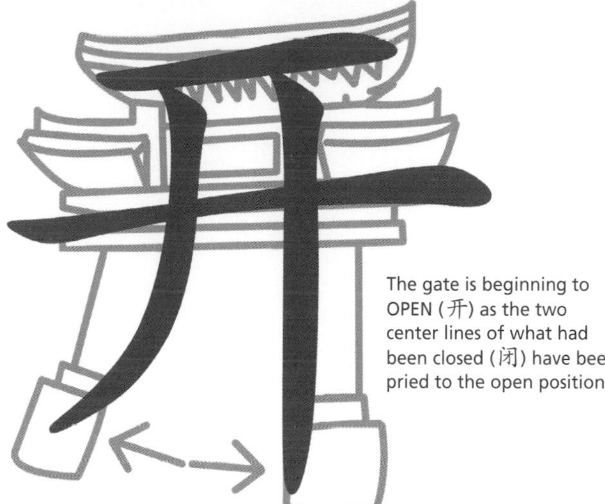

The gate is beginning to OPEN (开) as the two center lines of what had been closed (闭) have been pried to the open position.

6 strokes

 **shut, close, gate-way, connection** Traditional 

guān

关门 ***guānmén*** **to close, shut down [operations]**

海关 ***hǎiguān*** **customs [border crossing inspection]**

有关 ***yǒuguān*** **related, relevant**

A warrior stands ready to SHUT off the GATEWAY to the next region.

7 strokes

 **leisure** Traditional 

xián

悠闲 ***yōuxián*** **leisure, at ease**

空闲 ***kòngxián*** **idle, unwanted**

The tree (木) grew at its LEISURE in the enclosure.

6 strokes

  **closed, shut** Traditional 

bì

关闭 ***guānbì*** **to close, shut, shutdown**

闭嘴 ***bìzuǐ*** **Shut up! [rude]**

The gate is CLOSED as compared to when it is open (开).

7 strokes

 **extra, surplus, intercalary** Traditional 

rùn

闰月 ***rùnyuè*** **leap month**

Only on the INTERCALATIVE leap day would the antisocial king appear at the gate to greet his people.

Enclosures 口/冂/匚/凵

6 strokes

cause, factor, reason

yīn

原因 ***yuányīn*** reason, cause

因子 ***yīnzǐ*** factor, element

A big (大) FACTOR of rising support for the CAUSE was the state of men's conditions within the enclosure.

A powerful (力) little mouth is SURROUNDED in the criss-cross wires of a cage.

6 strokes

group, organization, association

Traditional

tuán

集团 ***jítuán*** group, organization

团结 ***tuánjié*** to unite, rally, join forces

A GROUP of dancers meet in a small enclosure though their ORGANIZATION has almost outgrown it.

7 strokes

surround, encircle

Traditional

wéi

包围 ***bāowéi*** to surround, encircle

周围 ***zhōuwéi*** surrounding, vicinity

7 strokes

sleepy, tired, become distressed, quandary

kùn

困倦 ***kùnjuàn*** sleepy, fatigued, tired

困难 ***kùnnán*** trouble, difficulty, problem

This tree is in a QUANDARY and IS DISTRESSED by being limited by its enclosure.

6 strokes

return, go back, revolve, turn

huí

回去 ***huíqù*** to go back, return

回家 ***huíjiā*** to go home

回来 ***huílái*** to come back, be back

I TURN round and round many TIMES looking for something.

8 strokes

 **map, drawing, plan, chart**

Traditional 

tú

地图 *dìtú* map

意图 *yìtú* intent, aim, plan, goal

Many need to sit at a table with a good PLAN or MAP for their lives to make it through cold winters (冬) without depression.

8 strokes

 **country**

Traditional 

guó

国家 *guójiā* country

中国 *Zhōngguó* China

A king keeps his jewels within the walls of his COUNTRY.

For a famous PARK or GARDEN, you often have to pay a few dollars (元) to walk (儿) within the walls (囗) of the property.

7 strokes

园 **park, garden**

Traditional 

yuán

花园 *huāyuán* garden

公园 *gōngyuán* park, public park

8 strokes

 **harden, solid, clot**

gù

坚固 *jiāngù* firm, hard, stable

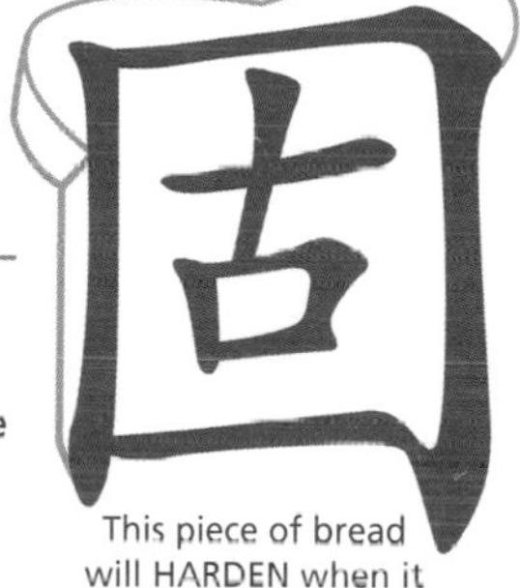

This piece of bread will HARDEN when it becomes old (古).

7 strokes

 **medical, doctor, cure, medicine**

Traditional 

yī

医疗 *yīliáo* medical treatment

医生 *yīshēng* doctor

医药 *yīyào* medicine, curative

As an archer in an open enclosure targets his mark, a DOCTOR targets illness.

4 strokes

 **area, region, district**

Traditional 

qū

区域 *qūyù* area, region, district

区别 *qūbié* difference, distinction

An "X" marks the spot on this corner of the DISTRICT map.

6 strokes

网 **net, web** Traditional 網

wǎng

网站 *wǎngzhàn* **website**

上网 *shàngwǎng* **go online [internet]**

网路 *wǎnglù* **network**

网球 *wǎngqiú* **tennis**

A couple of Xs connected together begin to form a NET

7 strokes

岗 **ridge, mound, post, position** Traditional 崗

gǎng

岗位 *gǎngwèi* **post, job, position**

站岗 *zhàngǎng* **to stand guard, mount guard**

The "X" marks the spot on this map where the RIDGE of the hill is at its peak

Framing the earth (土) TWICE (二), in mirroring positions, an artist paints the scene AGAIN.

6 strokes

 **again, twice**

zài

再见 *zàijiàn* **goodbye**

再会 *zàihuì* **to meet again**

6 strokes

刚 **just, barely, firm** Traditional 

gāng

刚好 *gānghǎo* **just right, exactly, to happen**

刚强 *gāngqiáng* **firm, unyielding**

The hiker had BARELY made it to the ridge (冈) when he dropped his knife over the side.

5 strokes

 **bundle, package, wrap, pack up, include, contain**

bāo

包扎 *bāozā* **to wrap, pack, bind up**

包裹 *bāoguǒ* **package**

The outer enclosure is already WRAPPED (巳) around private things to CONCEAL them.

CHAPTER 11

GARMENTS and SILK

6 strokes

衣 **garment, clothes**

yī

衣服 *yīfú* **clothing, apparel**

毛衣 *máoyī* **sweater (wool)**

Take the lid off of the box of GARMENTS so the person (亻) can pull the CLOTHES over their heads and legs to see how they fit.

Needles and threads are used to sew SILK garments.

5 strokes

丝 **silk**

Traditional 絲

sī

丝绸 *sīchóu* **silk, silk cloth**

蚕丝 *cánsī* **natural silk**

Garments 衣 and Silk 糸

12 strokes

装 install, clothing, pretend

Traditional 裝

zhuāng

安装 *ānzhuāng* to install

服装 *fúzhuāng* clothing

假装 *jiǎzhuāng* to pretend

You can hide behind fancy CLOTHING (衣) and PRETEND to be a warrior (士).

8 strokes

 表 outside, surface, chart/table, diagram

biǎo

表达 *biǎodá* to express

表格 *biǎogé* form, table

On the SURFACE, a warrior (士) with a very high rank steps OUTSIDE and looks impressive because of his fancy garments (衣).

7 strokes

纸 paper

Traditional 紙

zhǐ

报纸 *bàozhǐ* newspaper

折纸 *zhézhǐ* origami [paper folding]

As if they were silk (纟), pulp fivers are crisscross–layered (氏) to make PAPER.

8 strokes

 终 end, finish

Traditional  終

zhōng

终止 *zhōngzhǐ* termination, to finish/end

终结 *zhōngjié* finally, [with neg.] in the end

Like a long silk (纟) thread, days string together intil it all ENDS with winter (冬).

8 strokes

 组 organize, group, assemble

Traditional 組

zǔ

组合 *zǔhé* to combine, assemble

组织 *zǔzhī* organization

Leaders of a GROUP must keep their eyes open to see changes and also (且) ORGANIZE their policies so that things run as smooth as silk (纟).

9 strokes

络 **net, web, contact** Traditional 絡

luò

联络 *liánluò* to contact/call, connect

网络 *wǎngluò* network, Internet

A silken (纟) NET over a table can keep hungry little mouths out of CONTACT with the food we put on the table.

8 strokes

练 **practice, train, drill** Traditional 練

liàn

练习 *liànxí* practice, exercise

训练 *xùnliàn* training

教练 *jiàoliàn* coach

You must PRACTICE hard until your actions become smooth as silk (纟).

8 strokes

经 **sutra, expire, pass through** Traditional 經

jīng

佛经 *fójīng* [Buddhism] sutra

经过 *jīngguò* to pass/elapse, after

经营 *jīngyíng* to operate, manage

The threads of time continue as we PASS THROUGH each day, saying an evening SUTRA at the table daily.

6 strokes

级 **class, rank, grade** Traditional 級

jí

等级 *děngjí* rating, grade, rank

阶级 *jiējí* class, rank

Through a string of effort and luck, he was able to climb the shaky stairs to advance in RANK.

5 strokes

幼 **infant, childhood**

yòu

年幼 *niányòu* young

幼稚 *yòuzhì* naive, childish

幼儿 *yòuér* infant, baby

Childhood is one part of a thread (幺) of a life that makes us strong (力).

6 strokes

纪 **discipline, record, age** Traditional 紀

jì

纪律 *jìlǜ* discipline

记录 *jìlù* record, notes

年纪 *niánjì* age

HISTORY winds through the fabric of ourselves (己) and make us who we are.

7 strokes

纳 accept, admit, obtain, adopt

Traditional 納

nà

接纳 *jiēnà* acceptance, to admit

采纳 *cǎinà* adoption, to accept

出纳 *chūnà* cashier

To OBTAIN good silk (纟) from inside (内), the man ACCEPTS he might pay a lot.

9 strokes

给 give, grant, provide, supply

Traditional 給

gěi/jǐ

发给 *fāgěi* to grant, give, deliver

供给 *gōngjǐ* to supply, provide

If you speak (口) well, someone may PROVIDE you with a string (纟) of good luck.

6 strokes

约 approximately, agreement, contract

Traditional 約

yuē

约束 *yuēshù* constraint, to bind, restrict

预约 *yùyuē* reservation

契约 *qìyuē* contract, deed

When teaching others to dye silk, make an AGREEMENT to carefully use the ladle (勺) to remove it in APPROXIMATELY the required time.

14 strokes

缩 shrink, reduce, wrinkle

Traditional 縮

suō

缩小 *suōxiǎo* to shrink, reduction, curtailment

收缩 *shōusuō* to shrink/contract

For lodging (宿) in a string of hotels, it can be hard to SHRINK or REDUCE costs since you often pay one–hundred dollars for a night.

7 strokes

纯 pure, innocence, genuine, purity

Traditional 純

chún

纯粹 *chúncuì* pure, true

纯正 *chúnzhèng* genuine, pure

GENUINE silk of great PURITY can be found in that lidded pot that has been heated.

9 strokes

Traditional

统 **order, unite** 統

tǒng

系统 *xìtǒng* system

统一 *tǒngyī* unity, together

统治 *tǒngzhì* to govern, rule

I think that all is in ORDER when I have had a sufficient (充) amount time and everything runs as smooth as silk.

A THREAD (纟) between land (土) and sun (日) has bound us together since the BEGINNING.

8 strokes

Traditional

细 **dainty, get thin, narrow** 細

xì

详细 *xiángxì* detailed, thorough

仔细 *zǐxì* attentive, careful

Examining NARROW thread-like fields in many parts of rural China can be enjoyable.

11 strokes

Traditional

绪 **thread, clue, beginning** 緒

xù

就绪 *jiùxù* be ready, completed

头绪 *tóuxù* clue, lead

情绪 *qíngxù* mood, sentiment, emotion

12 strokes

Traditional

编 **weave, organize** 編

biān

编织 *biānzhī* to weave, knit

编排 *biānpái* to arrange, organize

Take this silk thread through that door to ORGANIZE each color in a row on a flat (扁) surface.

9 strokes

Traditional

绝 **cut off, absolute, refuse** 絕

jué

绝对 *juéduì* absolutely

断绝 *duànjué* to cut off, break off

拒绝 *jùjué* to refuse, reject

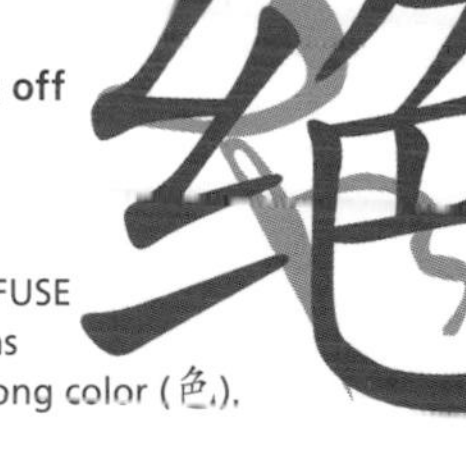

They decided to REFUSE the silk (纟) that was delivered in the wrong color (色).

7 strokes

系 system, series, department

xì

系统 ***xìtǒng*** **system**

中文系 ***Zhōngwénxì*** **Chinese Department (college department)**

系列 ***xìliè*** **series**

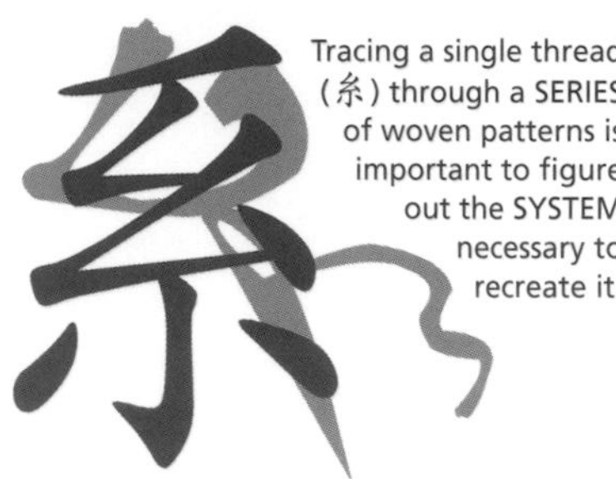

Tracing a single thread (糸) through a SERIES of woven patterns is important to figure out the SYSTEM necessary to recreate it.

10 strokes

tight, tense

Traditional 緊

jǐn

紧张 ***jǐnzhāng*** **tense, nervous**

紧急 ***jǐnjí*** **urgent**

要紧 ***yàojǐn*** **important, critical**

Two thick threads of silk are ready to be stretched TIGHT in a loom to make a cloth for this table.

11 strokes

ratio, rate, frequency

lǜ

频率 ***pínlǜ*** **frequency, rate of recurrence**

效率 ***xiàolǜ*** **efficiency**

Under a lid, silk (糸) has been piled up at a fast RATE but a RATIO of ten (十) to one they are small strands.

Cloth 巾

3 strokes

towel

jīn

毛巾 ***máojīn*** **towel**

围巾 ***wéijīn*** **scarf, shawl**

TOWELS and laundry can hang from a post such as this.

5 strokes

linen, cloth

bù

布匹 ***bùpǐ*** **cloth, fabric, textile**

麻布 ***mábù*** **linen**

This person jumped with joy after all of the CLOTH towels and LINEN sheets were hung out to dry.

7 strokes

hope, wish

xī

希望 ***xīwàng*** **hope, wish**

希腊 ***Xīlà*** **Greece**

I HOPE that where the X marks the spot is where I will find fresh linen (布) sheets.

As if hanging laundry from a line (巾), the long (长) piece of fabric was hung to make a tent for the night.

9 strokes

带 sash, belt, zone

Traditional 帶

dài

带子 ***dàizi*** **tape, belt, band**

地带 ***dìdài*** **zone**

A BELT is threaded through three loops of a man's trousers and he is on his way to the urban ZONE of the city (市) for business.

7 strokes

帐 tent

Traditional 帳

zhàng

帐幕 ***zhàngmù*** **tent**

蚊帐 ***wénzhàng*** **mosquito net**

In ancient times, large lanterns might mark the entry gates of the CAPITAL.

8 strokes

京 capital [city]

jīng

北京 ***Běijīng*** **Beijing**

东京 ***Dōngjīng*** **Tokyo**

南京 ***Nánjīng*** **Nanjing**

5 strokes

市 market, city

shì

都市 ***dūshì*** **city, metropolis**

市场 ***shìchǎng*** **[town] market**

市长 ***shìzhǎng*** **mayor**

In the CITY, we could use laundry (巾) facilities to wash clothing.

12 strokes

就 undertake, become, take position

jiù

成就 ***chéngjiù*** **achievement, success**

就任 ***jiùrèn*** **to take office, assume a post**

In the capital city (京) a person might be cut off at the neck if he UNDERTAKES a challenge to BECOME more than he is capable of being.

Below a dotted cliff, a city's (市) laundry is drying on part of a swing that waits for a child to take a SEAT.

10 strokes

席 **seat, occasion, place**

xí

出席 ***chūxí*** **to appear, attend**

缺席 ***quēxí*** **absence, non-attendance**

6 strokes

师 **teacher, master, expert** Traditional 師

shī

老师 ***lǎoshī*** **teacher**

律师 ***lǜshī*** **lawyer**

A TEACHER uses a knife (刂) to cut informational charts to size.

11 strokes

常 **often, frequent, common, regular**

cháng

常常 ***chángcháng*** **always, constantly**

非常 ***fēicháng*** **very, extremely**

Bits of knowledge were OFTEN passed by word of mouth (口) though later it became COMMON to write them down on hanging scrolls (巾).

3 strokes

干 **dry, parch** Traditional 乾

gān

干旱 ***gānhàn*** **drought**

烘干 ***hōnggān*** **drying [over a fire]**

DRY your clothes on this line.

5 strokes

刊 **publish**

kān

刊物 ***kānwù*** **publication, journal**

刊登 ***kāndēng*** **to print in a publication, publish (in a newspaper or magazine)**

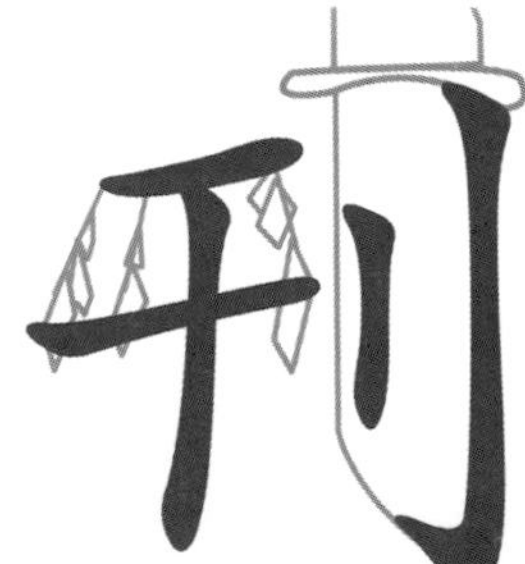

The engraving can be PUBLISHED after the plate is printed and cut with a knife after being hung to dry (干).

Shape or Form 形

The SHAPE of the open (开) gate doesn't change as much as the STYLE of hair (彡).

7 strokes

形 **shape, form, style**

xíng

形状 ***xíngzhuàng*** **shape, form, appearance**

形容 ***xíngróng*** **to describe**

5 strokes

央 **center, middle**

yāng

央行 ***yānghàng*** **central bank**

央求 ***yāngqiú*** **to beg, plead**

Here is a person holding a box in the MIDDLE of his body.

A board sits LEVEL on top of this man's FLAT head as he carefully balances it, slightly waving his arms up and down in a slow motion.

5 strokes

平 **even, flat, level, average**

píng

平面 ***píngmiàn*** **flat surface**

平衡 ***pínghéng*** **balance, even**

平常 ***píngcháng*** **ordinarily, generally**

15 strokes

影 **shadow, image**

yǐng

影子 ***yǐngzi*** **shadow**

影像 ***yǐngxiàng*** **image, portrait**

电影 ***diànyǐng*** **movie, film**

The sun tries to emerge over the walls of the capital (京) to remove the SHADOW that prevented the jewels on the hair comb (彡) from being clearly seen.

3 strokes

丸 **pill, pellet, round**

wán

药丸 ***yàowán*** **pills [medicinal]**

弹丸 ***dànwán*** **bullet, pellet**

In most countries, adding one more ROUND egg to nine (九) makes a standard carton of ten eggs.

4 strokes

in, inside, middle, center

zhōng

中间 *zhōngjiān* **intermediate, middle, among**

中部 *zhōngbù* **middle part, central section**

The arrow struck through the CENTER/ MIDDLE of the target.

6 strokes

danger, endanger

wéi

危险 *wéixiǎn* **danger/hazard**

危机 *wéijī* **crisis**

DANGER can happen after stepping into barbs atop a cliff that can internally cause oneself (己) to twist and writhe in pain.

When you use (用) ideas to wrap (勹) up projects, it is important to consider various ANGLES and not to cut CORNERS.

7 strokes

角 **angle, corner, horn**

jiǎo

角度 *jiǎodù* **angle, point of view**

号角 *hàojiǎo* **horn, bugle, antler**

COMPARE the two sides of this character, and see that they are slightly different.

4 strokes

比 **compare, contrast**

bǐ

比较 *bǐjiào* **to compare, contrast**

对比 *duìbǐ* **contrasting**

13 strokes

explain, untie

jiě

解释 *jiěshì* **to explain, interpretation**

解开 *jiěkāi* **to untie, undo**

了解 *liǎojiě* **to understand**

When hearding cows (牛) that turn the wrong corner (角), UNITE your powers (刀) to get them back or be able to EXPLAIN what happened.

3 strokes

大 large, big, great

dà

伟大 *wěidà* great, big, mighty

大学 *dàxué* college/university

This person looks BIG with outstretched arms.

8 strokes

奋 arouse

Traditional 奮

fèn

兴奋 *xīngfèn* excited, exhilarated

奋斗 *fèndòu* to struggle, contend, strive, combat

The large (大) jumping man AROUSED the attention of the workers in the fields (田).

4 strokes

太 too, overly, excessively, extremely

tài

太大 *tài dà* too big

太太 *tàitai* wife, married woman, lady, madam

The big (大) dog (犬) eats TOO many bones and becomes EXCESSIVELY fat.

8 strokes

奇 strange, odd

qí

稀奇 *xīqí* strange, rare

好奇 *hàoqí* curious

新奇 *xīnqí* new, novel

A large (大) tack may (可) point to an area that seems STRANGE until you understand the bigger picture and it is not actually that ODD.

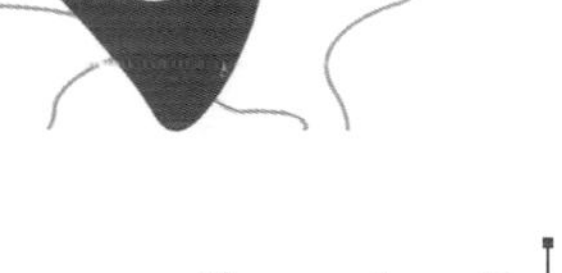

4 strokes

天 sky

tiān

天空 *tiānkōng* sky

天堂 *tiāntáng* heaven

A big (大) person stretches wide and tall and reaches to the SKY.

9 strokes

奏 play music, perform

zòu

演奏 *yǎnzòu* to give a music performance

节奏 *jiézòu* rhythm

演奏会 *yǎnzòuhuì* concert, recital

When she would PLAY MUSIC on her big (大) three (三) stringed instruments, it was like a gift from heaven (天).

10 strokes

高 tall, high

gāo

高度 *gāodù* height

高中 *gāozhōng* high school

Pagodas are TALL buildings used for religious purposes.

3 strokes

小 little, small, tiny

xiǎo

细小 *xìxiǎo* small, tiny, little

小学 *xiǎoxué* elementary school

A person crouches down to make himself look SMALL.

4 strokes

长 long, leader

Traditional 長

cháng/zhǎng

长度 *chángdù* length

校长 *xiàozhǎng* school principal

A LONG cloth is stacked on the ironing board.

4 strokes

少 less, few, little

shǎo

少数 *shǎoshù* minority, few

A small (小) quantity is cut in half and only a FEW are left.

Measurement 寸/尺

6 strokes

 **temple**

sì

寺院 ***sìyuàn*** **temple**

少林寺 ***Shàolínsì***
Shaolin Temple

A multi-storied TEMPLE on the land (土) that warriors had fought for has a large bronze bell hanging from the measured (寸) eves.

This vertical and horizontal square is used to take a MEASUREMENT of the dot on the inside.

3 strokes

寸 **inch, unit of measurement**

cùn

尺寸 ***chǐcùn*** **size, dimension, measurement**

5 strokes

 **opposite, versus** Traditional 對

duì

反对 ***fǎnduì*** **opposition, resistance**

相对 ***xiāngduì*** **relatively, comparatively, to resist**

They sat OPPOSITE each other at a table (又) and discussed the ideas of us VERSUS them and still, neither giving even an inch (寸).

On his or her BIRTHDAY, congratulate someone who is living LIFE right and seems to cut through a measured (寸) three decades and still looks younger.

7 strokes

寿 **life, longevity, birthday** Traditional 

shòu

寿命 ***shòumìng*** **life, lifespan, longevity**

寿辰 ***shòuchén*** **birthday**

寿司 ***shòusī*** **sushi**

6 strokes

 **guidance, leading, conduct** Traditional 導

dǎo

领导 ***lǐngdǎo*** **leader, guidance, to guide/lead**

教导 ***jiàodǎo*** **to teach, instruct**

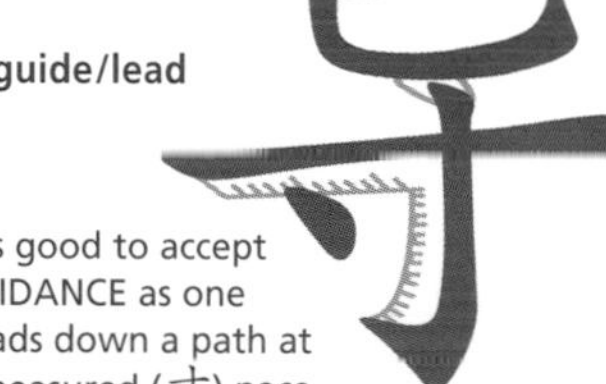

It is good to accept GUIDANCE as one heads down a path at a measured (寸) pace.

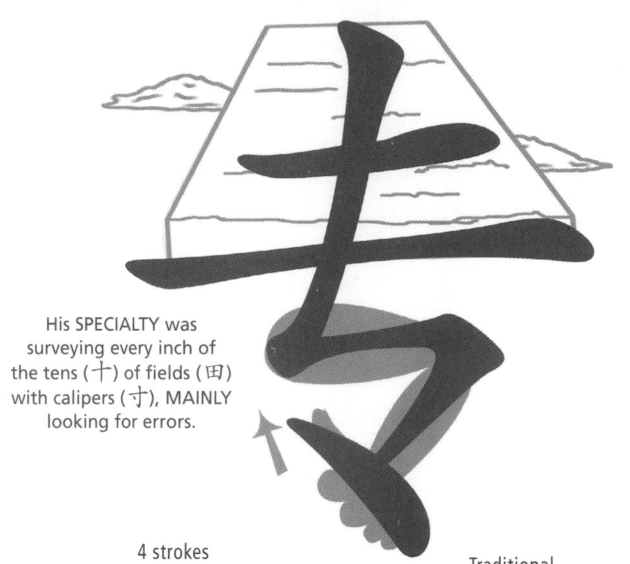

His SPECIALTY was surveying every inch of the tens (十) of fields (田) with calipers (寸), MAINLY looking for errors.

4 strokes

专 specialty, exclusive, mainly

Traditional 專

zhuān

专家 *zhuānjiā* **specialist, expert**

专一 *zhuānyī* **concentrated, single-minded**

4 strokes

尺 ruler, feet (for measurement)

chǐ

尺子 *chǐzi* **ruler (tool)**

尺寸 *chǐcùn* **size, dimension, measurement**

三尺 *sānchǐ* **3 feet**

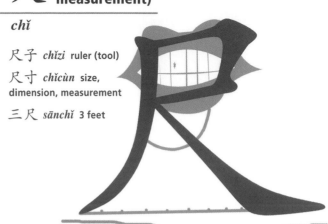

He used a RULER to measure how wide that gap was when he opened his mouth.

6 strokes

尽 entirely, exhaust

Traditional 盡

jìn

耗尽 *hàojìn* **to exhaust**

尽力 *jìnlì* **to try one's best**

尽量 *jìnliàng* **as much as possible**

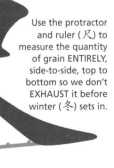

Use the protractor and ruler (尺) to measure the quantity of grain ENTIRELY, side-to-side, top to bottom so we don't EXHAUST it before winter (冬) sets in.

7 strokes

克 gram, restraint, overcome

kè

公克 *gōngkè* **gram**

克服 *kèfú* **to overcome, surmount**

克制 *kèzhì* **restraint, self-control**

OVERCOME old (古) traditions as you walk (儿) through life and exercise RESTRAINT in difficult situations.

INDEX